The Dual-Entity of Market Competition

The relationship between the government and the market lies at the heart of Economics as a discipline. This title approaches this issue with a new lens termed mezzoeconomics—A branch of modern economics that mainly studies regional economic entities and the allocation of regional resources after they are generated.

Combining mezzoeconomic theory with practice in the light of China's Reform and Opening-up, the author analyzes the regional governments' participation in market competition, the dual entities (enterprises and regional governments) of market competition, and a mature market economy featuring a strong form of effective government and efficient market. Three corresponding theories are proposed—the Regional Government Competition Theory, the Dual-Entity of Market Competition Theory (DEMC) and the "Double Strong Forms" Theory. The author hopes that these theories of mezzoeconomics can build a new, effective theoretical model and serve as a guide for regional governments to reform and innovate their governance philosophy and policies.

This book will be of keen interest to students and scholars of economics and regional governance.

Yunxian Chen is an economist in China. He is affiliated with Harvard University as an Associate in Research and a guest professor and doctoral supervisor at Hong Kong Polytechnic University, Peking University and Sun Yat-sen University, etc. He is also an honorary dean of the International School of Business & Finance and Advanced Institute of Finance at Sun Yat-sen University. His major academic publications in Economics include *Government Foresighted Leading: Theory and Practice of the World's Regional Economic Development* (2017), *Regional Government Competition* (2019), etc.

China Perspectives

The *China Perspectives* series focuses on translating and publishing works by leading Chinese scholars, writing about both global topics and China-related themes. It covers Humanities and Social Sciences, Education, Media and Psychology, as well as many interdisciplinary themes.

This is the first time any of these books have been published in English for international readers. The series aims to put forward a Chinese perspective, give insights into cutting-edge academic thinking in China and inspire researchers globally.

To submit a book proposal, please contact the Taylor & Francis Publisher for the China Publishing Programme, Lian Sun (Lian.Sun@informa.com)
Titles in economics include:

Macroeconomic Policy and Steady Growth in China
2020 Dancing with Black Swan
Edited by Zhang Xiaojing

Political and Economic Analysis of State-Owned Enterprise Reform
Huiming Zhang

Political Economy in the Evolution of China's Urban-Rural Economic Relations
Fan Gao

China's New Normal, Supply-Side, and Structural Reform
Cai Fang

The Dual-Entity of Market Competition
Establishment and Development of Mezzoeconomics
Yunxian Chen

A Study of Labor Mobility in China
Sun Wenkai

For more information, please visit https://www.routledge.com/China-Perspectives/book-series/CPH

The Dual-Entity of Market Competition

Establishment and Development of Mezzoeconomics

Yunxian Chen

Routledge
Taylor & Francis Group
LONDON AND NEW YORK

First published in English 2022
by Routledge
2 Park Square, Milton Park, Abingdon, Oxon OX14 4RN

and by Routledge
605 Third Avenue, New York, NY 10158

Routledge is an imprint of the Taylor & Francis Group, an informa business

Translated by Lin Ma

English Version by permission of Foreign Language Teaching and Research Publishing Co.,Ltd.

British Library Cataloguing-in-Publication Data
A catalogue record for this book is available from the British Library

Library of Congress Cataloging-in-Publication Data
A catalog record has been requested for this book

ISBN: 978-1-032-15586-9 (hbk)
ISBN: 978-1-032-15591-3 (pbk)
ISBN: 978-1-003-24483-7 (ebk)

DOI: 10.4324/9781003244837

Typeset in Times New Roman
by MPS Limited, Dehradun

Contents

Figures

Tables

Preface

I was very fortunate to be born at a time of great transformations. Forty years since the reform and opening up in China, I had the good luck to have spent over a decade learning, teaching and researching in universities, over a decade working in financial enterprises, and over a decade serving in local governments. Meanwhile, I also took chances of the time and studied successively at Harvard University, Yale University, University of Massachusetts USA and Toronto University Canada. My experiences, studies and thinking during this time constitute the foundation of this book.

The relationship between the government and the market is as complex as the Goldbach's conjecture in economics. In this book, I strive to explore breakthroughs on this issue, based on theory and practice, from three perspectives—Regional governments' participating in market competition, dual entities (enterprises and regional governments) of market competition and a mature market economy features a strong form of effective government and a strong form of market efficiency.

First, the Regional Government Competition Theory. I have come to realize through practice that regional economic development is constrained by the number of regional economic projects, how complete industrial chains are as well as trade volumes for imports and exports; policies and measures adopted by governments for the sound growth of the regional economy should focus on investing in infrastructure, supporting talent cultivation and scientific innovation and putting in place financial instruments; management efficiency of the regional economy is contingent upon how complete the set of supporting regional policies is, how sound the regional business environment is and how efficient the local administration is. Based on these, I creatively put forward a "Sheep's Horns Competition Theory" (for its shape, see below), or the Nine Factors in Three Categories Competition Theory (the "9-in-3" Competition Theory).

The essence of this theory is that the objective function of regional government competition is about government revenue and the indicator function is regional competitiveness. The core supporting the objective function and the indicator function resides in Category One, regional economic development level that consists of three factors—projects, industrial chains and imports and exports.

Category Two, regional economic policies and measures also consist of three factors—infrastructure investment policies, talents and science and technology support policies and fiscal and financial support policies. Category Three is about regional economic management efficiency, which covers policy system efficiency, environment system efficiency and management system efficiency. Among them, the latter two categories are the key supporting part of the entire system (for further details, see Chapter 5).

The author holds that broadly speaking, regional government competition is centered around supporting policies and measures for competition over operative resources (industrial economy), non-operative resources (livelihood economy) and quasi-operative resources (urban economy), which actually is a "9-in-3" competition. In essence, it is a competition over government revenue the objective function in industrial development, urban construction and social welfare. Narrowly speaking, regional government competition mainly refers to competition for investment, development and construction of quasi-operative resources (infrastructure resources), which substantially is a competition in investment strategies.

Regional government competition differs from enterprise competition in nine aspects: The objective functions they compete for, the way they establish their objective functions, the path they realize their objective functions, their investment and financing mechanisms, their price-determining mechanisms, competition orientations, areas of competition, their roles in competition as well as their management modes. The competitiveness of regional governments can be assessed quantitatively by comparing the input end (structure of fiscal expenditure) and the output end (regional performance) through the District Resource Planning (DRP) model. Through "9-in-3" competition, regional governments will benefit from the scale effects, cluster effects and neighborhood effects, and the urban economic development will follow the 80/20 rule (the Pareto's Law), which eventually will prompt investors to select regional governments by "voting with feet," which means through the flow of personnel, capital and goods, investors choose regions with favorable public environment and services to grow their business.

Second, the Dual-Entity of Market Competition Theory (DEMC). In the author's opinion, the horizontal market system consists of industrial economy, urban economy, international economy (such as space economy, marine economy, polar economy, earth exploration economy), etc. While the vertical market system includes market factor system, market organization system, market legal system, market supervision system, market environment system and market infrastructure as its six pillars. In the modern market system, enterprises are the major market players in the industrial economy and regional governments, the major market players in the urban economy as well as the principal investors in developing generative resources. Therefore, there are dual entities in market competition: Enterprises, mainly in the industrial economy; and regional governments, mainly in the urban economy. Enterprise competition centers on optimized resource allocation under the conditions of resource scarcity, while regional government competition strives for optimized resource allocation on the basis of resource generation. So competitions among both enterprises and regional governments can yield results of the 80/20 rule, which together form the double driving forces for the modern market economy (for further details, see Chapter 2).

The role of the dual entities in the modern market economy manifests three rules in the development practice of nations around the world, including the congregating effect of the 80/20 rule, the equilibrium law of gradient changes and the coordination effect of competition and cooperation that demonstrate an objective and inevitable trend in regional economic development and are given full play to their role in different development stages, respectively.

Finally, the "Double Strong Forms" theory of a mature market economy. On the basis of research results of economists around the globe, the author attempts to categorize efficient markets into three types, the weak form, the semi-strong form, and the strong form and also three groups of effective governments, the weak form, the semi-strong form and the strong form. Together, they can produce nine combinations (for further details, see Chapter 10).

The author believes that a mature market economy must be the combination of a strong form of effective government and a strong form of an efficient market, which shall be the target of economic breakthroughs and the necessary path for nations worldwide to follow for sustainable development. For a strong form of effective government, it should respect market rules, safeguard economic order and keep economic development on a stable track, and effectively deploy resources and participate in regional competition. A strong form of an effective market also has three criteria. It should allow full competition, feature orderly legal supervision and put in place a sound social credit system. The "double strong forms" mechanism in a mature market economy will help clarify the complicated relations between the government and the market so as to concretely improve industrial development, urban construction and social welfare in nations around the world.

All these three theories focus on studies in mezzoeconomics and are results of the author's own experience and practice in the process of China's reform and opening up. Especially in resolving the hardships met in practice, the author got much inspiration. From the theoretical perspective itself, at least six aspects of the core economic theory the author attempts to establish in the field of mezzoeconomics come from the forefront of China's practice in reform and opening up. First, the Resource Generation Theory and categorization of three kinds of regional resources that originated from the author's experience in serving the Foshan Municipal Government. As a regional government, Foshan partitioned and redefined the role of industrial economy, urban economy and livelihood economy, and made applications in practice accordingly in as early as 2004. Second, the establishment of the Government Foresighted Leading Theory (GFL). This theory can be traced back to achievements made by the Shunde District in Foshan in the process of reform and opening up and it was put into practice in 2005 for sustainable economic development of the district. Third, the Dual Attributes Theory of Governments. This theory is based on an analysis of the economic behavior of Shenzhen Municipal Government and has been further updated and improved as Shenzhen's reform and opening up constantly deepens. Fourth, the Regional Government Competition Theory, or the "9-in-3" Competition Theory. It is rooted in comparative analysis over cities in the Pearl River Delta and it is also an overview of their practice in reform and opening up. Fifth, the "Double Strong Forms" Theory. It not only originates from reasonable thinking over China's four-decade reform and opening up but is also backed up by the great achievements already made in China. Sixth, the New Economic Engine Theory. This theory is based on China's success in reform and opening up and sustainable development and puts forward concepts of new investment engines, innovation engines and rule engines that explores a new path for sustainable development of the world economy.

At present, the regional governments' competition in China can be seen in at least two fronts. First, the "9-in-3" competition, which outlines a clear picture of regional governments' contest in economic development, policies and measures as well as management efficiency. Second, regional governments tend to establish state-owned enterprises (SOEs) as the backbone in competing for projects, resources for building complete industrial chains and imports and exports. Such practice fuels up competition among various enterprises and helps reinforce competitive neutrality. From factor-driven to investment-driven, the driving force of China's reform and opening up is shifting towards innovation, and the major playing field of reform and opening up is also extending from coastal regions to the hinterland and from special economic zones to the whole nation. With the formation of dual entities in the market and as government foresighted leading comes into play, the socialist market economy with Chinese characteristics is making substantial strides to a mature market economy featuring a strong form of effective government and a strong form of an efficient market. The Chinese economy has already come under the global spotlight with its way of economic solution. The socialist economics with Chinese characteristics, combined with an effective government and an efficient market, will revolutionize the global economic system.

The relation between the government and the market in traditional economic theories is a focus of world economic research and also a tough nut in practice for countries worldwide. In fact, it has been a common problem for the whole world. The author hopes the discussions in this book, from the perspective of mezzoeconomics, can fill up some gaps in this regard by building a new economic model in theory and clarifying economic operation in practice, and eventually serving as a guide for regional governments around the globe in reforming and innovating their governance philosophy and policies and adopting the right policy instruments.

Abbreviation

"9-in-3" Competition Theory	Nine Factors in Three Categories Competition Theory; the "Sheep's Horns Competition Theory"
DEMC	Dual-Entity of Market Competition Theory
DRP	District Resource Planning
GFL	Government Foresighted Leading Theory

Part I

1 Principal market players in microeconomy, mezzoeconomy and macroeconomy and their behavior analysis

1.1 Principal market players in microeconomy and their behavior analysis

Microeconomics, as a branch of modern economics, studies the behavior of individual agents (producers, consumers and firms) as its subject of research. It mainly falls into three parts. First, microeconomics focuses on how to optimize the behavior of economic agents with individual producers maximizing profits and individual consumers maximizing utility. Second, it considers how an equilibrium price in a market is determined and the answer is it is the result of interactions of optimized economic behavior of all producers and consumers in the market. Third, it studies how equilibrium prices of all single markets are determined and concludes it as the result of interactions of optimized economic behavior of all the producers and consumers in the markets.

The fundamental issue in microeconomics is about how to allocate industrial resources and its basic principle is that supply and demand determine the relative price. Its essence is that free exchange tends to allow resources to be utilized to the fullest and resource allocation in such cases is considered to be Pareto Optimality. Thus, the main field of research of microeconomics includes consumer choice, manufacturer supply and income distribution, with the price theory as its core. Therefore, microeconomics, in many occasions, is also known as "price theory."

Microeconomics deals with the economic behavior of individual agents in the market and the relevant economic variables. Based on the condition that industrial resources are scarce, microeconomics holds that all individual behavior attempts to achieve maximum benefits with limited resources and examines conditions to do this. While for goods and services in the market, consumers first choose goods or services with their limited income according to the price and strive to obtain maximum utility and satisfaction from what they purchase. Second, manufacturers are suppliers of goods and services, who aim to maximize output and profits with the minimum costs. Third, choices made by consumers and producers are manifested through the relation of supply and demand in the market, which affects prices, and in turn, is adjusted by prices. Therefore, the interaction of market mechanisms, equilibrium prices, optimal

DOI: 10.4324/9781003244837-1

allocation of industrial resources, market failure as well as government intervention are all within the research scope of microeconomics.

Microeconomics has its roots in Adam Smith's *The Wealth of Nations* and Alfred Marshall's *Principles of Economics.* Since the 1930s, the British economist Joan Robinson and the American economist Edward Hastings Chamberlin put forward a firm's equilibrium on the basis of Marshall's theory of equilibrium price. With the proposal of theories on equilibrium price, consumer behavior, producer behavior, firm's equilibrium, welfare economics, etc., the microeconomic system is eventually established. (See Figure 1.1, demand relations in solid lines while supply relations in dotted lines.)

The development of microeconomics has roughly experienced four stages by far. From the mid-17th century to the mid-19th century it was the early or infant stage of microeconomics; From late-19th century to early-20th century, neoclassical economics emerged, which set the foundation of microeconomics; From the 1930s to the 1960s microeconomics was officially established; from the 1960s to present it has been a time for further development, expansion and evolution of microeconomics.

Major new developments in microeconomics in recent years worth mentioning are listed as follows:

1. A new theory of consumption, which covers issues such as revealed preference, consumer choice under risk and the view that "consumption is also household production."
2. A new theory of the firm, discussing the nature of firms, utility maximization model, principal-agent problem, internal organizational efficiency, non-optimizing theory of the firm, etc.
3. Unbalanced growth theory. Through studies on economic practice in reality, especially that of developing nations, this theory reveals that over a given period of time, the economic development of most developing nations, even some developed nations, are unbalanced, which casts doubts over, supplements to, and drives further development of the balanced growth theory.
4. The game theory is a game-changer in microeconomics. *Theory of Games and Economic Behavior*, co-authored by John von Neumann and Oskar Morgenstern in 1944, signified the formal establishment of the game theory. When John Forbes Nash Jr., Reinhard Selten and John Harsanyi were jointly awarded the 1994 Nobel Prize for Economics for helping develop the game theory, the theory had been substantially enriched and improved in this half of a century, which reshaped oligopoly theory in microeconomics. From Antoine Augustin Cournot, Joseph Bertrand to Edward Hastings Chamberlin, economists have come to realize that in real life, most of the market competition should be explained from the perspective of oligopoly theory, and key empirical researches should be conducted on oligopoly market under the framework of "structure, behavior and performance." Therefore, analytical techniques such as

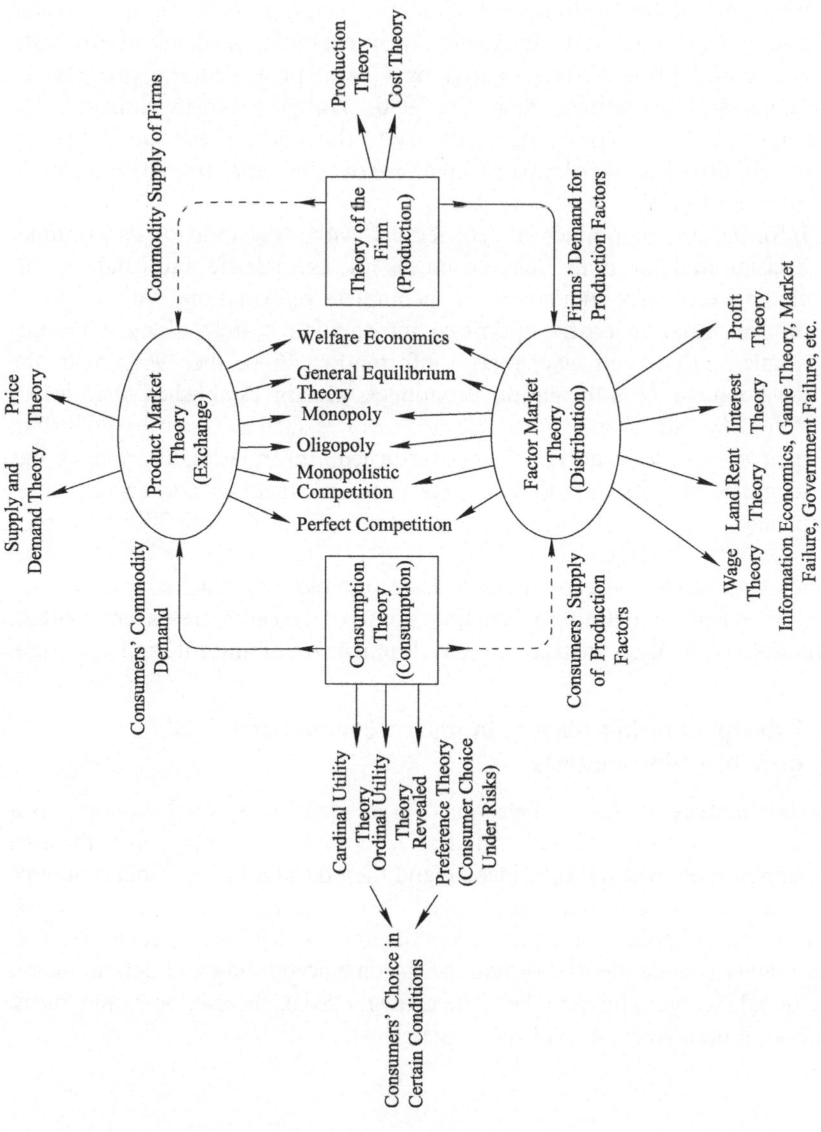

Figure 1.1 Theoretical system of microeconomics.

sunk cost, incomplete information model, individual rationality and collective rationality, and folk theorem are developed, which propel market analysis in modern economics to a new stage.

5. The public choice theory. Public choice economists represented by James M. Buchanan and Jr., Gordon Tullock pioneered the application of microeconomic principles in the analysis of demand and supply of public goods.
6. The new institutional economics (with the property rights theory as its core). Since the 1970s, the new institutional economics established by John Kenneth Galbraith, Karl Gunnar Myrdal and Ronald Coase has incorporated institutions, including laws, rules, property rights, customs and norms into microeconomics. For example, theories of property rights and firms as represented by Coase, propelled the progress of neoclassical economics. Since the 1980s, Douglass North pioneered the application of property rights theory to the study of economic history, which drove forward institutional innovation and transformation in microeconomics.
7. Information economics is concerned with the individuals' optimal decision-making under circumstances of asymmetric information, including economic analysis with incomplete information, with its focus on "information cost," optimized information search, along with economic analysis with asymmetric information. Since the 1960s, with the development of information economics, certain established theories of Alfred Marshall's and other relevant theories such as general equilibrium in a competitive market were overturned. Information economics has identified limitations with traditional economic theories, and hence further promoted the development of microeconomics in the late 20th century.

In fact, as a branch of economics, microeconomics has reached relative maturity in terms of definition, starting point of research, research content, methodology, analysis instrument, development trend and internal structure.

1.2 Principal market players in macroeconomy and their behavior analysis

Macroeconomics studies the behavior of a national or regional economy as a whole. It is concerned with understanding economy-wide events such as the level of unemployment, the national income and the utilization of national economic resources. In modern macroeconomics there are macroeconomic theories, macroeconomic policies and macroeconometric models. Macroeconomic theories mainly include theories of national income accounting and determination of national income, which can be further categorized as theories on employment, inflation, economic cycles and economic growth.

A nation is a community of people with a specific culture in a defined territory under the control of a government. A national government, as the symbol of a state, is the political authority controlling a nation and governing society. In economic fields, a government utilizes resources based on the national income determination mechanism and thus executing national economic policies and activities, which yields economic results accordingly. So it can be said that modern macroeconomics serves for national economic policies and economic activities and strives to identify the right path and model for stable national income and sustainable growth. It mainly focuses on economic growth, fluctuations of economic cycles, unemployment, inflation, national finance, international trade, etc., with research indicators concentrating on national income, ratios of aggregate social consumption, savings and investment to national income, the volume of currency in circulation and velocity of money, price levels, interest rates, population size and its growth rates, employment and unemployment rates, national budget and deficit, imports and exports, balance of international payments, etc. (See Figure 1.2).

French economist François Quesnay's *Tableau Économique* and British economist Thomas Robert Malthus's Theory of Population laid the foundation for macroeconomics. In 1933, Ragnar Anton Kittil Frisch, a Norwegian economist, first put forward the concept of "macroeconomics," which realized rapid development since the publication of John Maynard Keynes's *The General Theory of Employment, Interest, and Money* in 1936, who regarded national income and employment as the focus of his research and advocated the wide application of macroeconomics across the western world, which served well the policy of state intervention in the economic operation.

Macroeconomics has established itself as an independent branch of modern economics through years' development over mainly four stages. From the mid-17th century to the mid-19th century it was the early stage of macroeconomics or the era for classical macroeconomics; from the late-19th century to the 1930s, the foundation of modern macroeconomics was laid; from the 1930s to 1960s, modern macroeconomics was officially established; from 1960s onwards, macroeconomics has enjoyed further development and evolution.

The key points in modern macroeconomics are as follows. First, the acceleration principle, which suggests that to a certain extent, changes in investment are the causes and results of changes in national income, from which the theory of interaction between "accelerator" and "multiplier" is derived. Second, about price. Price, when discussed in macroeconomics, refers to the general price level. In the theory of determination of national income, the general price level depends mainly on the total demand, while changes in the total demand effect and are also greatly affected by monetary supply and demand. As changes in money supply and the general price level are closely associated, monetary analysis is crucial in macroeconomics. Third, the role of governments. Macroeconomics considers that governments should and in fact could adjust the aggregate

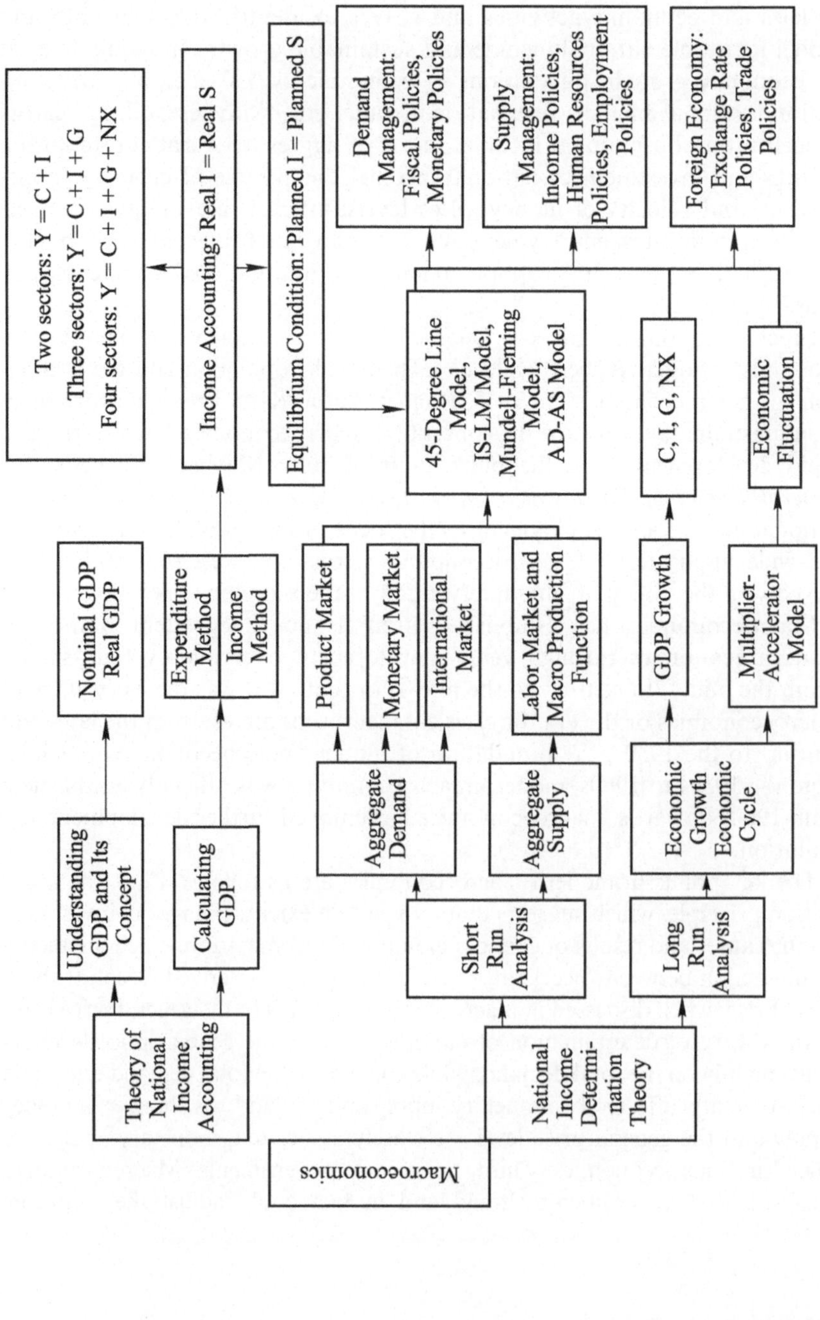

Figure 1.2 Theoretical system of macroeconomics.

demand through fiscal policies and monetary policies, etc., so as to ease cyclical economic fluctuations and attain full employment without causing inflation.

1.3 Effects and deficiencies of behavior analysis of principal market players in microeconomy and macroeconomy

The social science of economics usually regards the allocation and utilization of economic resources as a focus of research and assumes that all economic activities run under the conditions of resource scarcity in order to meet the insatiable needs and demands of human society. From this assumption come questions such as what to produce, how much to produce, how to produce, when to produce and for whom to produce. Based on all these derive the rules and mechanisms necessary for the orderly operation of economic activities, the right positioning and role of governments, the two major branches of economics, microeconomics and macroeconomics, with their respective functions and deficiencies.

With its focus on resource allocation under the condition of resource scarcity, microeconomics, which studies individual economic agents (families, enterprises and individual product markets), assumes resource utilization is not a problem. Through analysis at the micro level, microeconomics studies how to allocate resources, how economic variables change, the supply and demand of factors of production and products, changes and roles of prices in different markets (monopolistic ones or competitive ones), etc. In microeconomics, the driving force of economic behavior is to maximize profits or satisfaction at the lowest costs. In analyzing economic behavior at the micro level, there are empirical analysis and normative analysis, static analysis and dynamic analysis, partial equilibrium and general equilibrium, etc. Back from the assumption of "a rational economic man" to actual economic behavior, microeconomics constantly grows with the changes of the times and has yielded numerous outcomes.

However, microeconomics also has inherent defects. From Adam Smith's *The Wealth of Nations* (1776) to Alfred Marshall's *Principles of Economics* (1890) and John Richard Hicks's *Value and Capital* (1939), we can easily spot three fatal defects in microeconomics. First, it takes resource scarcity as the only prerequisite in resource allocation. However, with the development of human society, new resources are constantly generated, developed and capitalized on to meet the ever-increasing demands of human society. Therefore, nowadays, when working on resource allocation, we need to pay special attention to new resource generation. Second, it considers the industrial economy as the only form of market economy. But, as a matter of fact, with the progress of the society, new economic areas have been explored and exploited, such as urban economy and international economy (including space economy, marine economy and polar economy), which run differently compared with the industrial economy while playing a tangible role in the market economy. Third, it constrains the mechanism of resource allocation to enterprise behavior only, despite the fact that enterprises are only one type of market players. Apart from enterprises, there are other agents, who under market rules, also participate in resource allocation under the guidance of the "invisible hand" of the market.

For macroeconomics, it considers the utilization of resources and its optimal use. It assumes resource allocation is not a problem. With a nation in its entirety as the subject of research, macroeconomics analyzes the aggregate economy, how various economic variables change and how they interact. The key is about national income, as utilization of resources and its optimal use depend on the national income and its fluctuations. The basic driving force of macroeconomics lies in the pursuit of an optimal objective, so it strives to promote economic benefits through the introduction of economic policies and measures while taking into account factors such as social well-being, political considerations, culture, ethics and customs, with a view to cutting frictions and costs in economic activities, thus reducing uncertainties and enhancing the effectiveness of economic policies and measures. The theory of the determination of national income is the core of behavior analysis in macroeconomics, and through models, simple or complicated, abstract or specific, such as the income-expenditure model, IS-LM model and AD-AS model, fluctuations and adjustments of the national income of a nation can be illustrated. So by far, positive progress has also been registered in the development of macroeconomics.

However, macroeconomics also has deficiencies. From Keynes's *The General Theory of Employment, Interest, and Money* (1936) and neoclassical economist Paul Samuelson's idea on "mixed economy," to modern economics, it is not hard to identify three major limitations of macroeconomics. First, there is no clear-cut demarcation between a national government and a regional government. Actually, the economic policies of a nation are the aggregate of that of the national government and regional governments. A nation adjusts the primary distribution of wealth among firms through taxation and adjusts the primary distribution of wealth among regional governments by way of revenue sharing, which together constitute the national income. In economic operation, regional governments have functions at both the macro level and the micro level in order to perform governmental duties on behalf of the nation on one hand and grow the regional strength for industrial development, urban construction and social welfare on the other hand. The dual attributes of regional governments make them part of the market competition. Second, regional governments' services are mixed with their economic activities. The service function of regional governments is mainly manifested by their supply of public goods while their economic function is played out in the market competition. Traditionally, the role of the government was confined to "a night watchman" and "a small government," and government economic behavior was used to be interpreted from the administrative point of view, which not only stifles innovation in research on the role of the government in the economy but also makes it increasingly difficult to explain the dual functions regional governments increasingly tend to play in reality. Third, purely public goods and quasi-public goods are ill-defined. From the perspective of resource allocation, purely public goods are related to non-operative resources, which are provided by governments to guarantee basic needs and ensure fairness and justice. In contrast, quasi-public goods are associated with quasi-operative resources, whose operation right depends on regional budget, the maturity of the local market and social acceptability. In resource allocation in the reality, utilization of quasi-operative resources is the key in discussing the relations between the government and the market and behavior analysis in microeconomy, mezzoeconomy and macroeconomy.

In summary, first, the current microeconomics and macroeconomics both study resource allocation and utilization under conditions of resource scarcity. However, in the real life, in order to cater to the ever-increasing material and cultural demands of human society, we not only need to make good use of existing resources and optimize resource allocation but also need to consider how to constantly develop and capitalize on new resources. So it seems that breakthroughs are yet to be made in expanding the scope of research in economics. Second, mathematical tools should be applied in economic studies. After qualitative analysis, quantitative analysis is also necessary. Economic rules need to be revealed and proven with data and optimization of economic decision-making in real life also requires statistics. However, in reality, economic activities are after all practiced by humans, enterprises and governments whose minds, investment decisions, policy decision-making as well as changes are not subject to the manipulation of mathematical formulas. Therefore, we need to innovate the current research scope, system and methodology in economics. Third, economics is an applied science that affects the economic development of nations around the world. With rapid progress in high-tech, such as cloud computing, big data, the Internet of things, artificial intelligence and industrial chain, and the development of new forms of economy, like urban economy, international economy (space economy, marine economy and polar economy), the deficiencies of traditional market system and economic theories are all the more clear and breakthroughs are urgently called for.

1.4 Principal market players in mezzoeconomy and their behavior analysis

Mezzoeconomics is a branch of modern economics that mainly studies regional economic entities (regional governments), the institutional aspects of the economy that are not captured by micro or macroeconomics. Mezzoeconomics concentrates on the allocation of regional resources after they are generated.

Region is a relative term. For the whole world, a country is a region while for a country, a province or a state is a region. The principal market players in mezzoeconomy are regional governments. Regional governments' behavior is both "quasi-macro" (because of its role of "coordination" compared with a nation) and "quasi-micro" (with characters of enterprise behavior in pursuit of maximized interests). Thanks to the dual attributes or dual roles of regional governments, defects in traditional economic theories and traditional market theories can be rectified, and the modern economics and modern market system can be improved. According to the modern market system, not only enterprises, but regional governments are also a force in market competition. Besides, researches also show that, apart from microeconomics that studies individual economic agents and macroeconomics which focuses on a nation as a whole, there should also be mezzoeconomics, which looks at the role of regional governments in the modern economic framework.

The focus of mezzoeconomics is about the allocation of regional or urban resources on the basis of resource generation. Government administration over regional economic activities mainly serves for industrial development, urban construction and social welfare. Corresponding to economic development are industrial resources as operative resources, urban resources for urban construction, which are quasi-operative resources (with both public and commercial attributes), and public goods and public resources for social welfare, which are non-operative resources. Whether urban resources should be developed as public goods or as commercial goods is contingent upon government financial capabilities, market demand and social acceptability, and how scientific such resources are allocated determine how competitive the regional government is in the regional market.

Regarding the three types of resources and their relevant supporting policies in mezzoeconomics, three points need to be noted. First, putting in place relevant industrial, trade and human resources policies, operative resources (industrial resources) should be allocated based on the principle of "planning and guiding, support and coordination, supervision and management." With relevant supportive fiscal, financial and investment policies, quasi-operative resources (urban resources) shall be allocated based on the principles of "abiding by market rules, safeguarding economic order and participating in regional competition." Supported by relevant income, employment, and guarantee policies, allocation of non-operative resources (public resources) should follow the rule of "guaranteeing basic needs, ensuring fairness and justice, raising effectiveness and efficiency." Second, regional governments should exercise "foresighted leading" in resource allocation, which means to do what enterprises cannot do or cannot do well while allowing enterprises to play their own part. Government foresighted leading should follow market rules and rely on market forces to guide, adjust and forewarn the growth of the industrial economy, coordinate, participate in and maintain the order of urban economy and guarantee, safeguard and improve livelihood economy. Government foresighted leading requires governments to utilize policies on planning, investment, consumption, pricing, taxation, interest rates, exchange rates, legislation, etc, as well as conceptual, technological, organizational and institutional innovation to effectively push forward structural reforms on the supply side or the demand side with a view to forming a leading edge in economic growth and facilitating scientific and sustainable development of the regional economy. Third, conceptual innovation plays a substantial role in promoting allocation of regional resources in the factor-driven stage; organizational innovation can have a multiplier effect on the allocation of regional resources in the investment-driven stage; institutional and technological innovation plays a decisive role in allocating regional resources in the innovation-driven stage while comprehensive innovations in all fronts throughout a whole business cycle shall drive forward scientific and sustainable resource allocation in all stages of regional economic development.

The core of mezzoeconomic research is about regional government competition, including in projects, industrial chains, imports and exports, infrastructure investment, talents, science and technology, fiscal and financial support, policy system efficiency, environment system efficiency and management system efficiency.

Regarding research on mezzoeconomics, regional governments are its subject of research; efficient growth is the desired goal of regional governments; improving total-factor productivity is the main approach of regional government competition; the supply-side structural reform is the basic orientation of government reform while optimizing the allocation of regional resources through district resource planning (DRP) for sustainable growth of regional economy is the cutting edge of regional governments in competition. Mezzoeconomic research focuses on major economic variables affecting regional government competition, the revenue and expenditure of regional governments. Major theories in this field include the Resource Generation Theory, the Dual Attributes Theory of Governments, the Regional Government Competition Theory, the Theory of Resource Allocation in Four Development Stages, the GFL, the New Economic Engine Theory, the DEMC as well as the "Double Strong Forms" Theory of a mature market economy (see Figure 1.3).

Mezzoeconomics has a relatively short history of research and development. It was initially put forward by Dr. Hans-Rudolf Peters, a German professor of national economics in the mid-1970s. In the mid-1980s, Chinese scholar Mr. Shenzhi Wang published *Mezzoeconomics* (Shanghai People's Press, 1988) which elaborated upon Peters' idea and further expounded on the research scope of mezzoeconomics as sector economy, regional economy and collective economy. In 2011, the author published *Foresighted Leading: Theoretical Thinking and Practice of China's Regional Economic Development*, which was published by the German publishing company Springer in English two years later. In 2013, the author co-published with Jianwei Qiu *Government Foresighted Leading: Theory and Practice of the World's Regional Economic Development*, whose English edition was published by the British publisher Routledge in 2017. In 2015, co-authored with Wenjing Gu, the author's *Mezzoeconomics: Innovations and Developments in Theoretical Configuration of Economics* came out and was published in English by American Academic Press in 2018. In 2017, again co-written with Wenjing Gu, my *Regional Government Competition* came off the press and made its English publication by Routledge in 2019. These

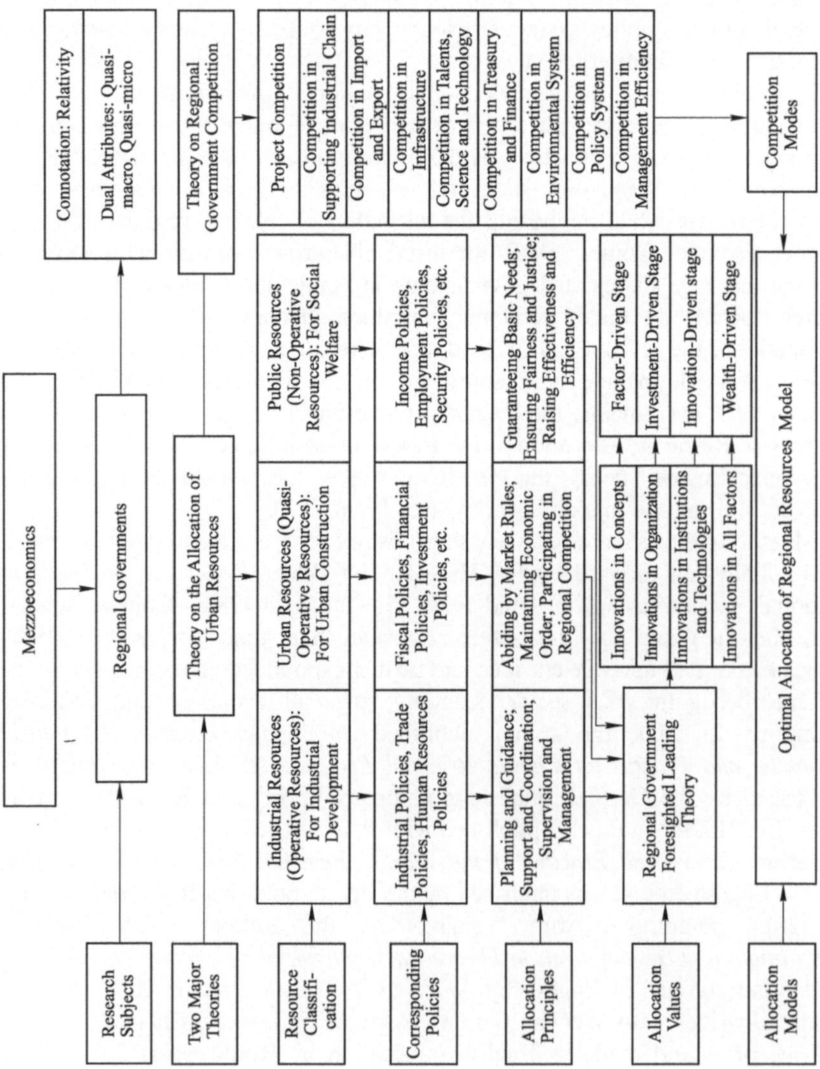

Figure 1.3 Theoretical system of mezzoeconomics.

publications have set up the theoretical framework of mezzoeconomics and opened up a broad space for further growth by elaborating on the GFL, the Dual Attributes Theory of Governments, the DEMC, and the "Double Strong Forms" Theory of a mature market economy. These mezzoeconomic theories have charted the course for global economic development and the establishment of a new global economic governance system.

2 Overview of economic behavior of regional governments

2.1 Principal market players in microeconomy, mezzoeconomy and macroeconomy and their behavior analysis in diagrams

From the analysis in Chapter 1, we know that microeconomics studies the economic behavior and its results of individual agents (producers, consumers and firms). The fundamental issue in microeconomics is about how to allocate resources under conditions of resource scarcity with its focus on price determination mechanism; its major theories include those on equilibrium price, consumer choice, price determination of production factors, perfectly competitive market and imperfectly competitive market, general equilibrium, the game theory and market failure. Mezzoeconomics concentrates on economic behavior and the results of regional agents (regional governments); its fundamental issue is about resource allocation on the basis of resource generation with the focus on major economic variables affecting regional competition, namely the revenue and expenditure of regional governments; major theories in this field include the Resource Generation Theory, the Dual Attributes Theory of Governments, the Regional Government Competition Theory, the Theory of Resource Allocation in Four Development Stages, the Government Foresighted Leading Theory (GFL), the New Economic Engine Theory, the Dual-Entity of Market Competition Theory (DEMC) as well as the "Double Strong Forms" Theory of a mature market economy. Macroeconomics studies economic behavior and relevant results of a national or regional economy as a whole. It considers the utilization of national resources and their optimal use with a focus on the mechanism of determination of national income. Its dominant theories include theories of national income accounting and determination of national income, which can be further categorized as theories on employment, inflation, economic cycles and economic growth.

The modern market system dominated by microeconomy, mezzoeconomy and macroeconomy can be illustrated as follows in Figure 2.1.

From Figure 2.1, we can grasp the following points.

First, we should have a holistic view over "the modern market system." Horizontally, it includes industrial economy, urban economy and international

DOI: 10.4324/9781003244837-2

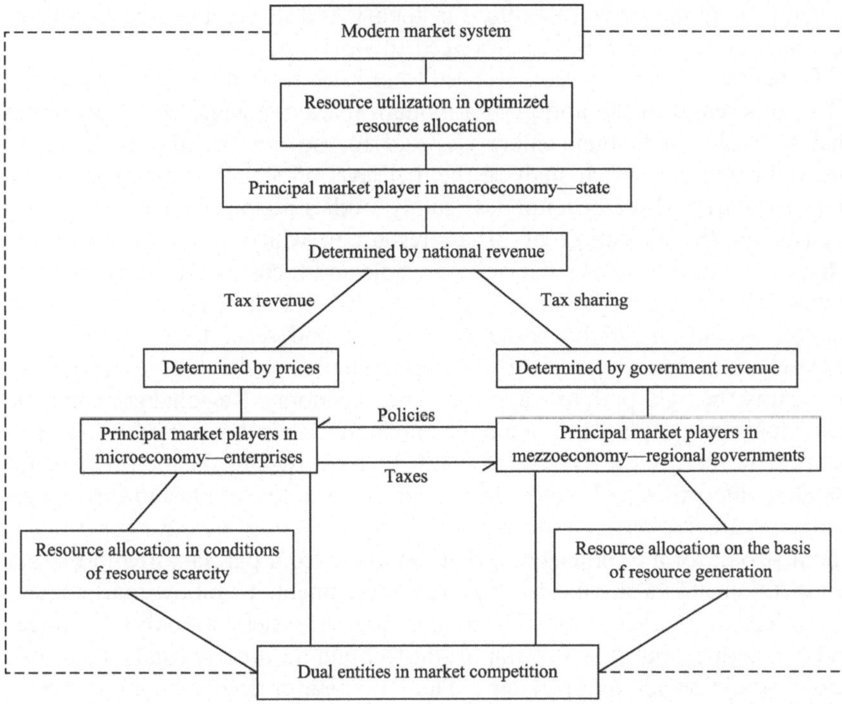

Figure 2.1 Modern market system dominated by microeconomy, mezzoeconomy and macroeconomy.

economy (such as space economy, marine economy, polar economy, earth exploration economy), while vertically, it consists of six pillars, including systems of market factor, market organization, market legal framework, market supervision, market environment as well as market infrastructure. "Large and comprehensive," the modern market system lacks clear and detailed theoretical division, which can lead to shortsightedness and ambiguity.

Second, we should bear in mind that there are dual entities in the modern market system. The growth of the modern market is not only fueled by competition among enterprises at the micro level but also by competition of regional governments at the mezzo level. Together, they are two engines driving forward modern economic development.

At last, it should be noted that a mature market economy consists of "a strong form of effective government" and "a strong form of efficient market." For "an effective government," there are three forms, "the weak form," "the semi-strong form" and "the strong form" and so does the efficient market. Together, they can result in nine combinations, among which "a strong form of effective government" and "a strong form of efficient market" is the best or the optimal mode, which shall be a target nations around the globe strive to explore in theory and in practice and also a research subject modern economics need to work on.

To realize the above target, we need to proceed from the following aspects. First, to strengthen the notion of a modern market system. Microeconomics mainly studies individual enterprises and focuses on the allocation of industrial resources, which shall be the first level of economic activities in the modern market. Mezzoeconomics mainly studies regional governments and focuses on the allocation of urban resources, which is the second level. Macroeconomics studies a nation as a whole and focuses on the allocation of industrial, urban and public resources, which is the third level. The modern market system should be based on the first and second levels while formulating and improving rules for market regulation at the third level. Second, to identify the right path to a mature market economy. Regional governments have dual roles to play, to pursue the maximum interests on one hand and to coordinate the overall interests beyond the local regions on the other hand. Besides, enterprises and regional governments are dual entities in the market and a mature market economy features a strong form of effective government and a strong form of efficient market. So apart from participating in market competition, it is also vital for regional governments to follow market rules and safeguard market orders. The modern market system not only encourages full competition but it is also important to build an orderly legal framework and a sound social credit system. Third, to reinforce coordination of economic activities at the micro-, mezzo- and macro levels. From factor-driven to investment-driven, to innovation-driven and wealth-driven, the key to a nation's economy resides in a sound distribution mechanism of the national wealth while allowing the market to play a decisive role in resource allocation and the government to play a better role.

When analyzing the national income mechanism as illustrated in Figure 2.1, let's assume the non-tax revenue of a nation is zero. Then regional governments' taxation will be the only source of national revenue. Because of tax sharing, regional governments will share their taxes from enterprises and individuals with the national government at a certain proportion while keeping the rest for their own expenditure. We can put the revenues of regional governments and the national government in a formula, as follows:

$$N = \delta \times T$$

In this formula, N represents the total financial revenues of the national government. δ stands for the proportion of tax sharing, which is a fraction between zero to one and the larger it is, the more taxes to be shared with the national government. T is the total taxes levied from enterprises and individuals.

From this formula, we can find two rules.

First, after δ is fixed according to laws and regulations of the national government and regional governments, N depends on T, which means the national

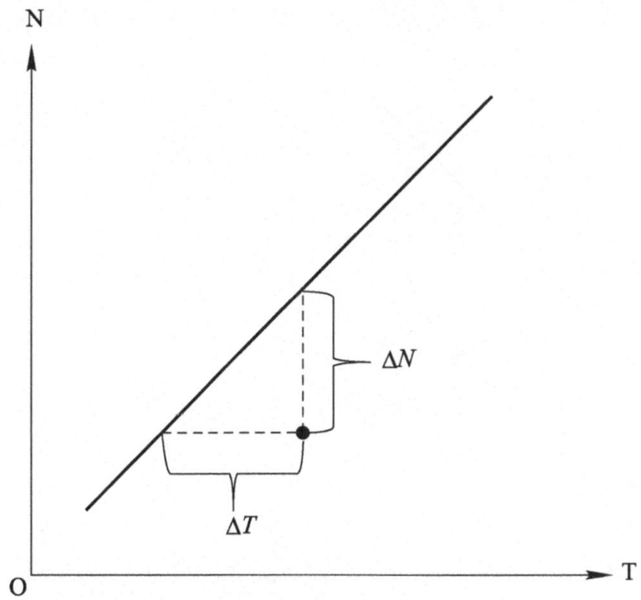

$$\delta = \frac{\Delta N}{\Delta T}$$

Figure 2.2 Relationship chart of *N* and *T*.

government has to encourage enterprise production and consumer consumption, expand tax base or increase tax rates to ensure high government revenues (Figure 2.2).

Second, when the national economy runs stable at the micro level and taxes levied from enterprises and individuals remain unchanged, *N* depends on δ. So to gain a high government revenue, δ will have to rise (Figure 2.3).

In summary, national governments, regional governments and enterprises and individuals are all important market players in economic activities at the micro-, mezzo- and macro levels. With the tax system, items of taxation and tax rates provided by the nation, enterprises and individuals pay taxes to regional governments, part of which goes to the national government through tax sharing. At the macro level, a nation's government revenue depends on both regional governments at the mezzo level and enterprises and individuals at the micro level. At the mezzo level, regional governments regulate local economy as an agent of the nation while also call for support of the nation for regional interests. At the micro level, taxes of enterprises and individuals are sources of income of both the national government and regional governments. So it is clear that in world economic development, activities at the micro-, mezzo- and macro level are closely related and nations should promote coordination among them.

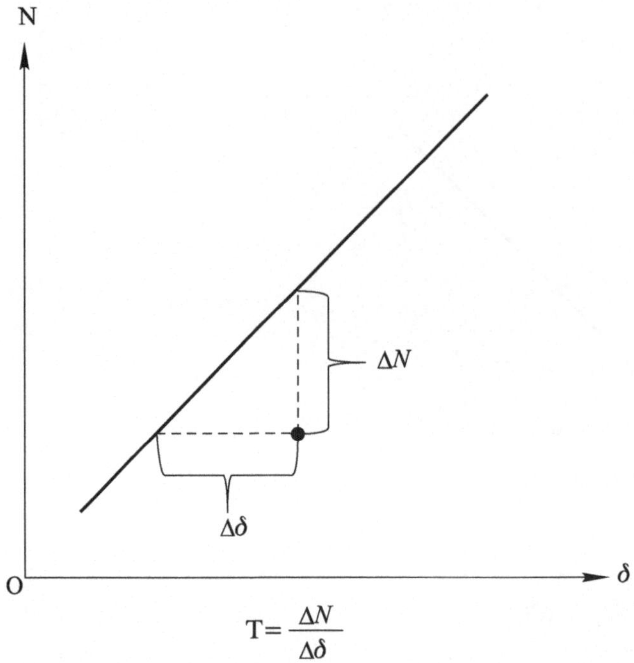

Figure 2.3 Relationship chart of N and δ.

2.2 Overview of economic behavior of regional governments

After the above analysis, we can move on to the relation of the government and the market, which is a key topic in economics that never ceases to be discussed, explored and argued.

2.2.1 Theoretical exploration on the relation of the government and the market

By the end of the 15th century, mercantilism that represented the interest of commercial capital, argued that the government should encourage exports and restrict imports through tariffs and non-tariff approaches so as to earn gold and sliver from other nations to strengthen its own wealth. In 1776, when *The Wealth of Nations* was published, Adam Smith advocated in his book the role of "an invisible hand" of the free market while the government should be "a night watchman" in order to protect every member of the society from injustice or exploitation. In *A Treatise on Political Economy* (1803), Jean-Baptiste Say, the best-known expositor of Adam Smith's views on free economy, put forward the far-reaching Say's law, which stated that the production of goods created its own demand and refuted the notion that "general overproduction" could exist.

By the mid-19th century when mechanized industry dominated in the UK, France and the USA, Marxism economics, inheriting and further improving the labor theory of value of Adam Smith, distinguished itself. It pointed out the contradiction between the unlimited production and the relatively reduced purchasing power of the working people as well as the contradiction between an organized and planned social organization in the individual factory and social anarchy in production as a whole, and held that such contradictions would lead to cyclical economic crisis because of overproduction, and so capitalist private ownership over means of production shall shift towards social ownership through reforms, so as to build a center of the society which can allocate resources to each production department at a certain proportion according to plans as demanded by socialized mass production. Alfred Marshall's *Principles of Economics* (1890) seemed to be a response to Marx's approach. Marshall believed free economy to be a more farsighted, cautious and liberal choice which represented the features of firms and industries at the age of mass production. Pareto Efficiency or Pareto Optimality, named after the Italian economist and political scientist Vilfredo Pareto (1848–1923), who succeeded his mentor, Leon Walras, as chair of economics at the University of Lausanne in 1893, gave a plain and classic depiction over the process of resource allocation and highlighted the decisive and irreplaceable role the market could play in resource allocation.[1]

Entering into the 20th century, economics started to pay more and more attention to market failure and the role of the government in economic activities. Arthur Cecil Pigou proved in *The Economics of Welfare* (1920) the Pareto Optimality of production and exchange while also revealed that the market could not realize the Pareto Optimality of social wealth distribution and held that fair redistribution of national income among all social members must rely on the government. During the Great Depression from 1929 to 1933, John Maynard Keynes proposed government intervention and advocated that the government should utilize financial and monetary policies to improve the marginal propensity to consume and the marginal efficiency of capital, increase consumers' consumption demands and firms' investment demands to stimulate economic growth and realize full employment. In 1954, Paul Samuelson put forward the concept of public goods, which he called "collective consumption goods," and believed it was the government's duty to serve public goods in the market because they were non-excludable and non-rival and the market could not possibly allocate resources for production of public goods. Later, economists of neoclassical synthesis represented by Samuelson put forward "mixed economy," which consisted of private sectors that could play a dominant role in the market and public sectors under the administration of the government. According to "mixed economy," the role of the market mechanism lies in rational allocation and utilization of resources to ensure economic efficiency at the micro level while the role of the government is to prevent and cope with economic recession and regulate economic operation at the macro level. According to economists represented by Alvin Hansen (1887–1975), an

American economist at Harvard, macroeconomic policies reverse to economic performance shall be adopted, which means to introduce expansionary economic policies during economic recession and tighten economic policies during economic expansion in order to effectively stabilize social demand, curb inflation and eliminate unemployment. Cambridge Keynesians, particularly Joan Robinson (1903–1983) and Nicholas Kaldor (1908–1986), while upholding Keynes' principle of effective demand, advocated cutting large government expenditure, strictly restricting imports and giving a full play to the role of taxation in narrowing income inequality. Meanwhile, neoliberalism economists, such as neoliberal London School economists represented by Friedrich August von Hayek (1899–1992), Walter Eucken (1891–1950), founder of the Freiburg School of Ordoliberalism, Milton Friedman (1912–2006), a leading proponent of monetarism, and Robert E. Lucas, Jr. (1937-), a Nobel laureate for his research on rational expectations, upheld for a complete and full role of the market mechanism and opposed government intervention into the economy. By the 1970s, with the emergence of supply-side economics in the USA, the role of Say's law was reaffirmed and it was a popular view that the government should refrain from stimulating demand. Instead, it should regulate supply, give a full play to the role of the market mechanism so that supply and demand of factors of production could reach an equilibrium and find an effective application.[2]

The above views and arguments regarding the relationship between the government and the market shows several features. First, economists in and prior to the 19th century tended to take the market as the only force in resource allocation and considered the government a guardian of free competition of the market while a bystander in the economy. Second, since the 20th century, doubts were raised regarding whether the market should be the sole force in resource allocation and discussions on the role of the government in conditions of market failure and in adopting relevant measures began. Third, the theoretical development of economics far lagged behind economic realities, and problems seen in economic operation were not all results of "market failure" or "government failure," which shows the deficiencies of traditional economic theories and traditional market theories, and indicates much space of growth for modern economic theories and modern market theories. This is where we need to make further explorations.

2.2.2 Case study of the USA

In the case of the USA, its relation between the government and the market has also undergone a long process of evolution. Now we uphold the view that the market should play a decisive role in resource allocation while the government a better role in leading, regulating and supervising economic development. However, such a consensus is not reached in one stroke.

Take the USA as an example. In March 1929, Herbert Clark Hoover took office as the 31st President of the USA. A staunch proponent of Alfred

Marshall's view on free market economic system, he insisted that legislative or administrative measures could not be adopted to deal with the economic depression and opposed government intervention in the economy. By March 1933, when Franklin D. Roosevelt replaced Hoover as the 32nd American President, there was a considerable shift in economic policies in the country. Roosevelt acted swiftly with his "New Deal," rapidly curbed banking crisis, effectively brought agriculture and industry back to life, provided jobs for labor instead of a dole, which drove forward government relief, employment and investment at the same time. The Social Security Act passed under the Roosevelt Administration also laid the foundation for America's modern social security scheme. The New Deal was pioneering in allowing the government to implement a proactive fiscal policy across the board to tackle with an economic crisis, which transformed the market economic system from a laissez-faire style to be led, regulated and supervised by the government.

The USA invited major western countries to the United Nations Monetary and Financial Conference in July 1944 at the Mount Washington Hotel in Bretton Woods, New Hampshire, where delegates from 44 nations gathered and created a new international monetary system known as the Bretton Woods system. Since then, the USA began to intervene and regulate the world economic development. Stagnation in the 1970s in the USA led to high unemployment, high inflation and low economic growth in the country. To cope with the economic instability, the Nixon Administration, the Ford Administration and the Carter Administration took a series of fiscal and financial policies and measures to stimulate economic growth, cut unemployment and contain inflation. By 1981 after Ronald Reagan was elected the 40th American President, he adopted measures to control money supply, lower individual income taxes, reduce the expenditure of social welfare, cut corporate income taxes, lift off or loosen regulations on enterprises once he took office. Then, the Reagan Administration introduced programs and policies to boost investment in science and technology, government expenditure and support industrial development to stimulate economic expansion. In 1985, President Reagan proposed the Strategic Defense Initiative (SDI), or "Star Wars," a strategic defensive system against potential nuclear attacks, another attempt to further the country's exploration and competition in space economy after John Kennedy's "decision to go to the moon" in 1961. In 1993, under the Clinton Administration, the American government fully capitalized on venture capital to build innovation parks, support start-up financing, grow the high-tech sector represented by information technology and information infrastructure based on information highway in the USA and the world at large.

During the Bush and Obama Administration, with the emergence of the sub-prime mortgage crisis in 2007 and 2008, the USA introduced a string of measures. First, the Federal Reserve adopted both the traditional radical monetary policy and unconventional currency policy, which played a key role in coping with the crisis and stabilizing the financial market through market approaches. Second, when the monetary policy of the Federal

Reserve failed to ease the widely influencing and increasingly serious crisis, the Bush Administration timely introduced government intervention measures. Created and run by the Treasury, the Troubled Asset Relief Program (TARP) was implemented under the funding of the government in aid of major financial institutions and some large enterprises. Third, after Barack Obama took office, he took a string of steps to stabilize the financial market, enhance supervision and regulation, rapidly cut taxes in numerous areas, increase government spending and deficits to boost economic growth, along with the rescue programs adopted by the Bush Administration. Fourth, in order to tackle the financial crisis, safeguard financial stability and reinvigorate the economy, both houses of Congress managed to build a sound legal environment through timely legislation. Fifth, under the Bush and Obama Administration, Congress passed a series of acts such as Emergency Economic Stabilization Act of 2008 (EESA), Economic Development Revitalization Act of 2008, Economic Development Revitalization Act of 2009, American Recovery and Reinvestment Act of 2009 (Recovery Act), as well as one of the most important economic reform and regulatory acts since the Great Depression in 1929, the Dodd-Frank Wall Street Reform and Consumer Protection Act (the Dodd-Frank Act), with a view to maintaining the stability of the financial market and driving forward economic growth[3].

Back to the topic of the relation between the government and the market in the USA, we can find the following features according to its development course. First, prior to 1933, laissez-faire dominated the American economic system. Second, after 1933, the American economic regime transformed from laissez-faire to a new system led, regulated and supervised by the government. Third, the Bretton Woods conference in July 1944 opened up the process of the American government's intervention into and regulation of the world economy. Fourth, the "moon shot" project of the Kennedy Administration in 1961 and the "Star Wars" initiative of the Reagan Administration in 1985 set the USA on the course to space exploration and space race. Fifth, in dealing with the ever-changing economic crisis, the American government initiated comprehensive government intervention by actively adopting currency, financial and supervisory policies, rolling out programs in science and technology investment, government procurement, and economic revitalization, and building an increasingly complete legal system to ensure sustainable growth of the national economy.

2.2.3 Case study of China

How to foster a proper relation between the government and the market is also a question faced in the entire process of China's reform and opening up. In the 1950s, China featured a highly centralized planned economy with the government as the sole force in resource allocation. In 1978, China initiated economic reform. From rural areas to cities, a series of programs rolled out, such as the Household Responsibility System in a small village called Xiaogangcun in Anhui Province, Central China, pilot programs to increase the autonomy of enterprises in companies such as Chongqing Iron and Steel Company in Sichuan Province, the tax reform program of levying taxes on enterprises' profits and allowing them to retain the balance for reinvestment and distribution to workers as bonuses rather than remitting all of their profits to the state as was normally done for state-owned enterprises (SOEs), as well as the contract management system of industrial companies of state ownership. Since the 1980s, the Chinese economy has accelerated its pace to marketization. Enterprises were allowed higher autonomy and could undertake industrial production from developed and newly industrialized countries and regions through "three processing and one compensation" (i.e. processing with customer-supplied materials, assembling customer-supplied parts, processing in accordance with customer-supplied samples and compensation trade) to attract foreign investment. Besides, with the emergence and expansion of joint-stock companies, Shanghai Stock Exchange was founded in December 19, 1990 and Shenzhen Stock Exchange also started operation since July 3, 1991. In 1992, regulations such as "Pilot Measures for Joint Stock Enterprises" and "Opinions on Regulations of Limited Liability Companies" were formulated. Since then, China's modern enterprise scheme was officially established, the ownership and management of SOEs as well as the role of the government and the market in resource allocation were clarified. As the consumer market, the labor market and the capital market grew mature, incentives for economic development at the micro level were fully activated in rural and urban areas.

Competitive enterprises and conglomerates grew to be the dominant players in market competition while regional governments also started to display their presence in the market. As the market played a fundamental and decisive role in resource allocation and was propelled by the national government, regional governments and enterprises, the Chinese economy shifted to a fast track. By the 1980s, the labor-intensive textile and other light industries enjoyed rapid growth. By the 1990s, the capital-intensive basic industries such as raw materials and energy as well as infrastructure construction, including transportation, municipal engineering and water conservation boomed. During the first decade of the 21st century, the capital-intensive and technology-intensive equipment manufacturing industry flourished and the ensuing decade saw the emergence and takeoff of strategic emerging industries. When taking an overall view over the entire process of China's economic reform, we can see that its core is to cultivate a proper relation between the government and the market so that the market can play a decisive role in resource allocation while the government can also play a sound role.[4]

From China's practice in economic reform, we have come to realize several key points. First, there are dual entities in market competition, enterprises and regional governments, which can be seen quite often in reality. Second, the government has its part to play in three economic areas: industrial development, urban construction and social welfare. Third, the government has three roles to play in economic development. It is a participant in the market with capital to invest in joint-stock companies and become shareholders, involve in market competition and regulate the national welfare and people's livelihood. It is a regulator that regulates the macroeconomy with financial, monetary and legal policies and instruments. Besides, it is also a supervisor who supervises the activities of various enterprises in order to safeguard the market order. Fourth, a mature market economy consists of a strong form of effective government and a strong form of market efficiency. An effective government not only concretely guarantees people's well-being to ensure social harmony and stability and improve the economic environment but can also lead, support and supervise the industrial economy, safeguard openness, fairness and equity of the market, effectively increase overall production efficiency of the whole society, directly participate in and regulate the urban economy to drive forward urban construction and comprehensive and sustainable development of the economy and the society. Market efficiency indicates the proper operation of basic functions of the market as well as an orderly and sound market structure and environment. With an effective government, market rules can be respected, economic order can be maintained and a level playing field can be built while with market efficiency, there can be full competition, an orderly legal and supervision framework and a sound social credit system. The combination of an effective government and market efficiency shall be and will be the future direction of a mature market economy.

2.2.4 Overview of economic behavior of regional governments

From the above analysis, we can see the theoretical evolution and its deficiencies regarding the relationship between the government and the market in economics and cases of the USA and China. Then, how can we draw up a diagram to illustrate the economic behavior of regional governments?

As said previously, a region is a relative term. For the world, a country is a region while for a country, a city is also a region. So hereby, we specifically focus on regional governments within a country as the center of our discussion. So an overview of the economic behavior of regional governments can be shown as follows in (Figure 2.4 and Figure 2.5).

Three types of regional resources → The role of the government → Three kinds of policies → Principles for adopting relevant policies → Policy instruments → Behavior subjects → Market competition → Code of conduct in the market → Features of resource allocation in different stages → New economic engines

Figure 2.4 Overview of economic behavior of regional governments.

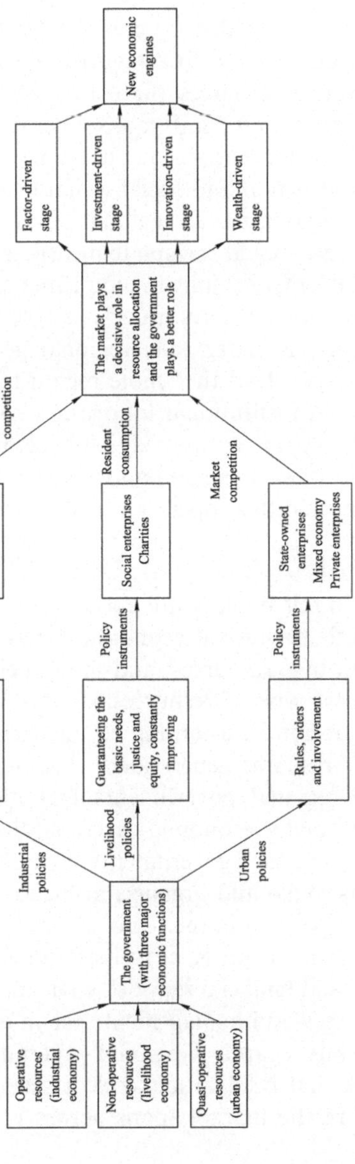

Figure 2.5 Detailed overview of economic behavior of regional governments.

So we can see the economic behavior of regional governments penetrate through all fronts and the entire process of economic operation. Especially in modern society, solutions to every economic problem could not be possible without researches on the role of regional governments. So behavior analysis over regional governments, which is to interpret, analyze and regulate the economic role of regional governments from the perspective of economics, is crucial.

2.3 Methodology and others

Regional governments are not an abstract concept, but concrete players in the market. Regional governments need to categorize the three types of regional resources, namely operative resources (industrial economy), non-operative resources (livelihood economy) and quasi-operative resources (urban economy), and based on the three economic functions in supporting industrial development, urban construction and social welfare, adopt industrial, urban and livelihood policies catering to the regional development needs. On this basis, regional governments should formulate measures, utilize relevant tools, support or build relevant organizations for implementing the policies. Based on the principle that the market plays a decisive role in resource allocation and the government plays a better role, regional governments should, in different development stages, lead the whole region for conceptual, technological, organizational and institutional innovation so as to boost regional sustainable growth and cultivate cutting edges of regional development. Key economic behavior, priorities of policies and relevant implementation principles, policy instruments and their operation and effects are not just subjects of research in economics, but also issues worth the attention of nations around the world in practice.

The core of research in this book is still about optimal resource allocation. However, compared with traditional economic views that divide resources into two groups—operative resources and non-operative resources—this book puts forward a new type of resources, quasi-operative resources and areas of "resource generation." According to analysis over quasi-operative resources and areas of "resource generation," this book concludes that the economic behavior of regional governments is both "quasi-macro" and "quasi-micro." Based on major economic variables, that is, government revenues and expenditures, regional governments introduce economic policies, select policy instruments, build and organize agencies to implement policies, and involve in direct competition in the regional market in terms of projects, industrial chains, imports and exports, as well as indirect competition such as in talents support, fiscal and financial support, environment system efficiency, and policy system efficiency and management system efficiency.

Before we go into details regarding regional governments' participation in market competition, we first need to make clear several points. First, governments' competition in the market spans across utilization of operative resources, non-operative resources and quasi-operative resources. Among them, quasi-operative resources are used for investment and construction of urban infrastructure as well as for developing smart cities, thus are the key to governments' competition. Second, governments' participation in the regional economic competition will overthrow the theory that enterprises are the sole forces in market competition. Because actually there are dual entities, both enterprises and regional governments, in industrial development, urban construction as well as people's livelihood, which play their due roles respectively. At last, governments are not only participating in economic competition themselves but they are also engaged in competition for industrial and urban projects through SOEs and as stockholders of enterprises (which will be further elaborated in this book). So government competition can make a difference in policymaking and implementation as well as affecting the market through SOEs. So if we leave individual households and international factors out of the picture, the national economy of a country is contingent on the economic activities of enterprises, regional governments and the national government.

Economic behavior and economic activities of regional governments are the focus of our research, which not only involves microeconomics and macroeconomics, but also the development of "operative resources," which belongs to the research field of industrial economics, the development of "non-operative resources," which falls into public economics and welfare economics, as well as the development of "quasi-operative resources," which concerns public finance and urban economics. Together, they constitute several major aspects of research on the economic behavior of regional governments. First, the three economic functions of regional governments on industrial development, urban construction and social welfare. Second, major economic variables of regional governments, namely government revenues and expenditures. Third, major influencing factors to government incomes and expenditures, or the "9-in-3" competition to be specific. Fourth, the rationality and necessity of regional governments' economic policies, policy instruments, policy coordination and effects in different development stages. Fifth, rules of economic behavior and economic activities of regional governments.

From a different perspective, we can discuss government economic behavior from the point of view of what should be done and what the governments have actually done. In terms of what governments have actually done, we need to first describe things as they actually are by explaining what government economic behavior is, which means we illustrate the three major economic functions of regional governments and make it clear regarding government revenues and expenditures, and how they affect the regional economy, the society and the regional governments. Then, we need to explain the process of government competition in the market and how it makes a difference to the regional economy, the society and the regional governments themselves. Besides, it is also important to illustrate the role of relevant economic policies and policy instruments and the possible development direction of economic behavior of regional governments. Such empirical analysis is complementary to normative analysis, which can be helpful to answer the question of what government economic behavior should be like. This means from the perspective of what should be done, we will, based on established rules and theories, analyze and appraise whether the existing government economic activities are rational and how to make adjustment if they are not.

So we can see in analyzing government economic behavior, we pay equal emphasis on empirical analysis and normative analysis. On one hand, in empirical analysis, certain established rules or theories are required to verify the analysis results while on the other hand, in normative analysis, empirical studies are necessary to testify the relevance of certain economic behavior and rules or theories. So in this book, empirical analysis and normative analysis are equally important and both will be adopted in analyzing government economic behavior.

Notes

1 Zhang, S. (Ed.). (2015). *Public economics*. Beijing: China Renmin University Press, pp.1–13; Chen, Y. (2018). *National finance*, Beijing: Peking University Press, pp.165–189.
2 See note 1 above.
3 See note 1 above.
4 See note 1 above.

3 Resource generation and categorization of three types of resources

3.1 What could the third book of Adam Smith be about?

3.1.1 Profile of Adam Smith

Adam Smith (1723–1790), a renowned Scottish social philosopher and political economist, is a towering figure in classical political economics.

Adam Smith's father was a comptroller of customs at Kirkcaldy, a small but thriving fishing village near Edinburgh, and his mother was the daughter of a substantial landowner. At the age of 14, in 1737, Smith entered the University of Glasgow, already remarkable as a center of what was to become known as the Scottish Enlightenment. There was a famous professor of moral philosophy called Francis Hutcheson, from whose economic and philosophical views Smith was profoundly influenced.

Graduating in 1740 from the University of Glasgow, Smith won a scholarship at Oxford. His years there were spent largely in self-education, from which Smith obtained a firm grasp of both classical and contemporary philosophy. In 1751, at the age of 28, he was appointed professor of logic at Glasgow.

In 1752, he transferred to the more remunerative professorship of moral philosophy, a subject that embraced the related fields of natural theology, ethics, jurisprudence and political economy. In 1759, Smith published his first work, *The Theory of Moral Sentiments*, which laid the psychological foundation on which *An Inquiry into the Nature and Causes of the Wealth of Nations* was later to be built.

In 1776, aged 53, Smith completed the famous *An Inquiry into the Nature and Causes of the Wealth of Nations*, which is still very influential today. This book looks deeply into market behavior and the complex political-economic system, which won Adam Smith a far-reaching reputation in the history of economic thought and his luster remained even to this day.

Upon completing this masterpiece, Smith spent more than over a decade exploring, thinking and investigating in an attempt to write a third book on jurisprudence and government. In 1790, he died at the age of 67, full of honors and recognition.

DOI: 10.4324/9781003244837-3

It was the custom of his time to destroy rather than to preserve the private files of illustrious men, with the unhappy result that much of Smith's unfinished work, as well as his personal papers, was destroyed, which leaves his unfinished third book and its core ideas much space of imagination for later generations.

According to *The Life of Adam Smith* by Ian Simpson Ross, Adam Smith was an absent-minded man who paid little attention to things other than his scholarly learning. For instance, when he was at a ball, he failed to recognize his dance partner. One morning, he took a piece of bread and butter, which, after he had rolled round and round, he put into the teapot and poured the water upon it; after some time he poured it into a cup and tasted it, he said it was the worst tea he had ever met with. An anecdote of his was that one Sunday morning, he walked 15 miles from Kirkcaldy in a fit of abstraction in his dressing gown. When he was appointed commissioner both of customs and of salt duties for Scotland, there was a tale that one day Smith was so mesmerized by the doorkeeper's salute that he returned it compulsively with his cane, to the servant's amazement. Besides, he had a stumbling manner of speech, until he warmed to his subject.

During Adam Smith's lifetime in the 18th century, the UK was undergoing a transition from the workshop handicraft industry to mechanical production. In the early-18th century, France and Germany remained at the backward feudal stage dominated by household handicraft workshops while the UK had entered into the capitalist stage where handicraft workshops had flourished in cities across the nation. Under capitalism, bunches of workers performed each of their own duties with simple tools according to the division of labor under the directive of a capitalist, which continued until 1760 when the Industrial Revolution began and machine manufacturing started to dominate in industrial production. At that time, the UK was not only the center of world trade but was also a leading industrialized country around the globe.

From the above passage, we can see that, first, Adam Smith lived in an age of transformation, thanks to the Industrial Revolution, when industrialization just emerged while urbanization was far within reach. Second, as the son of a customs comptroller and the daughter of a rich landowner, he grew up in a family with substantial wealth and social status. Hence, as the Industrial Revolution rolled out, Adam Smith was not eager in the pursuit of wealth, but was instead immersed in his scholarly learning and research without worrying about his livelihood. Third, for his three books, he committed to each book over a dozen years of endeavor. A university professor at the age of only 28, he completed his first book *The Theory of Moral Sentiments* at the age of 36, as an investigation of social behavior and moral sentiments of people. Subsequently, Adam Smith turned to research on commodity pricing, supply and demand, competition, market and enterprise behavior while hanging out with the business circle in London. Seventeen years later, aged 53, he completed his masterpiece *An*

Inquiry into the Nature and Causes of the Wealth of Nations. Not content with the fame and fortune brought upon him by *The Wealth of Nations*, Adam Smith started his profession in customs, just as his father did, which was acknowledged then as the true source of wealth, and more importantly where imports and exports among nations could be easily observed. According to the timeline, it can be speculated that after about 14 years of service in customs, during which time he personally performed government's duties, functions, powers, laws and regulations, Smith could have started his third book on law and government at the age of 67. Regrettably, the third book never came out. But no one can doubt that Adam Smith spent his lifetime learning, thinking, analyzing and revealing the attributes of the behavior of individuals, enterprises and states, as well as the principles and laws of the market and economy.

3.1.2 Analysis over Adam Smith's third book

Adam Smith's academic thoughts were not only subject to the feature of the times of booming industrial growth, but were also the results of the influence of theories of the physiocratic school, especially that of François Quesnay and Anne Robert Jacques Turgot, and David Hume's trade and monetary theories, and in particular, the philosophy of his mentor at the University of Glasgow, Francis Hutcheson. The philosophy proposed by Francis Hutcheson that "people could discover what is ethically good by discovering the actions that serve the good of humanity," had profoundly shaped Adam Smith's research on (benevolent) the behavior of individuals in society, (beneficial) behavior of industries in the market, and even his later attempt to analyze the (benevolent) behavior of the government.

3.1.2.1 Adam Smith's first book: The Theory of Moral Sentiments

The Theory of Moral Sentiments is made up of seven parts, with the first part on the propriety of actions, the second part merits and demerits or the objects of reward and punishment, the third tells about the foundation of our judgments concerning our own sentiments and conduct, and the sense of duty, the fourth is about the effects of utility upon the sentiment of approbation, the fifth part discusses the influence of custom and fashion on the sentiments of moral approbation and disapprobation, the sixth tells about the character of virtue and the seventh emphasizes the systems of moral philosophy.

In the book, Adam Smith regarded human sentiments and sympathy as the basic principle to decipher the roots of moral sentiments such as justice, benevolence and prudence, explained the nature and principles of moral evaluation and the characteristics of various virtues, and introduced and evaluated other schools of thoughts on moral philosophy, revealing the foundation on which the human society sustained and grew harmoniously, along with some basic moral principles human beings should adhere to.

Here, "human nature," "individual behavior," "self-preservation," "self-interest," "inner self," "impartial spectator," "self-command," "sympathy," "inner conflict," "profit seekers," "an invisible hand," "sympathy," "social animals," etc., are keywords in the book. Human sentiments, being an invisible hand, are regulating individual social behavior, promoting the organic integration of self-interest and sympathy, which constitutes the essence of human nature in Smith's theory. Through this book, Adam Smith, for the first time, presented and demonstrated the philosophy imparted by his mentor, Francis Hutcheson, that "people could discover what is ethically good by discovering the actions that serve the good of humanity."

3.1.2.2 Adam Smith's second book: An Inquiry into the Nature and Causes of the Wealth of Nations

The Wealth of Nations falls into five parts. Book One (11 chapters in total) describes the causes of improvement in the productive powers of labor, and the order according to which its produce is naturally distributed among the different ranks of the people. Book Two (five chapters in total) examines the nature, accumulation and employment of stock. Book Three (four chapters in total) distinguishes different progress of opulence in different nations. Book Four (nine chapters in total) elaborates on systems of political economy. Book Five (three chapters in total) discusses the revenue of the sovereign or commonwealth, which is closely related to the subject of this book. In Book Five, Chapter 1 is on the expenses of the sovereign or commonwealth. Specifically, Part I is on the expense of defense, Part 2 on the expense of justice, Part 3 on the expenses of public works and public institutions with Article 1 on the expenses of public works and institutions for facilitating the commerce of the society, Article 2 on the expense of the institutions for the education of youth, Article 3 on the expense of the institutions for the instruction of people of all ages, and Part 4 on the expense of supporting the dignity of the sovereign. Chapter 2 then probes into the sources of the general or public revenue of the society and Chapter 3 talks about public debts.

Important themes in *The Wealth of Nations* are the division of labor and value theory, which include division of labor, value theory (value in use and value in exchange and price of labor), three components of commodity price (wage, profit and rent), and market price and natural price; income and income distribution theory, which concerns wage, profit and rent; reproduction of social capital, which considers what is a reproduction of social capital, its prerequisite and its core.

The core idea presented by *The Wealth of Nations* can be summed up like this: A seemingly unrestrained and disorganized free market has in fact a self-adjusting mechanism that inclines to produce commodities of the right types and quantities the society needs most. It seems there is an invisible hand regulating everyone to follow the market rules through mechanisms of price, demand and supply. As Adam Smith puts it, "Every individual is continually exerting himself to find out the most advantageous employment for whatever capital he can command. It is his own advantage, indeed, and not that of the society, which he has in view. But the study of his own advantage naturally, or rather necessarily, leads him to prefer that employment which is most advantageous to the society." "He intends only his own gain, and he is in this, as in many other cases, led by an invisible hand to promote an end which was no part of his intention." "By pursuing his own interest he frequently promotes that of the society more effectually than when he really intends to promote it." Here, the mechanism of price, demand and supply, and competition, as part of the invisible hand, is regulating the social behavior of producers or enterprises, and leading to an organic integration of self-interest and altruism, which constitutes the essence of free economy. Adam Smith applied the concept of "an invisible hand" from *The Theory of Moral Sentiments* to *The Wealth of Nations* in explaining the role of self-adjustment and self-regulation of market economy, which again demonstrated his mentor Francis Hutcheson's philosophy that "people could discover what is ethically good by discovering the actions that serve the good of humanity."

Under the premise of economic freedom as endorsed by *The Wealth of Nations*, Adam Smith pointed out duties of the sovereign or commonwealth in a system of perfect liberty mainly in Chapter I of Book Five on fields like the expense of defense, the expense of justice and the expense of public works and public institutions (expenses of education included). So it appears the duties of the sovereign or commonwealth can be summarized as national defense, administration of justice and erecting and maintaining public works and public institutions. Among them, erecting and maintaining public works and public institutions such as roads, bridges, navigable canals and harbors, are of such a nature that the profit could never repay the expense to any individual or a small number of individuals, and which, therefore, cannot be expected that any individual or a small number of individuals should erect or maintain. Henceforth, the government plays the role of "a night watchman," which was touched on in Book Five of *The Wealth of Nations*, later called "the small government."

Thanks to this book, Adam Smith was hailed as the founding father of the discipline now known as economics and widely credited as the founding father of what is now known as capitalism. On this basis, later generations made up for the deficiencies in Adam Smith's theories such as the division of labor, value theory and market economy theory, hence came into being neoclassical economics, a mainstream branch of economics today. Besides, Smith's view on the role and duties of the government in the market economy is still influential today after over 240 years since it was put forward. Hence, from the perspective of traditional economics, "a small government," "a night watchman," and "a supplier of public goods" are still regarded as the roles of states in the modern market economy.

3.1.2.3 Analysis over the contents of Adam Smith's third book

Adam Smith completed his first book, *The Theory of Moral Sentiments* in 1759 and his second book, *The Wealth of Nations* in 1776 before he returned from London to Scotland, and worked at the customs as his father did, a place considered then to be the true source of wealth and a trading hub of imports and exports. During his time at the customs, he observed and contemplated while working in hope of composing a third book on the subject of "the general principles of law and government, and of the revolutions of them in different stages and periods of the society." However, he passed away before it was completed and all his manuscripts were later destroyed.

So what could Adam Smith's third book be about? Maybe this is the time to go back again to the philosophy instructed by his mentor, Francis Hutcheson, that "people could discover what is ethically good by discovering the actions that serve the good of humanity." In *The Theory of Moral Sentiments*, through observation over self-interest and sympathy of individuals in society, Adam Smith expounded on the basic essence of human nature and characteristics of morality. In *The Wealth of Nations*, through analysis on self-interest and altruism in the market, Smith dwelled on the basic essence of free economy and characteristics of enterprise behavior. Then, focusing on "government and law," would the third book of his elaborate on the basic economic functions of a nation and characteristics of management behavior of the government or the legal regime through discussions on national interests and individual interests? The concept of the "invisible hand" can be seen throughout the economic thoughts of Adam Smith. For moral behavior of individuals, self-interest and sympathy is the "invisible hand" that guides people's moral sentiments. For enterprise behavior, the "invisible hand" plays its part through self-interest and altruism by regulating prices, demand and supply as well as the competition mechanism. Based on this logic, what could be the "invisible hand" in the case of government administration? When we take into account Adam Smith's academic thoughts and the philosophy of his mentor, it seems that Adam Smith was studying "behavioral science" or he was perhaps attempting to reveal human nature, the essence of the market and government administration through "behavioral science" and "behavioral economics." But it was a great pity that he only managed to finish the first two steps out of the three.

However, at least we can say that if Adam Smith had the chance to finish his third work, his analysis on government functions and administration would not be confined to what was mentioned in Chapter I, Book Five of *The Wealth of Nations*. Apart from national defense and administration of justice, the government's public works and public institutions would go well beyond the range of the four types of infrastructure, roads, bridges, navigable canals and harbors, which were considered unprofitable by capitalists. However, it is a shame that even over 200 years later, today's economic theories barely make any breakthroughs on government functions and administration compared with Adam Smith's depiction in *The Wealth of Nations*.

There are of course limitations with Adam Smith's view on government functions and the characteristics of government behavior, which is quite understandable. First, he lived at the dawn of the Industrial Revolution, when the transformation of small handicraft workshops to large-scale mechanized production just began, while urbanization was yet to emerge and people still only had their eyes on industries, industrial resources and industrial revolution. Just like Adam Smith criticized mercantilism that took trade as the only source of wealth, and physiocracy which regarded agriculture as the only source of wealth, *The Wealth of Nations*, by pointing out that all departments of material production (industrial departments) could create wealth, had little touch on recognition of the role of urban infrastructure and urban resources and their application resources. Because of limitations of the times, Adam Smith could only restrain his view on government functions and administration under the framework of the industrial economy. Second, regarding the industrial economy, or more specifically on enterprises, commodities, prices, demand and supply, and competition, it was taken for granted that the government was nothing but a night watchman who ensured national defense, justice and order, and a sound market environment.

After *The Wealth of Nations* was accomplished in 1776, Adam Smith turned his study from individual behavior to enterprise behavior, and then to government behavior, and over a dozen years later, in 1790, he set about on his third book on government and law. So what confuses us is that why Smith chose a job at the customs after his masterpiece, *The Wealth of Nations*, already made his fame and fortune? Could it be just out of consideration to take care of his mother? Or to make money? From his life experience, we don't think either was possible. After the publication of *The Theory of Moral Sentiments* at the age of 36, Smith was invited by the then chancellor of the Exchequer, Charles Townshend, as tutor to his son and earned himself a life-long pension. In order to compose *The Wealth of Nations*, he socialized with people in the business circle in London and completed the masterpiece when he was 53. Thereafter, he decided to work at the customs, where he could closely observe import and export. It can be speculated that from here he had begun his study on domestic and international economy, and "government behavior" that originated from here. It seems his major choices in life were considerably related to his academic career. But why did the third book take him 14 years and was still left unfinished? Of course, during his research, Adam Smith must have also undertaken some school business of Glasgow. More importantly, however, in the author's opinion, is because he tried to apply the philosophy of his mentor, Francis Hutcheson, that "people could discover what is ethically good by discovering the actions that serve the good of humanity," into research on government administration and operation during his time at the customs.

If we say the essence of *The Theory of Moral Sentiments* resides in the guidance of "an invisible hand" to individuals and the society through self-interest and sympathy and the essence of *The Wealth of Nations* is about enterprises and the market regulated by "an invisible hand" based on self-interest and altruism, then what is the driving force behind government behavior? What is regulating the relations among countries? For a national government, it has its own national interests as well as international interests at heart. It is on its own, but also part of the world; It has partial demands (which is micro) while also expects overall equilibrium (which is macro). So its essence is an internal conflict of national interests of one country against another's, and even against that of the human race. Furthermore, in safeguarding or fighting for its own national interests, what can a state do economically, apart from by political and military means? How does a state pursue its own interests? Two paths seem possible, to protect its existing interests or to compete for more new interests. In protecting one's existing interest, commonly recognized rules are crucial, while in competing, what can you do? In what areas can you compete? These questions, I think, are what Adam Smith endeavored to answer in his third book. However, eventually, he didn't or did not yet answer these questions; hence, the deficiency of traditional economics and Adam Smith's market theory, which considered enterprises the sole players in the market, and there were only supply and demand relation or competition relation among enterprises in the market. This defect still exists today since many problems in modern economics are actually due to deficiencies of traditional economics rather than the market itself. There is no doubt that Adam Smith is highly admired even today, but questions he left unanswered and unsolved still prevail.

3.1.3 Deficiencies in Adam Smith's theory and emergence of John Maynard Keynes's theory

The founding father of economics and capitalism, the core of Adam Smith's theory and its deficiencies have a far-reaching influence over generations. Thanks to him, many economists, including the renowned Professor Alfred Marshall who published *Principles of Economics* in 1890, took "economics" as an independent discipline, proposed a series of new ideas and concepts, and promoted the study on economics to a new level through innovation, and hence the neoclassical economics. However, in my opinion, neoclassical economics, though a reform and innovation, and a conglomeration of the essence of previous theories, still ran within the framework of

Adam Smith's theory, with its focus on commodities, prices, demand and supply and competition from the perspective of industry, industrial economy and industrial resources and restraining the relation between the market and the government within industrial economy only. Though depth and range of research on the economic "Goldbach's conjecture" was improved and innovations were made, explorations on the relation between the market and the government were still chained to previous studies and the government was still deemed as the "night watchman" or "small government" who guarded national defense, maintained justice and order and supplied public goods.

The predominant contribution of *The Wealth of Nations* lies in its elaboration on the nature of the market, the nature of enterprises and their relationships with the government in the industrial economy, and the role of the market and the government were clarified under the guidance of "an invisible hand." This is the reason why Adam Smith's theory leaves a far-reaching influence on economics! However, Smith did not distinguish other forms of economies apart from industrial economy, did not specify a detailed and complete market system, the boundaries (or scope) of the market, and the effectiveness of the market, nor a clear relation between the government and the market. Limits of the times and the uncompleted third book contributed to the defects in Smith's theory.

Different from Adam Smith, John Maynard Keynes had the experience of both government employment and scholarly learning. His major works include *The Economic Consequences of the Peace* (1919), which was completed after World War I, and *The General Theory of Employment, Interest and Money* (1936), which was published in the context of the Great Depression during 1929–1933 and Franklin Roosevelt's "New Deal" in the USA. The deficiencies in Adam Smith's theory became the making of Keynes's success. However, Keynes's theory, though had made breakthroughs in economics, still had deficiencies and contradictions.

3.2 Contributions and deficiencies of Keynesian economics

3.2.1 Main experiences of Keynes

John Maynard Keynes (1883–1946), an English economist, journalist and financier, was best known for his economic theories (Keynesian economics) on the causes of prolonged unemployment. Born in Cambridge, he was highly proficient in mathematics and economics. From 1902 to 1906, aged 19 to 23, Keynes studied at Cambridge University. After graduation, from 1906 to 1908, Keynes worked as a civil servant taking a job with the India Office in Whitehall. Keynes returned to work in Cambridge University in 1908. In 1913, aged 30, Keynes published his first work, *Indian Currency and Finance*. From 1913 to 1914, he was appointed to the Royal Commission on Indian Currency and Finance.

From 1915, with the onset of World War I, Keynes returned to government employment, this time in the Treasury, where he studied relations with allies and recommended means of conserving Britain's scant supply of foreign currencies. In May of 1919, aged 36, he accompanied Prime Minister David Lloyd George to France as an economic adviser to the Versailles Peace Conference, during which he tried to reduce the huge amount of reparations to be imposed upon defeated Germany, but failed. Depressed, he resigned his post and returned to Cambridge University and published *The Economic Consequences of the Peace* in 1919. Thereafter, he published a series of articles and works such as *A Treatise on Probability* (1921), *A Revision of the Treaty* (1922), *A Tract on Monetary Reform* (1923), *Does Unemployment Need a Drastic Remedy?* (1924), *The End of Laissez-Faire* (1926) and *A Treatise on Money* (1930).

In October of 1929, after the Wall Street Crash, the Great Depression ensued. In 1930, Keynes joined the Economic Advisory Council. In 1931, at the invitation of the University of Chicago, Keynes traveled to the USA to discuss measures combating the economic crisis with American economists. From 1932 to 1933, Keynes relentlessly advocated stimulating economic growth through government intervention. In 1934, Keynes visited America again and met with President Roosevelt for the New Deal. In February 1936, *The General Theory of Employment, Interest and Money* was published.

In September 1939, World War II broke out. In 1940, Keynes served once more in the Treasury and became an all-purpose adviser. From 1942 to 1944, Keynes actively engaged himself in shaping the post-war economic order, from which the later International Monetary Fund (IMF), the World Bank and the Bretton Woods system were derived. In February 1946, Keynes made a trip to the USA to attend the first meeting of the World Bank and the International Monetary Fund. Two months later, John Maynard Keynes passed away.

3.2.2 Characteristics of Keynes's economic thoughts

Keynes's proficiency in mathematics and economics, coupled with his rich experience in academia and politics, made his ideas and research in economics special and unique. For example:

i In *The Economic Consequences of the Peace* (1919), Keynes elaborated on the pre-war Europe, the negotiations at the Paris Peace Conference, terms of the Treaty of Versailles, especially those on war reparations, as well as the prospect of Europe after signing the treaty and remedy measures to stop the problems, etc. He believed that the heavy claims the victorious Allied Powers demanded would devastate Germany's economy, thereby leading to further conflicts in Europe. He proposed revision of the treaty, the settlement of inter-Alley indebtedness, an international loan and the reform of currency, and the relations of Central Europe to Russia to remedy hidden troubles brought about by the treaty. Through his ideas in this book, we can see that first, Keynes made a grim prophecy over the severe consequences of government behavior that went against economic logic and tried to stop and rectify such situations. Second, Keynes analyzed government behavior and attempted to alter the possible consequences through government economic measures. In doing so, he endeavored to raise to a higher level the general public's awareness and acceptance of economics (especially of that time). Third, Keynes illustrated the role and duties of the government from the perspectives of state power and overall economic trend, which deviated away from traditional economic theories and presented an objective analysis over how government policies directly affected the national economy.

ii Faced with unemployment of over one million people in the UK in 1924, Keynes proposed in *Does Unemployment Need a Drastic Remedy?* that the government put in capital spending of £100 million per annum to stimulate the economy, specifically spending on housing, roads and electrical power distribution. He further proposed that national savings should be spent on works in Britain rather than invested overseas. He held that the important thing for government is not to do things which individuals are doing already, and to do them a little better or a little worse; but to do those things which at present are not done at all. Here it is clear that first, Keynes further suggested that the government's measures in stimulating economic growth should focus on increasing domestic investments in infrastructure such as housing, roads, and electrical power distribution. Second, the operation of such infrastructure should be put in the hands of semi-autonomous entities invested by private funds and administered by the government, which would significantly boost economic growth. Third, the important thing for the government is not to do things which individuals are doing already, and to do them a little better or a little worse, but to do those things which at present are not done at all. Such recognition reveals that Keynesian Economics already extended the role of the government to an investor in infrastructure for economic growth, and attempted to explain it under a theoretical framework and make breakthroughs.

iii Keynes published *The General Theory of Employment, Interest and Money* in 1936, which has six Books in 24 chapters. Book I is Introduction, explaining mainly the principle of effective demand. Book II, Definitions and Ideas, elaborates mainly on the definitions of income, saving and investment, and the significance of further investigation on them. Book III, the Propensity to Consume, mainly talks about the marginal propensity to consume and the multiplier. Book IV, the Inducement to Invest, investigates on marginal efficiency of capital, liquidity preference, etc. Book V, Money-wages and Prices, focuses on money-wages, prices and the employment function. Book VI, Short Notes Suggested by the General Theory, expounds on notes on trade cycle, mercantilism and the social philosophy towards which the general theory might lead. There are several key issues worth noticing here. First, Keynes, as a student of Professor Alfred Marshall in Cambridge, holds that the belief that the market naturally tends towards full employment and reaches equilibrium level of employment through self-regulation, as argued by the classical and neoclassical economic school represented by Adam Smith and Alfred Marshall, is a fallacy. Second, the level of employment in a country depends on the level of effective demand, which is the aggregate demand for goods and services in an economy when the aggregate demand price of output as a whole is equal to its aggregate supply price. As aggregate supply would not change significantly in the short run, the root cause of underemployment lies in insufficient effective demand. Third, effective demand or aggregate demand is the sum of consumption demand and investment demand. Insufficient effective demand or aggregate demand is thus due to insufficient consumption demand and investment demand. Fourth, therefore, Keynes advocates government intervention in the economy to stimulate consumption and increase investment for full employment. Keynes believes that as the propensity of consumption is relatively stable in the short run, to attain full employment, the government must focus on increasing investment demand. Changes in investment will result in a multiplier effect on income and output, boosting national income to grow by folds. Fifth, the government's expansionary investment advocated by Keynes is mainly through the form of fiscal policies rather than monetary policies. Especially during times of economic recession, the government should adopt expansionary fiscal policies to increase fiscal expenditure, cut taxes and issue bonds. Keynes also suggests that investment policies should be duly adjusted in accordance with consumption demand and the government should take a good commend of investment and prevent fluctuations of the economy brought about by it. Sixth, the government must take measures to increase effective demand, and increase consumption demand by improving equal increase in income.

Above all, in his *The General Theory of Employment, Interest and Money*, Keynes identified a new area of economic growth, which is neither in foreign trade advocated by mercantilism, nor in agricultural production championed by physiocrats, or in industrial economy as Adam Smith suggested, but in public works and institutions such as roads, bridges, navigable canals, harbors, housing and electric facilities that are of such a nature that the profit could never repay the expense to any individual or small number of individuals, and which, therefore, it cannot be expected that any individual or small number of individuals should erect or maintain but the government, as described by Adam Smith in Article 1, Part 3, Chapter 1, Book V of *The Wealth of Nations*. In addition, the government should intervene in the development of the national economy, especially in case of imbalanced aggregate demand and insufficient effective demand, through investment in infrastructure. Besides, government intervention is proceeded through proactive fiscal policies like increasing fiscal expenditures, cutting taxes and issuing government bonds so that more money would be put into the construction of public projects such as housing and roads. What's more, as an independent economic system, Keynes's economic theory has taken shape. Keynes's theory, along with classical economics dominated by Adam Smith and neoclassical economics dominated by Alfred Marshall, formed the two lines of economics. On one side, it is about supplying commodities, forming industrial economy with enterprises being the principal market players, among which all abide by market rules. On the other side, it is about supplying public works and public goods, forming infrastructure economy or urban economy. However, Keynes was not quite clear regarding the principal subjects in infrastructure economy or urban economy, the government, private investors or them together. As for the rules they follow, Keynes again was vague. Maybe also the market rules?

3.2.3 Roosevelt's new deal

As described above, Keynes made several trips to the USA during his lifetime. Particularly, in 1934, Keynes met with President Roosevelt, and discussed and promoted the New Deal. Though highly appreciated by President Roosevelt, Keynes's views also met with hostility from advocates of laissez-faire economy in the country.

The New Deal was a series of domestic programs under the administration of President Franklin D. Roosevelt in response to the Great Depression, with the core on relief, recovery and reform, known as the three Rs. Faced with the Great Depression, the administration of President Herbert Hoover advocated laissez-faire and opposed government intervention, which further exacerbated the crisis and the economy plunged to rock bottom. With public resentments rising, American voters voted in favor of the Democratic promise of a "new deal" championed by Franklin D. Roosevelt, which won him sweeping support across the nation and helped him defeat Hoover to be the 32nd President of the USA.

Apart from regulating banking and financial industries, revitalizing manufacturing industries and modifying agricultural policies, establishing a social security system and building emergency relief agencies, the most important part in Roosevelt's New Deal was to provide employment instead of aid through the construction of public projects in order to stimulate production and consumption.

The New Deal relief program hired young men, aged 18–25, to work in woods and fields to plant trees, prevent and control floods, fight soil erosion, build roads and buildings, construct forest roads and trails and fight forest fire on the federal land. In this way, federal relief provided by states was transferred to the hands in need through employment rather than aid. Such measures not only ensured relief, encouraged the unemployed to seek employment, but also propelled the construction and development of public utilities and civil works in the USA, which helped stimulate production and consumption, alleviate the economic crisis and social conflicts brought about by the Great Depression.

One of the earliest measures of Roosevelt's New Deal was the establishment of Civilian Conservation Corps (CCC) under the approval of Congress. The CCC recruited 250,000 people for its first patch who worked in 1,500 camps across the country. By the time the USA joined the battle of World War II, a total of over 2 million young men were employed in the CCC. Together, they worked on more than 7.4 million acres of national forests and parks. Each recruit worked for an average of 9 months each session and most of their salaries were used to support their families, thus expanding the scope of relief and correspondingly increasing the purchasing power across the whole society.

Under the New Deal, there were various institutions established to dispense relief and provide employment. Generally, they fell into two parts. The Public Works Administration (PWA) worked on long-term public works (with a total of $ four billion allocated by the government) while the Civil Works Administration (CWA) aimed at civil engineering (with a total investment of $ one billion), which were responsible for 180,000 small-scale projects across the nation, including school buildings, bridges, dikes, sewerage systems, post offices and buildings of administration agencies, providing employment for four million people successively, including a vast number of unskilled workers. Several new relief systems were also established subsequently. Among them, the most prominent were the Works Progress Administration (WPA), which received a grant of $ five billion from Congress and the National Youth Administration (NYA) which provided work training for the youth of the nation. It was estimated that a total of 23 million people were employed by WPA and NYA, over half of the nation's total working population back then.

On the eve of World War II, the Federal Government had already invested $ 18 billion for various projects and direct relief. Under the New Deal, the American government built nearly 1,000 airports, more than 12,000 sports fields, and more than 800 school buildings and hospitals, which not only created employment for craftsmen, unskilled laborers and architects, but also provided a variety of jobs for tens of thousands of unemployed artists, thus making it the grandest and most successful relief program the American government has ever implemented. Funds invested by the government, through various channels, stimulated resident consumption and individual investment.

The measures of Roosevelt's New Deal, especially a considerable number of public and civilian projects, such as that of Tennessee Valley Authority (TVA), not only greatly reduced unemployment and stimulated economic recovery, but more importantly, created a new model for economic growth through government intervention. Implementation of proactive fiscal policies, massive public works construction and provision of public goods provided a theoretical basis and practical means for government's intervention in the economy or explorations for a new model of economic growth. Investment, especially infrastructure investment in public works and public facilities brought numerous benefits to the American economy, establishing Roosevelt as the most popular American president after Abraham Lincoln.

3.2.4 Contributions and deficiencies of Keynesian economics

In recent years, the media often compared Donald Trump's economic policies with Roosevelt's New Deal and claimed they bore much resemblance. According to "The Essence of the Trump Administration is More like that of Roosevelt rather than Reagan," an economic review published on March 7, 2017 in Japan's weekly journalist, *Economist*, that "Although the Trump Administration is often considered similar to Reagan's, Trump's policies in fact bear more resemblance to Roosevelt's New Deal… During the election campaign, both Reagan and Trump put forward the promise to 'Make America Great Again' and ultimately achieved overwhelming victories. Furthermore, Reagan also championed tax cuts and deregulation. In terms of patriotic slogans and part of their economic policies, the Trump Administration and the Reagan Administration do have some similarities. However,…the economic policies of the Reagan Administration, apart from tax cuts and deregulation, also included hiking of interest rates, appreciation of dollar and fiscal… tightening. So in essence, Reagan's economic policies set store by the supply side rather than the demand side, which allowed full competition through thorough… deregulation. Compared with his predecessors, Trump's polices are more similar to the Democrat President, Franklin Roosevelt's New Deal, which was introduced following the global panic of the Great Depression in 1929. The New Deal aimed to ease the extreme shortage in demand and unemployment, so it was an economic program centered on huge public expenditures based on Keynesian demand-side …economics. During his election campaign, Trump publicly pledged $ one trillion on infrastructure spending in order to vigorously stimulate demand. Although the USA has now recovered from the crisis in 2008, and almost realized full employment, there are still mismatches in employment nevertheless. Trump's policies can be said to highly resemble the 'New Deal' in terms of its emphasis on demand side and …employment. As for the movement of interest rates under the Trump Administration, there might be a similar trend to that during the era of President …Roosevelt. Therefore, in order to maximize the effectiveness of his policies, Trump attempts to intervene in exchange rate fluctuations, curb excessive appreciation of dollar and high interest rates."[1]

From the Roosevelt Administration to the Trump Administration, the American government tends to stimulate economic growth through massive investment in infrastructure. The economic rationale behind this tendency originates from Keynes's theories, especially "*Does Unemployment Need a Drastic Remedy?*" (1924) and *The General Theory of Employment, Interest and Money* (1936). With his unique life experience in academia and politics and his pioneering idea of "government intervention," Keynes greatly contributed to the improvement of world economic theories and economic system.

Again, we will take *The General Theory of Employment, Interest and Money* as an example. It is generally agreed that if we say Adam Smith's *The Wealth of Nations* is the Bible of economic liberalism, then Keynes's *The General Theory of Employment, Interest and Money* is that of state interventionism. Key points worth noticing in this book are as follows. First, Keynes reinterpreted the concept of full employment and pointed out the three types of unemployment that existed in reality, voluntary unemployment, frictional unemployment and involuntary unemployment. The mere existence of involuntary unemployment signified the invalidity of traditional employment theories. Second, Keynes proposed the principle of effective demand and pointed out that the level of employment actually depended on the effective demand of the society, which was supposed to be in equilibrium with aggregate supply. Third, Keynes suggested a simple national income determination theory and held that the main factors affecting the national income and employment level were three psychological factors (marginal propensity to consume, marginal efficiency of capital and liquidity preference) and money supply. Fourth, Keynes summarized the law of the three psychological factors, namely, diminishing of marginal propensity to consume, diminishing of the marginal efficiency of capital, and the liquidity preference theory. Fifth, Keynes put forward the multiplier theory which held that increases in initial investments could lead to increased induced investments, and through the chain effect, would ultimately lead to expansion in effective demand in the society, multiple times of the initial investments, and vice versa. Sixth, Keynes put forward a theory of business cycles, and suggested that a business cycle mainly had four stages: Prosperity, depression, recession and recovery, due to fluctuations in investment rates, which were subject to the influence of changes in the marginal efficiency of capital. In addition, Keynes's study also spanned over price theory, wage theory, international trade theory, etc. Therefore, Keynes's revolutionary work in economic theory is also known as "Keynesian Revolution," comparable to the contributions of Nicolaus Copernicus in astronomy, Charles Darwin in biology, and Albert Einstein in physics.

Keynes's *The General Theory of Employment, Interest and Money* summed up a large number of economic concepts from the macro perspective, opening up a new chapter in the development of economics in the 20th century. As mentioned above, first, Keynes's unique experience in academia and politics allowed him to identify a new area of economic growth in the field of public works and public goods centered on infrastructure, instead of "foreign trade" advocated by mercantilism, or "agriculture and animal husbandry" championed by the physiocracy, or "production sectors of commodity goods" and "industrial economy" upheld by Adam Smith. Second, the government is the primary investor in infrastructure. Or in other words, the government is the principal force in intervening the economy and promoting economic growth in this field. Third, the government mainly utilized fiscal policies rather than monetary policies in infrastructure investment, hence, it seems Keynesian economics has gone beyond the limits of classical economics and neoclassical economics. Because classical and neoclassical economics centered on the logic of "formation of commodity prices, formation of industrial economy which centered on commodity production sectors, enterprises as main players in the free economy, and all abiding by market rules" to boost the economy. However, Keynesian economics followed the path of "government investment in public projects and public goods, infrastructure investment or urban economic expansion as priorities, the government as the principal investor in infrastructure, government adoption of proactive fiscal policies" to effectively propel economic growth. From the trajectory of economic growth, it is clear that Keynes and later advocates of Keynesian theories were indeed free from the shackle of the commodity-price model, which is the extremely successful and unique contribution of Keynesian economics.

However, with the development of Keynesian theories and related government policies, some problems revealed themselves. First, Keynes did not in essence strictly distinguish the difference between public works and public goods with material goods in basic economic theory. Instead, he intentionally or unintentionally placed public works and public goods into the framework of commodity-price analysis. Second, no strict distinctions between infrastructure and urban economy with material production and industrial economy were made. In fact, what motivated Keynes to put forward government intervention in the first place was to resolve unemployment and propel economic growth. Government intervention with proactive fiscal policies and in investing heavily in public works and public goods, especially in infrastructure, actually belonged to the research scope of urban economics, an area yet to be explored during the times of Adam Smith. Due to limitations of the times, Adam Smith only put infrastructure and urban economic expansion under the category of public goods, which private investors could not benefit from and so must be provided by the government. Hundred and sixty years later (from the publication of *The Wealth of Nations* in 1776 to the publication of *The General Theory of Employment, Interest and Money* in 1936), although Keynes categorized the operation of public works and public goods as a semi-autonomous area between private investors and the state, he did not specifically point out that they belonged to the urban economy instead of the industrial economy. The urban economy can be understood in both a broad sense and a narrow sense. In a broad sense, urban economy encompasses not only industrial economy (operative), livelihood economy (non-operative), but also public works and public goods such as infrastructure (quasi-operative). In a narrow sense, urban economy specifically refers to the economy of public works and public goods that centers on infrastructure investment and construction. Different from an industrial economy, it is a new economic field that can generate new resources. If the urban economy is mixed with the industrial economy, it would result in a series of contradictions in economics, especially in market economic theories. Third, Keynes did not strictly distinguish between the principal participants in infrastructure investment or urban economy and those in industrial economy. In the industrial economy, enterprises are the main players whereas in the urban economy or infrastructure investment, the government plays a dominant role while individual investors and investment alliances could also play a part. In the view of Keynes, effective demand consisted of investment demand and consumption demand. Insufficiency of investment demand was due to a decline in the marginal efficiency of capital, which meant the decline of interest rates in investment, and liquidity preference, which often was people's tendency to retain cash. In Keynes's analysis over the decline of interest rates in investment, investors in infrastructure obviously included both the government and private investors, who jointly invested following the rules of the market. Hence came the term of "return on investment (ROI)" in urban economy or infrastructure investment, with the government, individuals and groups as investors and the economy operating under market rules in the field of public works and public goods. However, Keynes and Keynesian economics did not distinguish between the government's participation or intervention in urban economy and enterprises' participation in the industrial economy, so it appeared that the government had a finger in the pie in the industrial economy or market economy, which triggered overwhelming oppositions from defenders of classical and neoclassical economics, or we should say advocates of market economy, against the so-called "government intervention." Henceforth, a series of disputes over theoretical and practical issues were generated. Fourth, furthermore, Keynes and Keynesian economics did not make it clear whether market rules were only valid in the industrial economy or commodity production. Were they also applicable to urban economy or infrastructure investment? No answer was given to this question and neither was the question of whether the government, as the dominant investor in infrastructure construction, should also follow market rules. Fifth, if we dig deeper, more questions will pop up. For example, is a government, as a participant in the urban economy and a principal investor in public works and public goods, in a competitive relationship with other regional governments, private investors and investment groups? How to define and distinguish a government's role in the development of industrial economy and urban economy? These questions were put aside, as after identifying the new area for economic growth, Keynesian economics concentrated on policy measures and effectiveness in this regard to resolve practical issues at the time. Such ambiguity and confusion in assumptions and later analyses created an "ambiguous zone" that led to endless disputes and contradictions in later generations.

To sum up, it is clear that first, Keynes's theory departed from Adam Smith's theory and built a unique system of its own, which somehow relied on Adam Smith's market theory as back up. For instance, Adam Smith put forward "an invisible hand" of the integration of "self-interest" and "sympathy" in *The Theory of Moral Sentiments* and "an invisible hand" of the integration of "self-interest" and "altruism" in *The Wealth of Nations.* Based on Smith's theory, Keynes identified a new field of economic growth, the development and utilization of infrastructure resources and urban resources. However, there seems to be an insufficiency of rationality in supporting discussions on the roles of a government and a nation. Or perhaps, Keynes was yet to work on it. Second, in regulating economic growth, Keynes and Keynesian economics manifested principles such as balanced supply, effective demand, optimal allocation of resources, and sound economic development. However, in theory, the fact that with the prosperity of a nation and progress of science and technology, more urban resources and international resources like space resources, marine resources and polar resources would be generated, is ignored. So the subject of "new resources" and "resource generation" in national economic growth deserves further study. Here, scarcity and generation of resources go hand in hand in the allocation of resources in economics. Third, the development of economic theories lags behind changes in reality. Keynes adopted Adam Smith's theory on the allocation of industrial resources, yet did not further work on problems of the generation of urban resources or infrastructure resources, thereby seemed narrow-minded. Keynesian economics, as a highly practical science at the time, addressed only the symptoms instead of the root cause of the problems, which in the opinion of the author, is the true defect of Keynes's theory. Fourth, generation and effective allocation of new resources require a sound mechanism, with which, the government, as one of the major developers and users of new resources, could possibly regulate the development and utilization of existing resources (industrial resources) as well as new resources (urban resources). The lack of such a mechanism is another flaw in Keynes's theory. Fifth, the basics of economic theories are subject to the regulation of "evolution paradigms." Therefore, we should draw on lessons and experience from reality and obey the rules of historical evolution in economics to further study and develop the modern market theory and modern economic system from the perspective of "resource scarcity" and "resource generation" in the key subject of resource allocation in economics.

3.3 Resource generation and categorization of three types of resources

3.3.1 Resource scarcity and resource generation go hand in hand in resource allocation

Faced with massive unemployment in the UK in the 1920s and the Great Depression in the USA and beyond to the whole world in the 1930s, John Maynard Keynes, with his unique experience in academia and politics, found an effective solution to such problems by identifying a new path and a new field of economic growth through enhancing effective demand by investing in infrastructure to effectively resolve unemployment and promote economic recovery and growth, apart from the traditional way of stimulating the industrial economy. However, implementation of such measures required the government to be the principal investor, which contradicted with Adam Smith's view on "the night watchman state."

Why couldn't Keynes and subsequent advocates of Keynesian economics explain and resolve this issue under the principles and framework of economics? To answer this question, we need to start with Adam Smith's *The Wealth of Nations.*

In *The Wealth of Nations*, Adam Smith put forward two assumptions when discussing the economic activities of human society, namely, the self-interest nature of economic activities and the fact of resource scarcity. Integration of egoism and altruism in commodity economy functions as an "invisible hand" in regulating commodities, prices, demand and supply, and competition, and eventually promoting market rules to take shape. Due to resource scarcity, economic regulation is universally aimed at optimizing the allocation of resources and sound development of the economy. Under the two assumptions, the "invisible hand" and market rules have long been established as the golden rule in classical and neoclassical economics, while "resource allocation" and "resource scarcity" have been taken as the starting point for research by both liberal economics and Keynesian economics. Just as Paul Samuelson said, "Economics is the study of how societies use scarce resources to produce valuable goods and services and distribute them among different individuals."[2]

Hence, when discussing resource allocation in traditional economics, it must be associated with resource scarcity. Resource allocation is in itself defined as the process of dividing up and distributing available, limited resources to competing, alternative uses that satisfy unlimited wants and needs. According to traditional economics, at a certain stage of social and economic development, compared to people's wants and needs, resources tend to be relatively scarce, thereby requiring rational allocation of limited and relatively scarce resources, so as to produce the most goods and services with the least resources and maximize benefits. Furthermore, rational allocation of resources has become an extremely critical factor in determining the success of a country's economic growth.

We will neither deny the importance of resource allocation, nor the absolute connection between resource allocation and resource scarcity, nor the fact that resource scarcity has become the cause for economic research. However, we cannot study resource allocation without thinking, discussing and exploring the problem of "resource generation," because things have changed quite a lot since the times of Adam Smith. First, when Adam Smith published *The Wealth of Nations* in 1776, the Industrial Revolution just started in the UK. At that time, what Adam Smith referred to as resource allocation was merely the allocation of industrial resources such as labor, capital and material in production, exchange and consumption of commodities and nothing else. Second, urban infrastructure in the UK around 1776 was still rather backward, with only roads, bridges, canals and ports, which could not be as advanced as that of the time of Keynes, thus unable to undertake the role of providing employment and promoting economic recovery. In addition, the construction of modern infrastructure in modern society not only involves a series of hardware and software investment projects but also numerous work in the development and construction of smart cities, which constitutes new fields of and generates new resources for a country's economic growth, hence comes the issue of resource generation. This new field of resource generation could be referred to as "urban resources," which is different from traditional industrial resources in terms of nature and way of allocation, and could promote economic growth from a different dimension.

The introduction of urban resources and resource generation in economics is crucial, for it can make up for the deficiencies in Keynes's theory, which identified a new field of economic growth, while restrained himself within the framework of industrial economy in analyzing it. Resource generation and resource scarcity go hand in hand in resource allocation. As two indispensable aspects in economics, they are closely associated with the economic development and progress of the times. Urban resources (including international resources such as space resources, marine resources and polar resources) differ from industrial resources of Adam Smith's time, in their nature, contents and functions, and each has its respective roles to play in economic practice and theories. However, by far, there has been no research on resource generation and its influence on economic growth as well as on economic theories, which deserves our due attention. Traditionally, economists tend to understand, analyze and interpret the new concept of resource generation through the principles and way of thinking of industrial economics, which emphasizes on efficient allocation of resources based only on resource scarcity and balanced or imbalanced distribution. Such practice results in deviation of economic theories from reality or lagging behind changes in economic reality, which leaves the area of resource generation and relevant institutional construction and regulation still a blank space in economics. These are the problems we should work on at the moment.

3.3.2 Resource generation—generative resources

Generative resources, derived from "resource generation," are also economic resources like industrial resources, but featuring as dynamic, economic, productive and risky ones.

Resources generated in resource generation are not produced as planned but are resources that already exist or resources generated with the progress of the times. They become dynamic from the original static state before they get economic and productive features. For instance, a mountain, when stands there, is a static natural being, but once developed, it becomes a dynamic resource, a factor of production, which is economic. Land, mines, rivers, forests, grasslands, etc., are natural resources when they are static landscapes while once developed, they are economic resources. This is common knowledge known to all. Urban infrastructure, including hardware, software and facilities for the development and construction of smart cities, are urban resources that also fall into the category of generative resources. Of course, there are other types of generative resources apart from industrial resources and urban resources, such as space resources (there are much more resources available in outer space than on earth). Just within the solar system, there are vast deposits of mineral resources on celestial bodies such as the Moon, Mars and other asteroids, abundant hydrogen energy on Jovian planets and comets, vacuum resources, radioactive resources and vast temperature-difference resources in planetary and interplanetary spaces as well as orbital resources and micro-gravity resources when spacecraft is utilized. In their static state, these are natural resources, but once developed and utilized, they are important and precious economic resources. Can national governments play a bystander role in the generation, development and utilization of such resources? Can we still explain and promote their development under the framework of traditional industrial economics? Obviously not. In reality, governments must play a different role in the generation, development and utilization of urban resources from that in an industrial economy.

Urban resources can be considered in a broad and a narrow sense.

First, cities are not set up randomly and most cities take shape gradually in the process of historic development. Second, cities are not static and unchanged. Most cities grow and expand through dynamic interactions with the progress of the times. What's more, cities have multiple functions as they build hardware and software infrastructure and even facilities for constructing smart cities through the process of development. All the makings of the building, construction and development of cities are urban resources.

Hence, from an economic perspective, urban resources in a broad sense include industrial resources, livelihood resources and infrastructure resources or public works resources. As for urban resources in a narrow sense, it is the focus of our discussion. Why did Keynes identify a new field of economic growth, but couldn't explain it with the commodity-price theory and the theories of industrial economics? Why did both the Roosevelt Administration and the current Trump Administration strive to resolve economic recession and promote economic growth through investment in infrastructure? (Infrastructure construction has become one of the measures taken globally to promote economic growth, for instance, China's endeavor in infrastructure investment in nations along the "Belt and Road.") All these questions could be answered through analysis over urban resources in their narrow sense. As important generative resources, urban resources in their narrow sense cover areas such as investment and construction of hardware and software infrastructure, as well as development and operation of smart cities in the process of further modernization. It is a new economic field that is worth efforts to develop its theories, explore its market rules and study the relationship between the government, and the market so as to fully utilize its potential as a new engine for national and even global economy. Research on it is related to but different from that of the theories of industrial economics. So modern economists really should endeavor to interpret and promote the development of urban economy and urban resources beyond the theories of industrial economics.

Urban infrastructure, as generative resources, refers to public facilities that serve the public good of social production and people's livelihood for the smooth operation of national and regional social and economic activities. It includes not only hardware infrastructure such as roads, railways, airports, communications network and public utilities but also software services such as education, science and technology, health care, sports and culture. Besides, with the progress of urban modernization, it also covers the development and construction of smart cities. To be specific, hardware facilities mainly refer to six major systematic engineering projects, energy supply system, including electricity, coal gas, natural gas, liquefied petroleum gas and heating; water supply and drainage system, covering water conservation, water plants, water supply, drainage and sewerage treatment system; transportation system, which can be divided into external transport facilities (aviation, railways, shipping, coaches, highways, etc.) and internal ones (roads, bridges, tunnels, subways, light rails, buses, taxis, parking facilities and ferries); posts and telecommunications system, such as postal service, telegraphs, landline phones, mobile phones, the Internet, radio and television; environmental protection and sanitation system, such as landscaping, garbage collection and disposal, pollution control; defense and disaster prevention system, for disasters such as fire, flood, earthquake, typhoon, sand storm, ground subsidence as well as air defense. Software infrastructure mainly refers to administrative management, culture and education, health care, commercial services, financial and insurance service and social welfare, etc. Meanwhile, with the progress of urban-rural integration, its range also expands to infrastructure for rural production, rural service, rural ecological conservation and rural social development. With the progress of urban modernization, the development and construction of smart cities has become a new highlight in urban infrastructure. Urban infrastructure, as new generative resources, is fundamental, non-trading and quasi-public goods in economics, which shall be a new field of economic growth and open up a new path for reform on economic theories.

3.3.3 Three types of resources in cities

The 21st century is a century when industrial development, urban construction and social welfare enjoy common growth and prosperity. In practice, the role of governments in the economy mainly resides in deploying and managing various resources, including natural resources, human resources, capital resources, industrial resources, urban resources and public resources, while also striving to optimize resource allocation and adopt relevant policies in this regard. For urban resources, there are three major types.

The first type of resources are related to industrial development, and so are known as "operative resources" in the market economy, which mainly refers to industrial resources in the regional economy in various countries. Due to differences in economic, geographical and natural conditions, regions tend to choose one from the primary industry, secondary industry and tertiary industry as the backbone of their economic development. Of course, in reality, there have been numerous successful cases of the tertiary sector, such as logistics, exhibition, finance, tourism, intermediary service and commerce and retail during the development of the primary or secondary industry. Traditionally, companies and enterprises are principal market players in the industrial economy, or in other words, companies and enterprises play the dominant role in the utilization of operative resources. In China, three types of governmental institutions are responsible for coordinating, supervising and administrating such resources. The first are departments in charge of development and reform, statistics and prices. The second type can be further divided into four groups: (a) Treasury, finance, taxation, industry and commerce; (b) industry, transport, security, energy and tobacco; (c) science and technology, information, private communications, intellectual property rights; (d) commerce, customs, maritime affairs, ports, postal service, quality inspection, foreign affairs and tourism. The third type is agencies specialized in audit, territorial supervision, food and pharmaceutical supervision and management. Institutions that coordinate, supervise and manage industrial resources in different countries may share some similarities or differ from each other in one way or another, but it has been a common consensus that the main principle over industrial resources is to "invigorate" them through planning and guiding, support and coordination, supervision and management.

The second type of resources are associated with social welfare, thus known as "non-operative resources" in the market economy, which is mainly resources catering to social well-being and people's livelihood in various fields, such as the economy (to guarantee basic social security), history, geography, image building, spiritual construction, cultivation of ideas, emergency response, security, disaster relief and other areas of social needs in regions. Traditionally, governments and social organizations are responsible for these resources or play a dominant role in the provision of social welfare and public goods. Institutions that coordinate, supervise and manage the allocation of such resources in China can also fall into three categories. The first can be further divided into five groups, including those in charge of finance, audit and planning; literature and history, counseling and archives; civil affairs, social security and poverty alleviation; women and children affairs, federations of disabled persons, the Red Cross, etc.; ethnic groups, religions and overseas Chinese affairs. The second are agencies in charge of affairs related to geology, earthquake and meteorology. The third are those working on emergency response, safety and security and air defense; people's armed forces, public security, judicial organs and supervisory agencies; fire control, armed police, border defense, coast guards, anti-smuggling, etc. Institutions governing these resources may have different names in different nations, but they perform similar duties and share the principle of "guaranteeing basic needs, ensuring fairness and justice, raising effectiveness and efficiency" in resource distribution.

The third type of resource is targeted at urban construction that is known as "quasi-operative resources" in a market economy. They are mainly urban resources that are utilized to safeguard smooth operation of national or regional social and economic activities, build software and hardware infrastructure to provide public service for social production and people's livelihood, such as transportation, posts and telecommunications, public utilities, landscaping, environmental conservation, education, science and technology, culture, health care and sports. The quality of such infrastructure has a direct bearing on the appearance, characteristics, taste, functions and roles of a nation or a region. A complete set of infrastructure can play an active role in promoting social and economic progress across nations and regions, and drive forward optimization of urban space and structure. The reason why the author calls these resources "quasi-operative resources" is because they are not clearly categorized in traditional economics, but stay in an overlapping zone of the government and enterprises, which means investment and development of urban infrastructure, as an undertaking to promote economic development and social welfare, can be undertaken by both enterprises and governments. Governmental institutions that coordinate, supervise and manage such resources in China are mainly five types, including those responsible for state-owned assets and major projects; land resources, environmental protection, urban and rural construction; human resources and public resource transactions; education, science and technology, culture, health care, sports, press and publication, radio, film and television, research institutions; agriculture, forestry, water conservation, marine fisheries, etc. Key points to be discussed in this book, such as "resource generation" and "infrastructure investment" and other relevant economic theories all center around this type of resource, quasi-operative resources.

Overall speaking, we can learn a few points from theory and in practice. First, in the allocation of operative resources, namely industrial resources in the industrial economy, the market should play a dominant role in distributing such resources to enterprises, the society, and various domestic and foreign investors through market approaches while governments should support the market with relevant policies in accordance with the principles of "planning and guiding, support and coordination, supervision and management." Second, for non-operative resources which aim to provide public goods and serve livelihood economy or areas beyond the capabilities of enterprises, governments should shoulder the responsibilities to supply, distribute, manage and develop such resources in an all-around way based on the principles of "guaranteeing basic needs, ensuring fairness and justice, raising effectiveness and efficiency." This is the reason why the national treasury, which derives its income from people and spends on people, should put more emphasis on public spending to improve peoples' livelihood. Third, for quasi-operative resources, namely urban resources in the urban economy (in the narrow sense), governments should decide whether these resources are to be developed and distributed as operative resources or as non-operative resources for public undertakings based on regional development, financial capabilities, capital flows, demands of enterprises and acceptability and affordability of the social public.

3.3.4 Objectives and rules of conversion of quasi-operative resources

There are two basic criteria in distinguishing operative resources and non-operative resources (which in essence are criteria in distinguishing private goods and public goods): Exclusivity and non-exclusivity, and competitiveness and non-competitiveness. Exclusivity means individuals or enterprises could be excluded from developing a certain kind of operative resources (goods or services). Once some individuals or enterprises pay to make investments in a certain type of resources, others are excluded from profiting from the same resources. As for competitiveness, it means increases in operative resources will lead to increases in production costs. So every unit of private goods produced additionally will increase production costs accordingly. Operative resources or private goods are exclusive and competitive. In contrast, non-exclusivity is the dominant feature of non-operative resources or public goods, which means when some develop non-operative resources or enjoy the benefits of public goods, it cannot exclude others from developing or benefiting from the same non-operative resources or public goods. For instance, every school-age child is obliged to receive compulsory education provided by the government and every citizen can enjoy safety and security guaranteed by the national defense. Non-competitiveness is the second feature of non-operative resources or public goods, which means the development of non-operative resources or production of public goods will not lead to an increase in production cost, which indicates that its marginal cost is zero.

Operative resources or private goods and non-operative resources or public goods can be illustrated as follows.

Operative resources or private goods:

$$x_j = \sum_{i=1}^{n} x_j^i$$

In this formula, x_j refers to the total sum of the No. j operative resources or private goods, n the total population or total enterprises in the economy, x_j^i the volume of the operative resources owned by the No. i individual or enterprise. So from the formula, we can see x_j is the sum of the volume of the resources possessed by every individual or enterprise (i) and operative resources can be divided among individuals and enterprises.

Non-operative resources or public goods (m kinds of them):

$$x_m^i = \sum_{k=0}^{m} x_k = x_m$$

This formula shows that every consumer i (individual or enterprise) has a share of non-operative resources or public goods at their free will and their total sum is x_m. Besides, non-operative resources could not be divided among individuals or enterprises.

Operative resources or private goods and non-operative resources or public goods are typically two opposites in the national economy and social products. In reality, with the development of the world economy and progress of the times, some originally non-operative resources or public goods gradually have the potentials to be transformed into operative resources, thus boasting the features of both public goods and private goods, which we call quasi-operative resources or quasi-public goods, such as hardware and software infrastructure and facilities for the construction of smart cities. Quasi-operative resources or quasi-public goods, a bridge or a school for instance, are not fully non-competitive nor non-exclusive. As for whether they would be transformed into operative resources or private goods, or non-operative resources or public goods, it depends on the economic development level, financial status as well as social acceptability of a nation or a region.

Let's suppose $\lambda(0 < \lambda < 1)$ represents the proportion of quasi-operative resources allocated in public sectors in society. Under extreme conditions in theory, if λ is zero, it means quasi-operative resources are all transformed into operative resources and utilized in private sectors; if λ is one, it means quasi-operative resources all belong to public sectors. When λ represents the extent of conversion of quasi-operative resources to non-operative resources and operative resources, it can be affected by the development level of the market economy (*Y*), financial status (including financial budget *B* and financial expenditure *FE*) as well as social acceptability (γ). Let's put them into one formula.

$$\lambda = F(Y, B, FE, \gamma) \tag{3.1}$$

Before further analysis into formula (3.1), we will first look at λ. First of all, the development level of the market economy, *Y*, is a variable between zero and one, which fluctuates between high-level underdevelopment and high-level development. The development level of the market economy can affect the level of disposable income, which can further influence the capital flow into areas of quasi-operative resources. If one economy is highly developed, people will have high disposable income, which indicates private sectors would be more capable and motivated to invest in quasi-operative resources. So λ will be small and the proportion of quasi-operative resources transformed into operative resources will be high. If originally λ is high, it means private capital in the market of quasi-operative resources is relatively small. So when the aggregate demand remains unchanged, the market will reward high returns to new capital, which will accelerate capital inflow from private sectors. So according to traditional economic theories, the increase rate of λ is negatively correlated with *Y*. Suppose a is a positive constant, the relation of λ and *Y* is:

$$\frac{\partial \lambda / \lambda}{\partial Y} = -a \tag{3.2}$$

Second, government input in quasi-operative resources is subject to the government's financial status. When the government budget *B* is lower than its financial expenditure *FE*, the government is in lack of capital, hence will promote the transformation of quasi-operative resources into operative resources to cut government spending. Besides, due to lack of capital, the government would like private sectors to yield high returns in order to attract investment, so capital inflow from private sectors will be sped up. Under such conditions, the proportion of transformation of quasi-operative resources to private sectors will increase, so λ will drop. Therefore, λ is negatively correlated with the ratio of financial expenditure to financial budget (*FE*/*B*). In addition, it should be noted that government expenditure is also subject to the influence of the level of λ. If λ is high initially, it means the proportion of financing from public sectors in areas of quasi-operative resources is high, indicating a high government budget. So suppose *b* is a positive constant, the relation between λ and financial status can be represented as:

$$\frac{\partial\lambda/\lambda}{\partial\left(\frac{E}{B}\right)} = -b \tag{3.3}$$

Moreover, private sectors' input in areas of quasi-operative resources is not only affected by capital supply, but also by social acceptability γ. What is worth attention is that social acceptability has different impacts over people's willingness to put in money in different stages of economic development. When the economy is backward, namely $Y < Y^*$ (Y^* stands for the threshold of economic maturity, which is set according to different standards of different nations), social acceptability to build infrastructure for economic growth will be high, so that people tend to invest in quasi-operative resources. In such cases, λ is negatively correlated with γ. If the economy is quite developed, namely $Y > Y^*$, people will come to realize the negative effects of infrastructure construction over environmental sustainability, so they would prefer to invest in other resources than in quasi-operative resources if returns on investment are of the same level. In such cases, λ is positively correlated with γ. So hereby, we introduce In (Y/Y^*) as the correction coefficient. In addition, it should be noted that the original level of λ has a significant influence over social acceptability. In a backward market, the higher λ, the higher preference of people to invest in public resources. On the contrary, in a mature market, the higher λ, the higher preference of people to control the scale of infrastructure construction, therefore investment in public resources are restrained.

So suppose c is a positive constant, the relation of λ and γ is:

$$\frac{\partial\lambda/\lambda}{\partial\left[\gamma\ln\left(\frac{Y}{Y^*}\right)\right]} = -c \tag{3.4}$$

Based on the above analysis, we can establish a simple formula of the relation between the proportion of quasi-operative resources allocated in public sectors λ, and the development level of market economy *Y*, financial status (including financial budget B and financial expenditure FE) and social acceptability γ:

$$\frac{d\lambda}{\lambda} = -aY - b\frac{FE}{B} - c\gamma\ln\left(\frac{Y}{Y^*}\right) \tag{3.5}$$

Formula (3.5) shows the relevance of the transformation of quasi-operative resources to operative resources and non-operative resources to several related variables. It should be noticed that in extreme conditions when λ is zero, which means quasi-operative resources are completely transformed into operative resources, such resources will have nothing to do with variables such as financial status and social acceptability. So under such circumstances, variables such as financial status cannot affect the utilization of quasi-operative resources.

Formula (3.5) is a differential equation of λ. Through Formula (3.4), we can adjust this formula so as to have a clear look at the relations between λ and the variables.

$$\lambda = e^{-\left(aY + b\frac{FE}{B}\right)}\left(\frac{Y}{Y^*}\right)^{-c\gamma} \tag{3.6}$$

Formula (3.6) shows how λ, the proportion of quasi-operative resources allocated in public sectors fluctuates in different economic periods.

From the above analysis, we can see that as a new area of resource generation, quasi-operative resources, or namely infrastructure, are dynamic, economic, productive and risky resources. Infrastructure construction, especially large-scale urban hardware and software projects, are basically capital-intensive, which have features such as large initial investments, long construction cycles, high costs and catering to only a small market and subject to losses and uncertainties. Therefore, conversion from quasi-operative resources to operative resources might come with some unique investment risks, operational risks and management risks as well as considerable limitations. First, non-governmental investments are usually made by independent legal entities such as enterprises or individuals in pursuit of wealth at the micro level. Second, when enterprises or individuals put in money with capital of their own or capital accumulated through social pooling, their investment scale is very much restricted. Third, enterprises or individuals could usually only focus on one field of industry rather than all social undertakings which are not economic for them. So even though sometimes, quasi-operative resources are transformed into operative resources and so are exclusive and competitive, it takes high costs and high risks, which is not plausible economically. Therefore, such resources will still be developed as non-operative resources and investment decisions will be made according to the governments' policy target in providing public goods to the society based on three standards. The first is to produce the minimum capital-output ratio (which means governments should choose investment projects that can yield the largest output when utilized capital remains unchanged). The second is to produce the maximum capital-to-labor ratio (which indicates governments should choose investment projects with the largest per capita marginal investment). The third is about job creation (which means governments should choose investment projects that can mobilize the largest labor when capital to be put in remains unchanged).

However, in reality, when governments provide public goods to society, due to the nature of non-exclusivity and non-competitiveness, two problems might arise. On one hand, there can be free-riders who benefit from resources, public goods, or services of a communal nature, but do not pay for them, and there might also occur the tragedy of the commons in which every individual has an incentive to consume a resource at the expense of every other individual with no way to exclude anyone from consuming. On the other hand, some governments, in the process of regional infrastructure construction and development, might have the problems of blindly providing free services and shared goods without considering yields, hands-off operation after construction is finished, paying attention only to social benefits while ignoring economic interests so that numerous urban resources are wasted due to low-level, low-grade and disorderly urban construction and management.

Therefore, in deciding how infrastructure is invested, developed, operated and managed, governments should pay more attention to the transformation of quasi-operative resources to operative resources with a view to maximizing fiscal revenues. To realize this goal, governments around the world usually will take the following measures. First, to make independent investment. Governments tend to set up SOEs and charge on projects on a yearly basis. Second, to yield returns on investment through ways such as build-operate-transfer (BOT) and transfer-operate-transfer (TOT). Third, to obtain payoff through public-private partnership (PPP) and port-park-city (PPC). Fourth, to establish joint-stock enterprises and earn profits through IPO. Fifth, to make social investment. For example, governments can yield returns through asset securitization. Sixth, other ways of investment, such as coupling infrastructure projects with other profitable projects.

Directly related to financial revenues and returns on investment are financial expenditure and investment expenditure. Government investment expenditure mainly comes from a few sources, like investment expenditure in the governmental budget, bank loans, government bonds, investment partners, and others. In such cases, the transformation of quasi-operative resources to operative resources can help facilitate the transformation of government functions, promote diversified sources of investment, disperse investment risks, attract social funds to participate in social infrastructure construction, and earn the maximum profits with the optimal financial expenditure structure through the market mechanism. Through this, governments can earn themselves investment profits through the leverage effect.

To realize this goal, in transforming quasi-operative resources into operative resources in infrastructure investment, governments can make some reforms on the property rights of existing infrastructure resources based on market rules and objective demands of the economic development so that such resources are suited to funding demands of the capital market, which means the ownership of the stock infrastructure resources to be transformed into forms such as state ownership yet private operation, joint stock, joint venture, cooperative partnership or even sold out to investors at home and abroad through auctions. But the basic principle is to transform the resources in accordance with the rules of the market economy and engage in market competition. Meanwhile, for new infrastructure, namely incremental resources, governments can follow the market rules in the first place in dealing with it and establish firms to work on infrastructure projects in forms of sole ownership, joint venture, cooperative partnership or joint stock, so as to participate in the competition in investment, development and operation of urban resources.

In investment, development and operation of urban infrastructure, governments mainly raise capital in the capital market through ways such as bonds or convertible bonds, stocks, funds, going public by buying a shell, asset securitization, coupling infrastructure projects with other projects, or through lease, mortgage, replacement or auction. In practice, governments can also raise money through rights of charge and pricing by way of design-build-operate (DBO), BOT, build-operate-own (BOO), build-own-operate-transfer (BOOT), build-lease-transfer (BLT), build-transfer-operate (BTO) and transfer-operate-transfer (TOT) on the basis of concession agreements. Besides, based on features and conditions of infrastructure projects, governments can adopt different methods of funding or use multiple financing tools at the same time. For example, through PPP or PPC, a complete economic circle of infrastructure, logistics, finance and industrial parks can be built, before it goes into operation through BOT or TOT. When the time is right, companies of the projects can even go public, and through issuing bonds or stocks, they can further develop infrastructure projects so that governments will have no worries about capital in improving investment, development, operation and management over urban infrastructure. In this way, governments can set on a path for scientific and sustainable development and satisfy people's increasing demands over public goods and public undertakings.

But it should be noted that there is a boundary for government regulation over operative resources (in the industrial economy). Governments should refrain from regulating competitive areas but instead should adopt relevant policies to guide the development direction, scale and structure of fields of non-governmental investment. Likewise, there is a boundary for government regulation over non-operative resources (in livelihood economy). Clarification shall be made over the range of public goods and public undertakings, and through finding the right balance in government revenues and expenditures, efforts should be made to properly guide the development direction, scale and structure of public goods and public undertakings. It is also true to quasi-operative resources (in urban economy). Through optimization of financial income and expenditure structure and renovating allocation of financial resources, the development direction, scale and structure of infrastructure investment can be improved.

To sum up, in transforming quasi-operative resources into operative resources, governments should strive to build a rational investment structure, form a proper investment scale and improve returns on investment by way of cooperation with others in investing, developing, operating, managing and competing for infrastructure projects based on the principles of openness, justice and competitiveness of the market economy. In developing countries, investment in infrastructure is vital to economic growth while in developed countries, fluctuations in infrastructure investment are closely associated with changes in economic growth, which has been a non-negligible trend in world economic development. Therefore, it is necessary to further study the duties and roles of governments in this regard.

Notes

1 See: Japanese Experts: Trump's Economic Policies Are like Roosevelt's "New Deal." (2017, April 1). *China News*. http://www.chinanews.com/gj/2017/04-01/8189095.shtml.

2 Samuelson, P. A., & Nordhaus, W. D. (2010). *Economics*. New York: McGraw-Hill/Irwin, p.4.

Part II

4 Dual attributes of government

4.1 "Shenzhen Miracle" reveals government's great potential in resource generation

A forerunner of China's reform and opening up, Shenzhen has developed from a remote and desolate small fishing village by the South China Sea into a modern international metropolis full of vitality. Back in 1979, Shenzhen's regional gross domestic product (GDP) stood at only 197 million *yuan*, per capita GDP 606 *yuan*, and local general public budget revenue 1,721 *yuan*. By 2017, Shenzhen's GDP reached 2.24 trillion *yuan*, per capita GDP 183,100 *yuan* (about 27,100 US dollars), and local general public budget revenue 333,213 million *yuan*. The four Asian dragons' growing at a rate of about 10% for 20 years was surprising enough, yet even they were dwarfed by Shenzhen's economy striding at an annual growth rate of 23% for nearly four decades, a rare achievement in the world that is known as "Shenzhen speed" and "Shenzhen miracle."

Shenzhen's development is even more astonishing under a closer look. Forty years ago, it was a small fishing village "in the corner of the province at the tail of the country" comprising only two small alleys, one named Zhuzai and the other Yuzai, and a 200-meter long street, and now the city has realized 100% urbanization with a real population of over 20 million, more than 6,000 kilometers of roads and nearly 1,000 skyscrapers that are over 100 meters tall. The transformation from a small fishing village with only a few "waterside sheds" into a modern and international metropolis full of charm, vitality and innovativeness, one on a par with China's "first-line cities" such as Beijing, Shanghai and Guangzhou, is truly a miracle of urbanization, industrialization and modernization.

Of the many "secrets" behind Shenzhen's miracle, the following are the most noteworthy. The first is concentrating efforts to construct urban infrastructure both hard and soft right after it was made a special economic zone and opened up. Examples were the development of urban areas including Luohu and Shangbu, the building of ports such as Shekou, Chiwan, Dongjiaotou and Mawan, development and construction of a number of industrial zones, the building of the eight major cultural facilities including

DOI: 10.4324/9781003244837-4

Shenzhen University and Shenzhen Library, formulation of the city's overall urban construction plan, and the building of supporting facilities. The second secret is opening to the outside world and being the first to utilize foreign capital to build a number of infrastructure facilities, such as Chiwan Port, Shekou Port, Dongjiaotou Wharf, Shekou Oil Depot, local telephone project, Shajiao B Power Plant, the Overseas Chinese Town, Daya Bay nuclear power plant and Guangzhou-Shenzhen Expressway. The third is reforming the management system starting also from infrastructure construction. The most typical case was the "four *fen* bonus" when the Shekou quay was first built. The measure was the first to break the practice of having everyone "eat from the same big pot," a metaphor referring to the then equalitarian income distribution system in China that allowed everyone to get an equal share regardless of the work done. With the incentive, each worker transported 80 to 90 barrows of building materials every day instead of the 20–30 barrows before the bonus was offered, and this helped realize the miraculous construction speed of "one story in three days." Shenzhen has seen concrete progress made in the field of resource generation with the mechanism of "government promotion, enterprise participation and market-based operation."

According to the government work report issued by Shenzhen in January 2018, the fixed asset investment in Shenzhen reached 514.73 billion *yuan* in 2017, exceeding 500 billion *yuan* the first time, after reaching 300 billion and 400 billion in 2015 and 2016, respectively. The city's investment growth rate in 2017 reached 23.8%, not only higher than that of Beijing, Shanghai, Chongqing, Nanjing and other large and medium-sized cities but also higher than the national and provincial average level by 16.6 and 10.3 percentage points, respectively. With regard to investment structure, the city's industrial investment in the year reached 91.59 billion *yuan*, up by 27.5% year on year, and private investment reached 267.93 billion *yuan*, up by 22.5% year on year. The scale of government investment that guides and drives private investment also reached a new level, with investment volumes at both municipal and district levels exceeding 100 billion *yuan* for the first time. According to the report, the investment scale of Shenzhen Government in 2017 in key zones and infrastructure was remarkable, which was made possible by the beginning of phase four construction of the rapid transit system (five lines including lines 12, 13 and 14), as well as the continued construction of phase three with its 12 projects. In 2017, the city's infrastructure investment totaled 116.35 billion *yuan*, increasing by 29.2% year on year, with investment in the production and supply of electricity, heat, gas and water as well as investment in the management of water conservancy, environment and public facilities achieving higher increase rates than the previous year. In addition, investment in the city's 17 key zones totaled 146.3 billion *yuan* (excluding Yantian River Lingang industrial belt), up by 48.5% year on year and reaching 104.3% of the target set in the annual plan.

In 2018, fixed asset investment in Shenzhen increased by another 20% to exceed 600 billion *yuan* and reach 644.3 billion *yuan*. The investment was in five areas: First, completing a new round of urban master planning with high standards; second, speeding up the integration of the city as a special economic zone; third, speeding up infrastructure construction; fourth, building a first-class smart city; and fifth, promoting urban renewal. The growth rate of fixed asset investment in Shenzhen was over 20% for three consecutive years from 2016 to 2018. The steady progress and positive prospects of Shenzhen's economy are closely related and attributable to the rapid growth of effective investment and sound implementation of major projects across the city. Using major projects as the engine to sustain the vitality of private investment is not only a prominent feature of Shenzhen's existing fixed asset investment but also a fundamental driving force behind its rapid economic growth.

Even more noteworthy than Shenzhen's investment amount and growth rate are the structure and benefits of the investments. On the working conference on fixed-asset investment and major project construction of Shenzhen held at the beginning of 2018, the goal of increasing the city's fixed-asset investment by 20% to realize a total amount of over 600 billion *yuan* in 2018 was set. It was also emphasized on the conference that the key to high-quality development of fixed asset investment was to optimize investment structure, specifically, by building the International Science and Technology Innovation Center, constructing the Guangdong-Hong Kong-Macao Greater Bay Area, facilitating the integration of the special economic zone, working on relatively weak areas in social welfare, focusing on the supply-side structural reform of infrastructure, and speedily improving the system and mechanisms for investment and financing. Shenzhen has attached equal importance to expanding investment scale and raising investment effectiveness and has been endeavoring to expand effective supply through optimizing investment structure, and has, as a result, well-realized coordinated progress between urban quality improvement and economic growth, as well as between industrial upgrading and social welfare improvement.

4.2 Dual attributes of government

Looking back at Shenzhen's experience, we could see clearly that over the four decades since China's reform and opening up, the city has realized coordinated progress and prosperity in industrial development, urban construction and social welfare, and Shenzhen Government has been a vital contributor to the achievements.

First, with regard to the industrial economy, Shenzhen Government allows enterprises to give full play to their role in the market economy and designs policies and measures in accordance with the principles of "planning and guiding, support and coordination, supervision and management."

Second, with regard to livelihood economy, Shenzhen Government fulfills its responsibility of supplying public goods to the society and designs policies and measures related to social security following the principles of "guaranteeing basic needs, ensuring fairness and justice, raising effectiveness and efficiency."

Third, with regard to urban economy, which belongs to the field of resource generation, a hybrid economic field mainly comprised of quasi-operative resources that could be developed by both enterprises and the government, Shenzhen Government plays the role of "formulating overall plans, participating in construction and conducting orderly management."

Of the three domains we'll mainly look into government's function in the urban economy, and since the marketization of quasi-operative resources, that is, investment into and development and construction of urban infrastructure, present two problems in practice, one being determining the investment carrier and the other being operating the investment fund, we'll focus our attention on Shenzhen Government's measures in the two aspects.

Pertaining to the problem of determining the investment carrier, Shenzhen Government has been making tremendous efforts to attract foreign capital since the beginning of the reform and opening up. It promulgated the provisional regulations on encouraging private enterprises early in 1987 and later issued *The Master Plan of Shenzhen City*, which placed the development, operation and management of urban infrastructure investments into the market system. Specifically, Shenzhen Government invests in urban construction projects in various ways, such as sole proprietorship, joint venture, partnership, joint-stock company and even state-owned privately run enterprise, and in the meanwhile constantly optimizes the city's development structure in accordance with actual changes of market supply, social demand and urban development, so as to avoid massive losses by preventing problems otherwise common in urban construction and development, mainly "huge wastes of urban resources, wasteful repeated construction of urban infrastructure, and low-level, low-standard and disorderly operation of urban economic management, which arise from the government providing for society public goods as free and shared services, investing without profiting, constructing without operating, focusing on social benefits only but ignoring economic benefits, and focusing on public welfare only but ignoring efficiency."

Regarding the operation of investment funds, tapping the city's potential as one of the earliest places in China to have a capital market, Shenzhen Government takes the initiative to use fiscal funds to leverage social capital into urban infrastructure construction. Specific steps taken include issuing bonds or convertible bonds, issuing stocks, setting up project funds or investing in projects by local and foreign funds, back-door listing projects as entities, securitization of project assets, project merger and acquisition, and leasing, mortgage, swaps, auction, etc. Shenzhen Government, making use of its charging and pricing power, also uses Build-Operate-Transfer (BOT) and Transfer-Operate-Transfer (TOT), amongst others, to implement capital operation of franchise rights, uses the Public-Private Partnership (PPP) model, etc. to build equity carriers and uses Port-Park-City (PPC) as a development model, and have in these ways built one after another rather perfect economic zones integrating infrastructure, logistics, finance and industries. The measures have enabled the government to overcome the construction fund bottleneck and achieve multiplied effects with limited public finance.

Shenzhen has established an effective mode of "government promotion, enterprise participation and market-based operation" for the investment, development, operation and management of urban infrastructure. The city's success implies that regional governments are one of the main participants in urban economy, that governments should and must rely on and act according to market rules in the investment, development, operation and management in this field, and that governments should take on the macro functions of guiding, coordinating and supervising in the field. Shenzhen Government has been following these principles to design its policies and measures for the development and construction of quasi-operative resources or urban infrastructure.

The above analysis shows that Shenzhen Government has dual attributes. On the one hand, its actions show a micro attribute. Its planning, guidance and support of operative resources (industrial economy) and its investment, operation and participation in quasi-operative resources (urban economy), namely, urban infrastructure, have led it to become the centralized agency of micro stakeholders in the regional economy. In the meanwhile, Shenzhen Government competes with other regions to realize maximum regional economic benefits through innovations in concept, technology, organization and institution. At such times Shenzhen Government is playing the quasi-micro role. It is different from yet also closely related to enterprises. The differences are in their behavioral purposes, development modes, regulatory factors and assessment criteria, and the relations are that both Shenzhen Government and enterprises are resource distributors and effective innovators to certain degrees, that competition mechanism applies both to the government's regional development and to the enterprises' market development, and that the economic behaviors of both must abide by market rules. At this point, Shenzhen Government's regional jurisdiction power shifts towards regional management power. It distributes resources to maximize regional benefits, with a focus on the solicitation of funds, investment, development, operation and management of urban infrastructure projects. Therefore, Shenzhen Government's actions are subject to both political and economic constraints, and its "effective actions" can raise the region's competitive advantage and complete the region's economic transition and social transformation in advance. In this sense, the Shenzhen Government possesses a certain degree of micro attribute.

On the other hand, Shenzhen Government's actions also present a macro attribute. Its regulation, supervision and management of operative resources (industrial economy) and its provision of non-operative resources (livelihood economy), that is, public goods or public welfare undertakings, under the principles of "guaranteeing basic needs, ensuring fairness and justice, raising effectiveness and efficiency," make it the agent of the national government in its local region. Shenzhen Government regulates and controls the economy through the means of planning, investment, consumption, price, taxation and law, while upholding social stability by providing basic social guarantee, public services, etc. When doing these, Shenzhen Government is playing a quasi-macro role, performing the political, economic, urban and social functions in its region with the public nature and coercive force bestowed on it. Specific steps taken include: studying and formulating the medium- and long-term plans for the region's economic and social development; promoting the dynamic balance between the aggregate supply and aggregate demand in the region; formulating economic policies, industrial policies and technological policies; investing vigorously in infrastructure construction; providing public goods and services; effectively adjusting income distribution and redistribution; and maintaining regional aggregate economic growth, dynamic equilibrium of economic structure and effective urban upgrading while upholding market rules and order of the region, regulating prices, curbing unemployment rates and promoting harmonious and sustainable development of society.

In practice, Shenzhen Government's quasi-macro role manifests mainly in its fiscal revenue and expenditure activities. It uses revenues from tax collection, transfer payments, equity and others to maintain its own operation and perform various functions by purchase expenditures and transfer expenditures. Fiscal purchase expenditures comprise social consumption expenditures and fiscal investment expenditures, the former including education and culture expenses, science expenses, health service expenses, as well as administrative expenses in industry, transportation, commerce, agriculture and other departments, and the latter including investment in infrastructure, investment in scientific and technological research and development, and policy-based financial investment to support industries in urgent need of development. Transfer expenditures are mainly for providing social security and fiscal subsidies. Among government expenditures, social consumption expenditures and fiscal investment expenditures, as purchase expenditures, directly affect the allocation of social resources and various factors. Their scale and structure give a general picture of the strength and scope of the Shenzhen Government's direct engagement in resource distribution and reflect its ability to directly regulate social resources and the degree of its impact on the social economy within a given period of time. Transfer expenditures, whereas, have an indirect impact on the distribution of social resources and various factors and assist in the implementation of social equity policies.

The dual attributes of the Shenzhen Government are rooted in the government's inherent purpose, that is, achieving the best outcome in economic development, urban construction and social stability with the lowest cost.

The dual attributes manifest in two aspects, the first being institutional supply, which includes the provision of policies, laws and regulations aimed at ensuring fair, just and effective supply of various public goods and public welfare services, and the second being economic regulation, which includes support for industry development and input for urban infrastructure construction, aimed at effectively guiding the transformation and upgrading of industries and the modernization and development of the city. It could be said that such dual attributes demonstrated by Shenzhen Government correct a deficiency of traditional economics system or traditional market theory, and are the theme of a new episode of the modern economic system and modern market theory. Shenzhen's practice over the four decades since the reform and opening up tells us that enterprises are the main competitors in the industrial economy whereas regional governments are the main competitors in the urban economy. Modern economics has also revealed that apart from microeconomics, which has enterprises as the object of study, and macroeconomics, which has the nation as the object of study, there should also be mezzoeconomics that takes regional governments as its object of study.

4.3 Government participating in regional competition

The public nature of the Shenzhen Government's role in regional management is mainly manifested in two aspects, guaranteeing regional public expenditure and maintaining regional market and social stability through taxation, industry and commerce, public security and supervision measures, and in the meanwhile ensuring these are conducted in an open, fair and just manner through administration, legislation, judiciary and other means. The coercive nature of the Shenzhen Government in regional management manifests itself both in the government's super-economic coercive powers such as legislation, judiciary and administration and in its economic coercive powers such as its control over money and affairs. From an external point of view, Shenzhen Government's regional management is embodied in its three major functions of industrial development, urban construction and social welfare, while from the internal point of view, the government's regional management is in essence its effective distribution of the various tangible and intangible resources, existing and potential ones alike, in the region.

The regional management practice across the world and the success of China's reform and opening up have already told us that, on the basis of ensuring the supply of social welfare services and public goods for the region with the principles of "guaranteeing basic needs, ensuring fairness and justice, raising effectiveness and efficiency," the government would, through the market mechanism, in all probability leave part or most of the urban infrastructure to the private sector for investment, development and management. The purpose is to prevent urban resources, especially urban infrastructure, from laying idle or being wasted and to avoid poor-quality urban construction and disorderly urban management. During this process, that is, the process of transforming quasi-operative resources into operative resources, the nature and equity structure of the carrier of urban infrastructure investment, that is, of the infrastructure project company (sole proprietorship, joint venture, partnership, joint-stock company and even state-owned privately run enterprise) must conform to market rules, and the capital operation of urban infrastructure investment—whether through BOT, PPP or other franchising modes, or through the issuance of bonds or stocks—must pass the test of market competition. It could be said that from the very beginning the "government promotion, enterprise participation and market-based operation" mode of Shenzhen has bestowed the city's government with the possibilities to compete with other regions in urban economic construction and development, and the dual attributes of Shenzhen Government along with its regional competitiveness arising therefrom means that its participation in the competition is inherently inevitable.

By analyzing the economic behaviors of the Shenzhen Government, we have pinpointed its three economic functions, distinguished between the city's three types of economic resources, clearly demarcated the different positions of Shenzhen Government and enterprises in urban economy and industrial economy, and explored Shenzhen Government's dual roles and special functions at both the micro and the macro levels. The analysis on the one hand directly exposes the existence of two competitors in the modern market system, namely, enterprises and regional governments. Competition of the enterprises takes place mainly in the industrial economy while that of regional governments occurs mainly in the urban economy. There's no competition between enterprises and regional governments in the field of the industrial economy. The analysis on the other hand shows that regional governments' competition is mainly concentrated in urban infrastructure construction. Its nature is the competition for various tangible and intangible resources in urban economic development, its main objective is to optimize the resource allocation, raise the economic efficiency and increase the rates of return of cities in the region, and the government, when designing supportive policies and measures, take advantage of the leading edges of the region's urban economy and have in mind the sustainable development goals of the region. Regional government competition and enterprise competition, taking place in different fields, together constitute a double-tier competition system of modern market economy system. As the competitors in the double-tier market competition, regional markets and enterprises co-exist and complement each other.

4.4 Objective function of regional government competition—theory of fiscal revenue determination

Fiscal revenue refers to the sum of all money collected by the government in return for its fulfillment of functions such as implementing public policies and providing public goods and services. It is expressed as the monetary revenue obtained by the government in a given period (usually a fiscal year). Fiscal revenue is an important indicator of a regional government's financial capabilities as the scope and quantity of public goods and services a regional government is able to provide in social-economic activities largely depend on its fiscal revenue status.

Internationally commonly used classification of fiscal revenue categorizes the revenues based on the form in which they are obtained by the government into tax revenue, income from state-owned assets, national debt revenue, fee income and other revenues. Tax revenue, the most important form and main source of the fiscal revenue of modern nations, is a form of compulsory and free revenue that the regional government obtains by virtue of its political power and according to specific standards. Income from state-owned assets is a collective term for the profits, rents, dividends, bonuses, fund use fees and other incomes obtained by the regional government by virtue of its ownership of state-owned assets. National debt income mainly refers to the paid income obtained by the state through credit. Fee income refers to the use fees and regulation fees the regional government collects from the beneficiaries when providing public services, doing administrative management or supplying specific public facilities. Use fees are the fees the regional government charges from users of public facilities according to certain standards, such as the fees charged from vehicles using the highways, bridges and tunnels constructed by the government. Regulation fees are the fees charged by the regional government for providing specific services or specific administrative management for individual citizens and include administrative fees and judicial regulation fees.

The prime determinant of a region's fiscal revenue is tax revenue. When income from state-owned assets and national debt revenue is fixed, fee income also carries a certain weight in deciding fiscal revenue.

Let's first look at the most important factor, tax. Tax revenue, being the primary source of funds for the regional government to perform its political, economic and social functions as well as to produce, purchase and provide public goods, is of vital importance for the regional government to fulfill its functions of maintaining social order, carrying out social management, investing in infrastructure, making economic planning, adjusting the industrial structure, developing science, education, culture and health, providing social security, etc. Keynes and Keynesianism refer to the state's taxation function and its mechanism of making tax policies depending on the circumstances as "artificial stabilizer," meaning that the government may decide what policy to adopt according to the fluctuation of the economic cycle, specifically, responding to the economic recession by reducing tax (increasing spending) to stimulate effective demand, raise employment and increase citizen income so as to promote national economy recovery, and in case of economic expansion, increasing tax (reducing spending) to restrain economic overheating and reduce demand and price in order to stabilize national economy

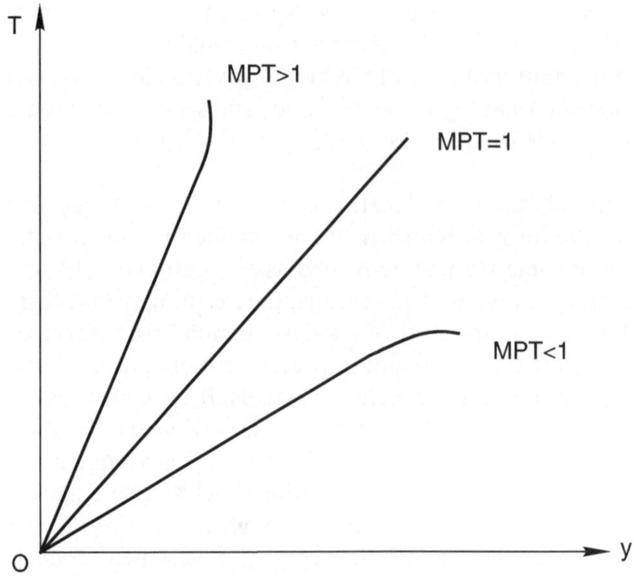

Figure 4.1 Graphic representation of tax's effect as automatic stabilizer.

development. Meanwhile, Paul Samuelson terms taxation as an "automatic stabilizer," believing that under the premise of stable taxation scope and tax rates, tax revenue changes with the change of national income, and plays a regulatory role in periodic fluctuations of the economy[1] (Figure 4.1).

T represents tax revenue, y represents national income and MPT represents marginal propensity to tax, namely, the fraction of the tax growth rate to the national income growth rate, as indicated by the following formula:

$$MPT = (\triangle T/T_O)/(\triangle y/y_O) = (\triangle T/\triangle y) * (y_O/T_O)$$

According to the formula:

> When a progressive tax system is adopted, MPT > 1. When income is below the exemption limit, the tax rate is zero and the tax is zero. As taxable income increases, the tax rate also rises, the proportion of national income that is levied as tax revenue gradually increases, and MPT > 1. When the economy expands, the growth rate of tax revenue is higher than the growth rate of national income. As tax revenue goes up, effective demand decreases and economic growth slows down. When the economy contracts, the decline rate of tax revenue is higher than the decline rate of national income. As tax revenue decreases, effective demand goes up and economic growth picks up speed.

When a proportional tax system is adopted, MPT = 1, that is, there is a linear relationship between tax revenue and national income. When the economy expands, tax revenue and national income grow at the same rate, and the inhibition effect of tax increase on effective demand is weaker than that under a progressive tax system. When the economy contracts, tax revenue and national income decline at the same rate and the stimulation effect of tax decrease on effective demand is weaker than that under a progressive tax system.

When a regressive tax system is practiced, MPT < 1. When the economy expands, the growth rate of tax revenue is lower than the growth rate of national income, and the inhibition effect of tax increase on effective demand is weaker than that under a progressive tax system or under a proportional tax system. When the economy contracts, the decline rate of tax revenue is lower than that of national income, and the stimulation effect of tax decrease on effective demand is weaker than that under a progressive tax system or under a proportional tax system.

It could be seen that in different stages of the economic cycle the increase or decrease of tax revenue changes with the increase or decrease of national income and in this process serves as a "stabilizer" in regulating total social demand and stabilizing economic development. So governments of all countries make use of this "stabilizer" to increase fiscal revenue and stabilize regional economic development, specifically, by promoting economic growth, improving management efficiency, formulating various taxation scopes and tax rates and using an optimal combination of different taxes.

Second, let's examine the impact of fee income on fiscal revenue. Fee income is the charges regional governments collect in return for public goods by simulating the pricing of private products. The purpose is to recover all or part of the cost of the special goods and services provided. In reality, it is sometimes difficult to clearly distinguish fee income from tax, but there are obvious differences between the two. First, fees are directly associated with particular goods and services provided by regional governments and the income from particular fees is used for particular purposes, while tax revenue has no direct association with the goods and services provided by regional governments and is allocated and used by the government from one pool instead of being designated for any specific purpose. Second, fee charging is usually regional governments' means to raise fund for specific purposes while taxes are the general financing means of governments. The third difference is that relatively speaking fee income is not strictly required to be included in the regional fiscal budget to be used all together, while tax revenue must be strictly managed and used in accordance with the fiscal budget. And fourth, fee income is generally speaking subject to relatively weaker legal and normative regulation while tax revenue is subject to higher levels of legislative supervision and administrative management.

Fee charging could not only improve the efficiency of public goods allocation and thus help avoid "tragedy of the commons" but also remedy the market failure and help lessen the negative spillover effects of private goods. These benefits make fee income, primarily made up of use fees and regulation fees, another important determining factor of regional governments' fiscal revenue. Governments of countries around the world endeavor to elevate fee income by promoting economic development, perfecting policies and measures and raising management efficiency. An analysis of the current fiscal revenue of countries in the world shows that generally speaking, fee income accounts for a larger proportion in the fiscal revenue of low- and middle-income countries, while for high-income countries the situation depends—for countries with relatively centralized distribution system fee income accounts for relatively lower proportions and for countries with decentralized distribution system fee income accounts for higher proportions.

How regional fiscal revenue in a certain period is determined gives a comprehensive picture of a region's economic strength, for it not only reflects the region's economic development level, but it also indicates how well the regional government is doing in distributing the region's operative resources, non-operative resources and quasi-operative resources, in supplying public goods and services with appropriate varieties and scales, and in improving the environment for regional economic development.

The structure of a region's tax revenue and fee income depends on the region's economic structure, and the scale of the region's revenue primarily depends on the "9-in-3," namely, regional economic development level covering projects, industrial chains, and imports and exports, economic policies and measures comprising infrastructure investment policies, talents and science and technology support policies, and fiscal and financial policies, and economic management efficiency, specifically, the efficiency of the policy system, the environment system, and the management system.

On the basis of the above analysis, we will discuss the determination mechanism of fiscal revenue, that is, the objective function of regional government competition (fiscal revenue maximization) from the standpoint of fiscal expenditure (FE) and from the standpoint of fiscal revenue.

From the standpoint of FE, the total expenditure of a regional government during a specific period is predetermined by the fiscal budget. So the government's FE is constant. But the government may adjust the distribution and allocation of expenditure in different fields to achieve maximum benefit. To facilitate analysis we'll extract three types of spending from the two large categories of regional governments' FE (purchase expenditure and transfer expenditure) to discuss their functional relationship: (1) Consumption Expenditure (CE) is mainly for improving the environment, policies and management system that support a region's economy, and indicates the management efficiency of the regional government. (2) Investment Expenditure (IE) is mainly used to improve the infrastructure, such as roads, bridges and power grids, in a region, and reflects the effectiveness of the regional government's economic policies. (3)

Transfer Expenditure (TE) is mainly used to improve the talents quality, science and technology, and financial support of the regional economy, and like investment expenditure, also reflects the effectiveness of the regional government's economic policies.

As mentioned above, the three always have the relationship below:

$$CE + IE + TE = FE \tag{4.1}$$

Consumption, investment and transfer, the three types of expenditure act upon the development level of the regional economy by their influence on the regional government's management efficiency and economic policy. Specifically, investment expenditure will elevate the local infrastructure level and lead to more investment projects in the region, and consumption expenditure and transfer expenditure will improve the local industrial chain and import and export conditions. Therefore, with other conditions unchanged, the level of regional economic development Y could be written as a function of CE, IE and TE in the following manner:

$$Y = g(CE, IE, TE) \tag{4.2}$$

Formula (4.2) does not give a clear functional form because in common economic systems different kinds of expenditure are complexly related and mutually restraining. For the purpose of this simplified discussion we are having, it could be assumed that the economic effects of the three types of expenditure do not have an obvious linkage and could be superimposed. This allows us to simplify formula (4.2) into the form below, with which we may look into the impact of each item:

$$Y = \varphi_1(Y_1, Y_0) * CE + \varphi_2(Y_2, Y_0) * IE + \varphi_3(Y_3, Y_0) * TE + Const1 \tag{4.3}$$

The first three items represent the economic effects of the three types of expenditure, and Const1 represents the sum of economic effects of elements other than FE, such as those of factor endowment and capital accumulation. The three coefficients, namely, φ_1 (y_1, y_0), φ_2 (y_2, y_0) and φ_3 (y_3, y_0), respectively, describe to what degree regional economic development is influenced by changes in consumption expenditure, investment expenditure and transfer expenditure. As variable and sensitive coefficients, their value is related to the stage of regional economic development. Y_0 represents the economic level at the beginning of the period, and Y_i (i = 1, 2, 3; the same below) represents the threshold or target value for different economic development stages. Variable coefficient $\varphi_i(.)$ represents the different degrees of impact the three kinds of expenditure have on the economy in the factor-driven stage, investment-driven stage and innovation-driven stage. Therefore, the following factors need to be taken into account when the variable coefficient $\varphi_i(.)$ is set. First, as the economy develops, the economic effect of the three types of expenditure generally overlaps with the growth curve, that is, in the early stage of economic development, the boosting effect of increasing FE on the economy is very obvious, but as the economy develops further, the economic effect brought by marginal unit expenditure will gradually go down. Second, the type of expenditure playing the dominant role differs in different stages of economic development. In the early stage of economic development, that is, the factor-driven stage, soft facilities are the most essential for attracting enterprises and talents, and at this time, consumption expenditure has the strongest economic effect. When it comes to the middle stage of economic development, that is, the investment-driven stage, investment expenditure has the strongest economic effect thanks to its good multiplier effect. In the late stage, the economy enters the innovation-driven period, during which qualified personnel, science and technology, and financial support come to be vital, and the strongest economic effect is created by transfer expenditure.

The above is an analysis from the standpoint of the government's FE. Next, we will further look into the determination mechanism of fiscal revenue from the point of view of the government's Fiscal Income (FInc). As mentioned above, the government's fiscal income consists of national debt revenue, income from state-owned assets, fee income, tax revenue and other revenues. It could be assumed that fee income is proportional to the level of infrastructure construction and tax revenue is proportional to the level of economic development. Income from state-owned assets, national debt revenue and other revenues are barely affected by the factors discussed here and are therefore assumed to be constant. Then we can get the following formula:

$$\text{FInc} = \tau\text{CumP(IE)} + \omega\text{Y} + \text{Const2} \tag{4.4}$$

CumP(IE) is the capital stock of infrastructure projects brought by investment expenditure over previous years, τCumP(IE) represents the income fee the government obtains from infrastructure projects, ωY represents the tax revenue the government gets from the total economic output, and Const2 represents the sum of national debt revenue, income from state-owned assets and other revenues, which could be regarded as constant over a period of time.

The expenditure budget of the government is based on the fiscal revenue projection of the next year. Under the conditions that Fiscal Income is larger than FE and that formula (4.1) is conformed to, the government could maximize Fiscal Income by adjusting the three types of expenditure, namely CE, IE and TE. The optimized formula is as follows:

$$\begin{aligned}
\max_{\{\text{CE, IE, TE}\}} \quad & \text{FInc} = \tau\text{CumP(IE)} + \omega[\varphi_1(\text{Y}_1,\ \text{Y}_0) * \text{CE} + \varphi_2(\text{Y}_2,\ \text{Y}_0) * \text{IE} \\
& \qquad + \varphi_3(\text{Y}_3,\ \text{Y}_0) * \text{TE} + \text{Const1}] \\
& \qquad + \text{Const2} \\
\text{s.t.} \quad & \text{CE} + \text{IE} + \text{TE} = \text{FE}, \\
& \text{FInc} \geq \text{FE}, \\
& 0 < \omega < 1.
\end{aligned}$$

As shown by the formula, the growth-boosting effect of the three types of expenditure, consumption, investment and transfer, differs in different stages of economic development. Thus, in each stage, the government should allocate more funds for the expenditure type that's the most effective in promoting the economy in that stage.

Specifically, when the economy is in the factor-driven stage, consumption expenditure has the highest contributing power to economic development, and the government should focus on improving the environment, management and policies that support the regional economy by raising the region's consumption expenditure. During this stage, $\varphi_1(Y_1,Y_0)$ is bigger than $\varphi_2(Y_2,Y_0)$ and $\varphi_3(Y_3,Y_0)$, meaning that the increase of fiscal income brought by higher consumption expenditure will offset and surpass the revenue decrease brought by lower investment expenditure and transfer expenditure.

If the economy is in the investment-driven stage, investment expenditure has the highest contributing power to economic development, and the government should focus its spending more on infrastructure construction, raising the region's investment expenditure. During this stage, $\varphi_2(Y_2,Y_0)$ is bigger than $\varphi_1(Y_1,Y_0)$ and $\varphi_3(Y_3,Y_0)$, that is, the elasticity of investment expenditure is higher than that of consumption expenditure and transfer expenditure. So the increase of fiscal income brought by higher investment expenditure will outweigh the fiscal income decrease resulting from lower consumption expenditure and transfer expenditure.

When an economy develops into the innovation-driven stage, the innovative ability of talents and enterprises make the greatest contribution to economic development, and the government should accordingly raise input into the scientific and technological level of personnel (human resources subsidy) and input into fiscal and financial support (financial subsidy), which would require higher transfer expenditure. In this stage, $\varphi_3(Y_3,Y_0)$ is bigger than $\varphi_1(Y_1,Y_0)$ and $\varphi_2(Y_2,Y_0)$, that is, transfer expenditure has the greatest elasticity and its increase will bring a fiscal income rise that outweighs the decrease of fiscal revenue caused by decreasing consumption expenditure and investment expenditure.

When the economy reaches the wealth-driven stage, the impact of the three types of expenditure on fiscal income would be almost the same and the government should flexibly distribute expenditure according to the region's development characteristics and advantageous industries.

To sum up, the scale of fiscal revenue in a region depends on the region's economic development, policy measures, management efficiency and other relevant factors. The above discussion of the determination mechanism of fiscal revenue reveals that key strategies of regional government competition are to follow the fiscal policy of "spending based on revenue" and "planning revenue based on expenditure," and to take effective measures to adjust FE structure according to the change of elasticity coefficients in the formula of fiscal revenue growth so as to promote normal growth of fiscal revenue.

4.5 Function of fiscal expenditure and investment expenditure of regional government

Fiscal revenue is the prerequisite of FE and FE is the purpose of fiscal revenue. First of all, fiscal revenue provides financial guarantee for the regional government to fulfill its functions—the regional government must possess a certain amount of social products in order to perform its functions and fiscal revenue is an important means for it to raise the funds needed. Secondly, fiscal revenue is an important mechanism for straightening out the relationship among the government, enterprises and individuals in terms of material interests. In practice, the obtainment methods of fiscal revenue and the amounts collected are related to the interests of many parties. Only when these various interests are properly handled can the government fully mobilize the enthusiasm of all parties in the region and achieve the purpose of optimizing resource allocation and coordinating distribution relations. Lastly, the amount of fiscal revenue determines the possible scale and maximum amount of FE. The former is the guarantee of the latter. Conversely, fiscal distribution is a two-sided process involving both income and expenditure. Only by optimizing the structure of FE and improving its effectiveness can the regional government boost economic growth and eventually raise fiscal revenue in return.

From another point of view, FE is the total amount of various expenses the regional government makes to perform its functions. The amount and structure of FE reflect the scale and depth of the government's involvement as well as the government's position and role in the region's economic development and social life.

To examine FE in detail, there are two ways to classify it, one by fiscal function and the other by economic nature. By fiscal function, regional government's expenditure could be put into five categories, namely, economic construction, social, cultural and educational undertakings, national defense, administrative management and others, and such classification will clearly reveal how much weight the regional government gives to the five categories and the change of its expenditure structure over time. By economic nature, FE could be classified into purchase expenditure and transfer expenditure, the former comprising social consumption expenditure (mainly expenses in administration, national defense, education, culture, scientific research, health care, etc.) and fiscal investment expenditure (mainly covering natural monopoly industries, infrastructure, agriculture, etc.) and the latter referring to expenses incurred by regional government's one-way transfer of the ownership of part of its income (used for social insurance, social relief, poverty alleviation, etc.)

The International Monetary Fund's functional classification and economic classification of FE represent the common expenditure classification approach used by regional governments around the globe (Table 4.1).

From the standpoint of economics, the regional government's two approaches to expenditure classification point to the policy measures, purposes

Table 4.1 IMF's Classification of Fiscal Expenditure

By functions of government	*By economic nature*
1 General public services	1 Current expenditure
2 Defense	1 Expenditure on goods and services
3 Education	1 Wages, salaries and other items
4 Health	2 Other purchases of goods and services
5 Social security and benefits	2 Interest payment
6 Housing and community amenities	3 Subsidies and other regular transfers
7 Other community and social services	1 To public enterprises
8 Economic services	2 To lower governments
1 Agriculture	3 To households
2 Mining	4 To other residents
3 Manufacturing	5 To abroad
4 Electric power industry	2 Capital expenditure
5 Roads	1 Purchase of existing and new fixed assets
6 Water transportation	2 Inventory purchase
7 Railway	3 Purchase of land and intangible assets
8 Communication	4 Capital transfers
9 Other economic services	3 Net loan
9 Other expenses that cannot be classified	
1 Interest on the public debt	
2 Others	

and methods it adopts to deal with the three types of resources in the region, namely, operative resources, non-operative resources and quasi-operative resources.

For operative resources (industrial economy), the government, following the principle of letting the market allocate resources, hands resources to enterprises, the private sector and other domestic and foreign investors as far as possible by means of capitalization. Playing the role of "planning and guiding, support and coordination, supervision and management," the government formulates appropriate tax policies, fiscal subsidies, depreciation policies, etc. to guide and restrict the direction, scale and structure of non-governmental investment. Of the measures, fiscal subsidies, such as price subsidy, foreign trade subsidy and fiscal discount, are a type of transfer expenditure. Either cash or in-kind subsidy, they act on the entire process of industrial economy, from production to circulation, distribution and consumption.

Fiscal subsidy is a worldwide economic phenomenon. Regional governments all over the world regard this special form of FE as an important means to regulate industrial economic activities. In order to maintain a world trade order featuring non-discrimination, freedom, transparency and fair competition, the World Trade Organization (WTO) formulated the Agreement on Subsidies and Countervailing Measures ("SCM Agreement"). The Agreement defines subsidy as a governmental act or measure where a government or any public body within the territory of a Member grants financial assistance to a certain enterprise or an industry or provides support to them in terms of price or income, resulting in the direct or indirect increase in the export of a certain product from the Member's territory or the decrease in the import of a certain product into its territory, or thus causing harm to the interests of other Members. Here fiscal subsidy is defined as an international trade means to promote exports and restrict imports. The Agreement states that recipients of fiscal subsidy are mainly domestic enterprises engaging in production and sales, that subsidy methods are various, and that the result is the subsidized party gaining benefits from the increase/decrease of income, cost or tax amount. The Agreement also points out that subsidies have specificity and that their primary purpose is to raise the competitiveness of certain industries or products in domestic and foreign markets. Put in simple terms, fiscal subsidies as a special kind of regional government expenditure can stabilize economic development, promote industrial restructuring, and boost foreign trade growth, but excessive fiscal subsidies will lead to unfair competition and damage to the market environment.

For non-operative resources (livelihood economy), regional governments should fully take on the supply, distribution and management responsibilities, and design relevant social safety and security policies in accordance with the principles of "guaranteeing basic needs, ensuring fairness and justice, raising effectiveness and efficiency." Here we'll focus on two kinds of FE related to non-operative resources. The first is expenses for regional administration and national defense, which belong to fiscal purchase expenditure. These expenses are to meet purely public needs with products and services provided to maintain social security and social order and enjoyed by all citizens free of charge. Among them, administration expenses include those incurred by administrative management organs, judicial organs, procuratorial organs, foreign affairs organs, etc. when performing their functions, and national defense expenses include those spent for national defense construction and military construction. From one point of view, administrative management and national defense are unproductive labor that do not directly contribute to the production and consumption of social wealth. In this sense, expenditures for them are purely "wasteful use" of social wealth and should be kept at a minimum. Yet from another point of view, the two are prerequisites for the production and consumption of social wealth as national defense protects people's production and life safety and administrative activities maintain people's production and life order. In this sense, the two kinds of expenses are not "wasteful use" of social wealth, but a necessary part of the production and consumption of the whole society. In this book, we will focus the discussion of livelihood economy on social security and thus government administration and national defense expenditures are regarded as an established factor and will not be discussed for the time being.

The other kind of FE related to non-operative resources we'll focus on is social security expenditure, one of the most important transfer expenditure items in regional FE. An important means of redistribution, social security expenditures are free and one-way payments the regional government makes with fiscal funds according to certain laws and regulations to provide essential basic life security and social services to members of society faced with life difficulties due to unemployment, old age, disease, injury suffered on the job, childbirth and other situations. Regional social security comprises four components, namely, social insurance (endowment insurance, medical insurance, unemployment insurance, maternity and disease insurance, injury and disability insurance, funeral and wills insurance, etc.), social welfare (social subsidies, social welfare facilities, social services, employee welfare, etc.), social relief (covering citizens who are helpless and have no livelihood, citizens who temporarily live in straitened circumstances due to natural disasters, citizens who have sources of income but whose living standard is lower than or only equivalent to the national legal minimum poverty standard, etc.) and favorable treatment and pension (pension, social preferential treatment, employment of veterans, settlement after retirement, social services for favorable treatment, etc.). As a type of transfer expenditure regional government makes to improve people's welfare, social security expenditure can not only remedy the problems caused by failures of the market mechanism but also serve as an "internal stabilizer" to regulate the economy when the region's economic cycle changes. A sound regional social security system, one that features well-established standards of social security projects, proper collection and distribution of social security funds, and an effective management system and supervision mechanism, will lay a solid foundation and provide a good environment for the sustainable development of the regional economy.

For quasi-operative resources (urban economy), that is, the investment into and development and construction of hard and soft urban infrastructure, the regional government should decide whether to distribute and develop such resources with the same principles guiding the handling of operative resources or to operate and manage them following the principles of public welfare undertakings, and the decision should be made based on the fiscal conditions of the government itself, the demand of the market and the degree of acceptance of the public. This is a major topic this book intends to look into and the following is a detailed discussion.

We'll first look at hard urban infrastructure (see Chapter 3 for details), which could be put into two main categories, economic infrastructure, namely, permanent projects, buildings, equipment and facilities, and social infrastructure, that is, facilities for culture, education, medical care and social security. Investment expenditure, one of the two major parts of the fiscal purchase expenditure of regional government, is primarily put in hard urban infrastructure. Hard urban infrastructure is in the "upstream" of a region's economic development chain, which means that generally speaking, the development of the three main types of industries in a region all require

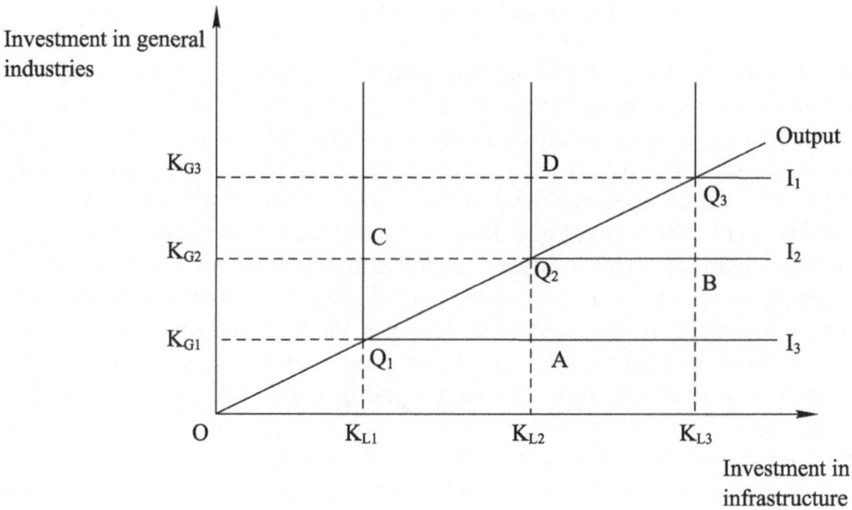

Figure 4.2 Model diagram of output.

expanding scale, increasing speed and even moderately outstripping growth of the investment into and construction of hard urban infrastructure. The price of products and services generated by hard urban infrastructure will form part of the product cost of other industries and the price change of hard urban infrastructure will cause a series of chain reactions, notably cost fluctuations of other industrial products. The relationship between investment into and construction of hard urban infrastructure and investment in general industries can be demonstrated with the following model diagram of output (see Figure 4.2).

The vertical and horizontal axis of Figure 10 respectively represents general industry investment and infrastructure investment. The ray starting from the origin is the output line, and I_1, I_2 and I_3 are lines indicating the relationships between infrastructure investment and general industry investment at certain values. When infrastructure investment is K_{L1} and general industry investment is K_{G1}, the output is Q_1. If general industry investment increases to K_{G2} and infrastructure investment remains at K_{L1}, the intersection point is C, that is, the output cannot reach Q_2. Conversely, if infrastructure investment increases to K_{L2} and general industry investment remains at K_{G1}, the intersection point will be A, that is, the output cannot reach Q_2 either. If the output is to rise to Q_2, infrastructure investment and general industry investment must be increased to K_{L2} and K_{G2} respectively, and so on and so forth. In other words, to achieve a certain output, infrastructure investment and general industry investment must maintain a certain matching relationship and both increase at a certain rate. Results of empirical analysis indicate that most of the developed countries in Europe and America started by increasing investment in general industries, and then went on to increase infrastructure investment. Their growth path could be roughly mapped as $Q_1 \rightarrow C \rightarrow Q_2 \rightarrow D \rightarrow Q_3$. Countries such as Japan and the Republic of Korea, contrarily, first increased infrastructure investment and then increased general industry investment. So their growth path is, roughly, $Q_1 \rightarrow A \rightarrow Q_2 \rightarrow B \rightarrow Q_3$.[2]

Then let's look at soft urban infrastructure (see Chapter 3 for details). Of a regional government's expenditure items, investment in soft urban infrastructure, specifically, expenses, research fees and subsidies in education, science, culture, health, sports, publishing, earthquake, ocean and other sectors, is social consumption expenditure, which belongs to fiscal purchase expenditure. Regional governments all over the world place expenditures for education, science, culture and health in the non-productive domain, believing that input in these sectors only constitutes direct consumption and does not directly create material wealth. Yet from the standpoint of their economic nature, most of the activities in education, science, culture and health are not purely public goods provided by regional governments—they also include a part that's directly invested, built and developed by private enterprises. Throughout the progression of world history, in the sectors of education, science, culture and health, the investment of regional governments and that of private enterprises have long been coexisting and growing together. It can be said that the education, science, culture and health sectors are only partially, or are not entirely, public items of regional society.

In terms of economic nature, urban infrastructure has the characteristics of quasi-operative resources and belongs to the field of resource generation. The investment, development and construction of its soft and hard facilities can be undertaken by the government, by private enterprises, or by both in a mixed economic mode (see Chapter 3 for details).

Here we will mainly look into regional government's investment expenditure, the amount of which puts a limit on the scope and scale of the government's investments. The total amount of the government's FE is limited by its total fiscal revenue, which is relatively fixed. This means the amount of investment expenditure depends on the structure of the government's FE, specifically, first the proportions purchase expenditure and transfer expenditure respectively account for in the FE, and second, the proportions investment expenditure and social consumption expenditure respectively account for in purchase expenditure (here, investment in soft urban infrastructure, that is, regional government's social consumption expenditures in the sectors of education, science, culture, health, etc., is not regarded as an investment in urban infrastructure). In a given period of time, under the condition of a fixed amount of total regional fiscal revenue, regional government's purchase expenditure and transfer expenditure come from the same pool of total FE, that is, one being higher would inevitably lead to the other being lower, and the same relationship exists between investment expenditure and social consumption expenditure, which together make up a total amount of purchase expenditure.

Then we can go on to discuss the functional relationship between the regional government's investment expenditure and total FE. If the proportion of purchase expenditure in FE is λ_1, the proportion of transfer expenditure in FE will be $1-\lambda_1$. If the proportion of investment expenditure in purchase expenditure is λ_2, the proportion of social consumption expenditure in purchase expenditure will be $1-\lambda_2$. Then the relationship between investment expenditure represented by I and total FE represented by G could be expressed with the following formula:

$$I = \lambda_1 \lambda_2 G$$

With FE fixed, the proportion of investment expenditure in FE will be limited by transfer expenditure and also by social consumption expenditure. According to the above formula, if investment expenditure is to be increased, either λ_1 or λ_2 will have to be raised. The rise of λ_1 will reduce the proportion of transfer expenditure, and rise of λ_2 will reduce the proportion of social consumption expenditure.

Let's look into two situations. The first situation assumes the proportion of purchase expenditure in FE to be fixed, that is, λ_1 is constant (the proportion of transfer expenditure in FE is also fixed). In this situation, fiscal investment expenditure will increase if the government raises λ_2 by allocating more funds to investment expenditure instead of social consumption expenditure. In this way, the government will be able to prioritize infrastructure development. But the rise of λ_2 means social consumption expenditure is reduced and the government's construction of various supporting systems for the regional economy will be undermined to some extent. When the contributing power of investment expenditure to fiscal revenue is stronger, the increment of fiscal revenue brought by the rise of investment expenditure will make up for or even outweigh the decrease of fiscal revenue resulting from the decline of social consumption expenditure, in which case increasing investment expenditure is conducive to fiscal revenue rise.

The other situation assumes the proportion of investment expenditure in purchase expenditure to be fixed, that is, λ_2 is constant (the proportion of social consumption expenditure in purchase expenditure also remains unchanged). In this situation, if λ_1 rises, that is, if the government raises purchase expenditure and reduces transfer expenditure, investment expenditure will also go up, but the reduction of transfer expenditure will undermine the government's subsidies for talents introduction and social financing.

Investment expenditure is an important part of FE because it determines how much the government invests in infrastructure construction. Moreover, since infrastructure construction is an important source of fiscal revenue, investment expenditure builds a bridge between FE and fiscal revenue. This is why the government needs to make choices and decisions based on the particular development stage the economy is in and pay special attention to the proportion of investment expenditure in FE so as to raise fiscal revenue by optimizing the allocation of FE. For example, when the economy is at the investment-driven stage, investment expenditure has high elasticity, and in this case, reducing transfer expenditure to increase purchase expenditure or lowering social consumption expenditure to raise investment expenditure are both important ways to push up fiscal revenue while keeping the total amount of FE at the original level.

Regional governments' practice of expanding investment expenditure around the world reveals the following. Seen from the supply side, such investments improve enterprises' production conditions, save their production costs and transaction costs, and lead to continuous increase and generation of new organic combinations of various production factors, thus creating new or greater regional economic benefits, expanding fiscal revenue, and promoting the sustainable development of the regional economy. From the demand side, investment expenditure fuels urban infrastructure construction, which involves various production factors that themselves harbor a huge market demand, and such demand triggers a series of economic reactions. The economic effect of such a circle repeating itself tallies with the multiplier effect or acceleration principle of investment on regional economic growth as described by Keynes: From a dynamic point of view, the series of chain reactions brought by the increase of investment will push up income at a rate that's several times higher than the increase rate of investment, and the increase of income will in return speed up the increase of investment, hence promoting sustained growth of the regional economy.

Last, it should be noted that there is a relationship of mutual promotion and co-growth between *i.* the amount of regional governments' investment expenditure and the amount of social capital input driven by it, and *ii.* the fiscal revenue determination mechanism and economic growth in the region. Fundamentally, when making decisions about the structure, scale and scope of fiscal investment expenditure, regional governments still need to work towards an effective combination of social benefits and economic benefits, for only in this way can they achieve optimal allocation of resources during the transformation of the region's quasi-operative resources into operative resources.

Notes

1 Zhang, S. (Ed.). (2015). *Public economics.* China Renmin University Press, pp.112–114.

2 Chen, G. (2017). *Public finance* (9th ed.). China Renmin University Press, pp.104–105.

5 Regional government competition

5.1 Determination of prices in the field of resource generation

In traditional economics, there's a lack of research and understanding about the field of resource generation, which actually is a field with increasing importance in real-life economic development. The field at least includes three categories of resources. The first is primordial resources, such as space resources, deep-sea resources, polar resources and deep earth exploration resources. When not developed these are static natural resources. When being invested in and developed, they turn into dynamic, economical and productive primordial resources. Primordial resources are risky because they require large investments, take long development terms and involve lots of uncertainties, which is also why governments around the world must be the primary party to invest in them in order to gain an advantage for their country or region in world economic competition. The second type is derivative resources, notably the infrastructure resources in the urban economy. Urban infrastructure resources turn into derivative resources in the field of resource generation when they transform from quasi-operative resources into operative resources. Investing in and developing such resources also have the four features of being dynamic, economical, productive and risky, which is why governments around the globe must be their primary investors too. The third is inverse resources, a special kind of generative resources that do not exist in the first place and are formed reversely by the external spillover effects in the development of regional economy, such as carbon emissions trading resources. The government must be the primary responsible party for the exploration, management and control of such inverse resources.

Now we will take carbon emissions trading resources, a kind of inverse resources that are relatively unfamiliar to most readers, as an example to analyze the goods price determination in the field of resource generation, and to distinguish it from the commodity price formation mechanism in the industrial economy.

In December 1997, in response to the situation that greenhouse gas emissions in the atmosphere were increasing year by year, bringing serious

DOI: 10.4324/9781003244837-5

pollution and harm to human beings, parties to the United Nations Framework Convention on Climate Change proposed for the first time in human history to limit greenhouse gas emissions in the form of laws and regulations in Kyoto, Japan, leading to the signing of a protocol to the United Nations Framework Convention on Climate Change—the famous Kyoto Protocol.

According to the definition of the Kyoto Protocol, greenhouse gases refer to six gases, specifically, carbon dioxide, nitrous oxide, methane, hydrofluorocarbons, perfluorocarbons and sulfur hexafluoride, whose emission needs to be artificially controlled. These gases are what the "carbon" in "carbon emission entitlement" refers to, and the so-called "carbon emission entitlement" is materialized in the form of greenhouse gas emission quota or emission permit. Countries that are parties to the Protocol split its carbon emission reduction target to be achieved in a certain period of time to different domestic enterprises in the above forms. Carbon emissions trading (hereinafter referred to as "carbon trading"), that is, trading of emission quotas or emission permits, gives rise to a series of carbon goods in international trade, brings about the carbon commodity in international trade and turns environmental resources into tradable commodities.

To encourage countries to achieve their emission reduction targets, the Protocol allows governments to adopt the following four ways of emission reduction. First, emission quotas may be sold and bought between developed countries, that is, "emissions trading"—countries finding it hard to meet emission reduction commitment may buy the extra quota finished from countries that have over-fulfilled their commitment. Second, greenhouse gas emissions are calculated with "net emissions," that is, the amount of carbon dioxide absorbed by forests is deducted from the actual emissions of the country. Third, the clean development mechanism could be adopted to encourage developed and developing countries to jointly reduce emissions. Fourth, the "group approach" could be adopted. For example, many countries within the EU may be regarded as a whole to meet their overall emission reduction goal when in fact some countries might fail to meet their targets while some overachieve their targets.

The Kyoto Protocol established three flexible means of cooperation for emission reduction, namely, international emissions trading (IET), joint implementation (JI) and the clean development mechanism (CDM). These mechanisms allow developed countries to flexibly meet emission reduction commitment through the carbon trading market and at the same time enable developing countries to obtain relevant technologies and funds through carbon trading. To have a deeper understanding of the carbon emissions issue, we will introduce the rules of the three mechanisms in detail in this chapter.

The first is international emissions trading (IET). The main idea is to allow annex I parties to acquire allowed emission units through transaction transfer or cross-border cooperation in a cost-effective way. The mechanism can reduce the negative impact of emission reduction activities on the economy without affecting the integrity of the global environment, and achieve the best cost-effectiveness of global emission reduction. The mechanism mainly works for developed countries.

The second mechanism is JI. This is a project-based cooperation mechanism among annex I countries. Its aim is to help annex I countries meet their quantified emission reduction commitments at a lower cost. Specifically, an annex I country with higher emission reduction costs may execute an emission reduction project in another annex I country with lower emission reduction costs. The investing country can obtain the emission reduction units generated by the project to help meet its emission reduction commitment, while the host country can obtain through the project certain amounts of funds or advanced technologies beneficial to the environment so as to promote its own development. The characteristic of this mechanism is that the project cooperation mainly takes place between countries with Economies in Transition and developed countries.

The last is the clean development mechanism (CDM). Its essence is to allow annex I countries with emission reduction commitments to invest in emission reduction projects in non-annex I countries to earn Certified Emission Reductions (CERs), which count as credits towards meeting their reduction targets under the Kyoto Protocol. This mechanism is mainly used between developed countries and developing countries.

As emission reduction became an international trend, there have emerged various regional and voluntary reduction plans, and transaction tools in the carbon trading market are also increasing, bringing wide development prospects to the field. It could be said that carbon emissions trading resources, as a kind of inverse resources in the field of resource generation, are gradually entering the economic development of all countries in the world.

Carbon emission entitlements, as original trading products, are in essence environmental policy tools created by the government. Parties to the Kyoto Protocol, based on the reduction targets set for them, put a limit on the total amount of greenhouse gases that could be emitted within their territory during the emission reduction period, allocate the allowed emission quantity to emission control enterprises in the form of emission permits or quotas, and allow enterprises to sell their unused emission permits or quotas to enterprises with excessive emissions. This is the basic form of carbon trading. The carbon trading market and its operation mechanism are built mainly by the government. The running of the market, including the generation of carbon assets, transfer of ownership and performance of commitment, requires the protection of strong laws and regulations formulated also by the government.

From an economic point of view, carbon commodity has the attribute of global public goods—the strong liquidity and long duration of greenhouse gases determined it is difficult to reduce greenhouse gas emissions and mitigate global warming through the efforts of individual countries. In the meanwhile, carbon commodity is also a kind of contingent or intangible commodity, that is, the object being sold and bought is carbon emission entitlements. The price of carbon commodity mainly depends on the supply and demand of the current carbon market.

The carbon trading market can be divided into the allowance-based transaction market and the project-based transaction market. Allowance-based transactions refer to the trading of emission reduction units generated when the total allowed emission quantity is controlled. The trading objects are mainly initial quotas allocated to enterprises by policymakers, such as the Assigned Amount Unit (AAU) in the Kyoto Protocol and the European Union Allowance (EUA) used by the EU Emissions Trading System (EU ETS). Allowance-based transactions are mostly spot trades. Project-based transactions, on the other hand, refer to the trading of emission reduction units generated by emission reduction projects. The trading objects are mainly emission reduction credits earned through the implementation of projects that reduce greenhouse gas emissions, such as the Certified Emission Reductions (CERs) in the clean development mechanism and the Emission Reduction Units (ERUs) of the joint implementation mechanism. Such transactions are usually futures trading.

As the most mature and influential carbon trading market in the world, the EU emissions trading system has been a unified market participated by many countries since its birth in January 2005. It has launched various derivatives including carbon futures, carbon options and carbon funds, forming a multi-level carbon market system with trading of actuals, futures and options. The carbon trading market formed with the Regional Greenhouse Gas Initiative (RGGI) of the USA has been prepared to connect with other carbon markets and carbon derivatives markets since its formation in 2005, laying a solid foundation for the future shaping of a unified market.

Let's take the Certified Emission Reduction (CER) trading as an example. Globally there are about 50 buyers of CERs, including carbon funds and other purchasing agencies, whose management methods vary. Some are set up and managed entirely by the government (mainly in Finland, Austria, etc.), some are set up jointly by an international organization and the government and managed by the international organization (mainly the cooperation between the world bank and governments), some are set up by the government and operated in an enterprise mode (such as the carbon funds in the UK and Japan), some are established by the government and enterprise in cooperation and managed in a commercial mode (typically the carbon funds in Germany and Japan), and some are funded by enterprises and managed in an enterprise way (mainly engaging in intermediate transactions of CERs).

As mentioned before, carbon emissions trading resources are a kind of inverse resources, a product of the negative externalities of regional economic development, and a natural condition faced by human beings in the struggle for survival and development. They have the two characteristics of public resources: for one, they do not belong to any one individual or enterprise, and for two, members of society can use such resources for free and there's no way to stop them. Naturally, the public goods generated from this kind of resources also have non-competitive and prominent non-exclusive characteristics. Yet under certain conditions, they also have the features of quasi-public resources with a certain degree of competitiveness and exclusiveness. This is because competitiveness and exclusiveness arise from resource scarcity. When the carbon emission management in a region takes the form of regulating, controlling and restricting, carbon emission right to some extent becomes scarce, and such scarcity creates conditions for such public resources to transform into quasi-public resources, that is, when regional carbon emissions exceed a certain critical point, their non-competitiveness and non-exclusiveness disappear—each additional ton of carbon emission in the region will bring additional carbon emission costs. When the market mechanism fails in curbing regional carbon emissions, the intervention of the regional government becomes inevitable. Governments' procedures and actions to curb carbon emissions create costs or fees, which in effect determine the price of carbon emission right as a kind of tradable quasi-public goods.

In the carbon emissions trading market, those being priced are emissions generated by the public sector as well as emissions generated by the private sector. In terms of pricing policy, besides pure public pricing, governments more often adopt regulatory pricing, especially in the quota trading market, that is, the spot trading market. The purpose of carbon emission pricing is not solely to curb the emissions of the six harmful gases represented by carbon dioxide, but ultimately to conserve the ecological environment, guarantee the living standards of the people and create conditions for them to live and work in peace. Therefore, regional governments usually weigh the advantages and disadvantages of the following three pricing methods to choose the one most suitable for their region. The first pricing method is based on the average cost, that is, the regional government sets the price towards the maximum economic benefits while maintaining emitters' balance of income and expenditure. The second is the two-part pricing method, that is, a pricing system composed of two elements, one being a basic fee not linked to carbon emissions that are paid by month or year, and the other being an ad valorem fee paid based on emission quantity. The third method is pick-load pricing, that is, setting different prices for different time periods according to needs, resulting in the highest charge at the peak of carbon emissions and the lowest charge when carbon emissions are the lowest.

To sum up, government actions and market mechanisms both play a part in the price setting of goods in the field of resource generation or quasi-public goods. That is to say that while letting the market decide the allocation of resources, the government should endeavor to play its role better, so as to achieve effective integration of the market and the government. The government should participate in the investment, development and construction of regional generative resources and participate in the competition of the regional market.

5.2 Characteristics of regional government competition

As touched upon before, "region" is a relative concept. Worldwide, a country is a region. Countrywide, a city is a region. Not only do commonalities and similarities exist between regions, so do individualities and differences. A regional government refers to the governmental organization that manages the administrative affairs of such a region, one that has a relatively stable territory, relatively concentrated population and its own governance institutions. Regional governments are public and coercive.

Regional competitiveness refers to the region's strength supporting its sustainable survival and development amid competition with other regions, that is, its ability to attract, compete for, possess, regulate and transform resources as well as its ability to compete for, possess and regulate the market, in a nutshell, its ability to optimize the allocation of resources compared with other regions. Put simply, it is the region's ability to attract resources and compete for the market, an ability required for its own development. An index system can be established with the methodology of comparative economics to analyze and evaluate regional competitiveness, pinpoint problems with development and find factors with room for improvement so that competitiveness could be enhanced. Through studying the ways to raise regional competitiveness, we could create competitive advantages, optimize resource allocation, promote scientific and sustainable development of regional economy and maximize regional fiscal revenue.

It is mainly for the following reasons that fiscal revenue determination mechanism is used to formulate the objective function of regional government competition. First, the constant expansion of regional governments' functions, notably economic regulation function, needs the support of large fiscal revenue. Over the course of the economic development of all countries in the world, governments have been taking on more and more functions. The role of regional governments has gradually evolved from a "night watchman" that only keeps up the operation of political power, sustains social stability, defends against foreign invasion, and maintains judicial justice, into a regulatory, interventional and managerial system adapted to the modern market economy and socialized mass production. One of the important ways of regional government regulation and management is to expand fiscal expenditure. Therefore, as both government functions and fiscal expenditure expand, the scale of regional fiscal revenue also needs to grow. Second, the constant growth of the regional population increases the total demand for public services, which requires the support of larger fiscal revenue. Increasing population requires the regional government to upgrade its governance in a multitude of aspects including education, health care, culture and sports, vocational training, social environment, regional management, and people's basic life needs of food, clothing, housing and transportation. Higher population mobility and population aging will also have an impact on the structure and amount of fiscal expenditure. In one word, the change of population and its structure brings a change of demand, and fiscal revenue has to be increased accordingly to provide support. Third, expansion of city scale and growth of public investment call for the support of sufficient fiscal revenue. The city is a dynamic concept. With the construction of hard urban infrastructure, the improvement of soft urban infrastructure, the development of smart cities, the acceleration of urban-rural integration, the expansion of existing cities and the formation of new ones, there emerges a great demand for municipal construction and along with that, for the investment, which also requires continuous growth of regional fiscal revenue as a source of funding. Fourth, the continuous progress in science and technology enables regional governments to constantly explore new scientific and technological fields and production fields, which also needs the support of larger fiscal revenue. For instance, the primordial resources in the field of resource generation, that is, resources discovered through space exploration, ocean development, polar exploration, research, etc., and the inverse resources in the field of resource generation, including carbon emissions trading resources, all need regional governments to increase investment to build advanced personnel, capital and property systems for the high-tech industry. Fifth, the expansion of social welfare needs the support of larger fiscal revenue scale. The government has to narrow the gap between the rich and the poor and reduce the polarization of social distribution in the region, so as to lessen the conflict between the rich and the poor and eliminate contributors to instability. Moreover, as the economy develops and people's income grows, regional governments have to constantly improve the professional, cultural and healthy levels of the public, so as to raise the total-factor productivity in the region, and this also requires growth of fiscal revenue. These are all important reasons that regional governments take fiscal revenue determination mechanism as the basis of the objective function of regional competition.

There are significant differences between regional government competition and enterprise competition.

First, the objective function of the two types of competition is different. The objective function of regional government competition is fiscal revenue determination mechanism while that of enterprise competition is price determination mechanism. Within the scope of its governance, a regional government's capability in terms of supporting and subsidizing the industrial economy, investing in and promoting the urban economy, and providing public goods and services in a livelihood economy is to a large extent dependent on the region's fiscal revenue. Fiscal revenue is an important indicator of regional governments' ability to carry out various social and economic activities. When a region's national debt revenue and income from state-owned assets are fixed, its fiscal revenue mainly depends on tax revenue and fee income, which mainly depend on the region's economic development level, economic policies and measures and economic management efficiency. That's why regional governments, with the aim of maximizing fiscal revenue, endeavor to attract investments with preferential policies and facilitation measures in the region's project construction, industrial chain supporting, cluster development and market development at home and abroad. This is different from enterprise competition which revolves around micro factors such as cost, quality, supply and demand that determine the price of goods.

Second, the two types of competition use different means to achieve goals. While enterprises attempt to raise labor productivity to influence the cost, supply and demand of commodities, regional governments strive to improve total-factor productivity to promote sustainable economic growth. This is because regional governments promote economic development with the goal of increasing fiscal revenue, and to achieve this goal the primary measure is to optimize fiscal expenditure structure to obtain maximum economic and social benefits, such as by adjusting investment expenditure, consumption expenditure and transfer expenditure to the best proportions. Generally speaking, after the simple expansion of tangible factors such as land, projects and capital, the bottleneck shaped by diminishing marginal return on capital will make such "extensive" mode of economic growth unsustainable. With the amount of input in relevant tangible factors remaining unchanged, regional governments can focus on investing in, enriching and improving intangible factors, distributing resources and adjusting structure around technological progress with innovation at the core, and providing support in terms of institution, policy, law and environment. Optimization of regional fiscal expenditure structure brings about a series of positive changes in the regional policy environment, which will then become a new driving force for regional economic development and urban construction.

Third, the paths taken to achieve goals are different. The performance of regional governments is led by efficiency-oriented growth, while that of enterprises is led by input-oriented growth. Experience of regional governments across the globe shows that the path of regional economic growth often goes through in succession the three stages of factor-driven stage (also known as resource allocation stage), investment-driven stage (also known as efficiency enhancement stage) and innovation-driven stage (also known as sustainable growth stage). Regional governments promote efficiency-oriented growth by optimizing the combination of tangible and intangible resource factors and encouraging and guiding capital input from the whole society. The elevation of enterprise performance, on the other hand, comes from continuous input of production factors including capital, labor, land, technology and entrepreneurship. The strategy of enterprise input is a quantitative expansion in the initial stage, gradually developing to the quality improvement stage, and then to the stage of expansionary management where sustainable and effective input becomes the key.

Fourth, the investment and financing mechanisms are different. The investment and financing activities of regional governments should consider both fairness and efficiency, while those of enterprises are conducted in pursuit of profitability and efficiency only. For the most part, regional governments invest and finance to remedy market failure. With regard to investment, in addition to appropriating funds for free to ensure social equity, regional governments are increasingly adopting diversified investment methods combining direct and indirect investment such as paid loans, public-private joint ventures and joint-stock cooperation. Regarding financing, in addition to the monetary financing adopted by the state when necessary, regional governments more often use debt financing to expand investment scale and boost the regional economy.

Fifth, the price determination mechanisms are different. The price of quasi-public goods is mostly determined by regional governments in the way of regulatory pricing with market economy rules as a basis, while the pricing of enterprise commodities is entirely done by market competition. Regional governments usually weigh the advantages and disadvantages and choose one from or combine two or more of the three pricing methods of average-cost pricing, two-part pricing and pick-load pricing, and take the lead in promoting the investment into and development and construction of quasi-public goods projects, with the participation of the private sector as a complement. It has become a common practice all over the world for governments to take part in the investment, development and construction of quasi-public goods in the field of resource generation and regulate and control the pricing of quasi-public goods, meaning that it's only natural that the price determination mechanism in this field would not be the same as that of enterprise commodities.

The sixth difference is competition orientation. Regional government competition is oriented towards optimizing supply while enterprise competition is oriented towards satisfying demand. To fulfill their purpose of developing economy, building cities and improving social well-being, regional governments invariably have to appropriately arrange the supply of tangible resource factors such as land, capital, projects, technologies and talents, effectively adjust the supply of intangible resource factors such as planning, investment, consumption, price, taxation, interest rate, exchange rate and law, and promote supply-side structural reform through innovations in concept, technology, organization and institution. Enterprise competition, on the other hand, has to be based on market demand, and the key to an enterprise's success or failure lies in whether or not its strategies and tactics can meet market demand in terms of both quantity and structure.

Seventh, the areas of competition are different. Regional governments mainly compete in urban economy and urban resource allocation, while enterprise competition focuses on industrial economy and industrial resource allocation. The two types of competition are relatively independent from each other, yet the two systems co-exist and complement each other. Regional governments are the research object of mezzoeconomics. Competition between regional governments occurs mainly in the factor market of urban economy, including the market for hard and soft factors such as land, projects, capital, personnel, property rights, technologies and information. Regional governments need to not only grasp the quantity, quality, structure and distribution of the urban resource factors but also formulate systems and policies to coordinate the allocation of urban resource factors in the region, and attract foreign resource factors, thereby optimizing resource allocation and raising regional competitiveness. Regional governments' competition in the factor market affects the competition of enterprises in the commodity market. Enterprises are the research object of microeconomics. Enterprise competition occurs mainly in the commodity market and in the allocation of industrial resources in the industrial economy. Market equilibrium theory with manufacturers as the subjects of study is the dominant theory of traditional classical economics. The ultimate goal of enterprises is maximizing profits and major factors affecting the competition amongst enterprises are supply, demand, market equilibrium price, perfect competition, monopolistic competition, oligopoly and different competitive strategies in different market structures. Enterprise competition is the precondition and foundation of regional government competition.

Eighth, regional governments and enterprises take different roles in competition. While enterprises belong to the micro economy domain and are micro players in the market economy, regional governments, the principal players in mezzo economy, play a dual (quasi-macro and quasi-micro) role in the development of the regional economy. On the one hand, the regional governments' planning, guidance and support for the industrial economy (operative resources) and its investment into and development and operation of urban economy (quasi-operative resources) make it the central agent of all micro stakeholders in the regional economy, granting a quasi-micro attribute to its behaviors. On the other hand, the regional government's regulation, supervision and management of the industrial economy and its supply of public goods and services (non-operative resources) make it the representative of the state in the regional economic society, and this gives a quasi-macro attribute to its behaviors. Such dual attributes of the regional government mean that it plays a dual role of competition and cooperation in the development of the regional economy, which is different from the purely competitive role of enterprises in the micro economy domain.

Ninth, regional government competition and enterprise competition use different management modes. Regional governments mainly use the District Resource Planning (DRP) system while enterprises mainly use the Enterprise Resource Planning (ERP) system. The ERP system enables enterprises to manage materials, capital, information, customers and other resources in an effective and integrated manner, assists enterprises to achieve effective cross-regional, cross-sectoral and cross-industrial coordination and allocation of the flow of materials, personnel, money, information, so as to, with market as its orientation, integrate resources effectively, adjust functions expeditiously and improve productivity markedly, ultimately raising enterprise competitiveness. The DRP system, on the other hand, enables regional governments to appropriately distribute various resource factors within their regions such as land, population, finance, environment, technologies and policies and predict market changes and distribute regional resources based on the layout of regional planning and strategies with systematic management philosophy and methods, so as to raise regional competitiveness. The adoption of the DRP management mode is conducive to the optimization of the region's total-factor productivity and thus to the region's sustainable socio-economic development.

5.3 Forms of regional government competition

The competition between regional governments and the competition between enterprises each forms a competition system of its own level. Mutually independent yet interrelated, the two together constitute the dual competitors in the modern market economy. First, competition at the enterprise level is the basis of all competition in the market economy and it is enterprise competition that drives the competition among regional governments. Regional government competition, mainly involving optimizing resource allocation in terms of institution, policies, environment, projects, etc., is another kind of competition on top of enterprise competition and one that in return influences, supports and promotes enterprise competition. Secondly, the enterprise competition system exists only among enterprises, meaning that every regional government can only play the role of a guide and planner in the industrial economy or industrial resource allocation, supporter and coordinator in commodity production, and supervisor and manager of market order, and has no right to directly intervene in the micro-affairs of enterprises. The regional government competition system, similarly, exists only among regional governments, which should, observing the laws of market economy, compete in projects, policies and measures in the sectors of urban resource allocation, industrial development, urban construction, social welfare, etc.

As aforementioned, the objective function of regional government competition is the determination mechanism of fiscal revenue. When debt revenue and income from state-owned assets are fixed, a region's fiscal revenue depends on tax revenue and fee income. At a given stage of economic development, the amount of a region's tax revenue and fee income mainly depends on its economic development level, economic policies and measures, and the regional government's economic management efficiency. Economic development level is determined by the number of economic projects in the region, the soundness of supporting industrial chains and import and export volumes. Economic policies and measures are reflected in the regional government's input in urban infrastructure, the innovativeness of talents and science and technology, and the strength of fiscal and financial support. Economic management efficiency finds demonstration in the soundness of the region's policy system, environment system and management system. These "9-in-3" directly or indirectly determine a region's fiscal revenue scale and the region's competitiveness. Therefore, regional government competition could be summarized as mainly taking place in the "9-in-3" (see Figure 5.1).

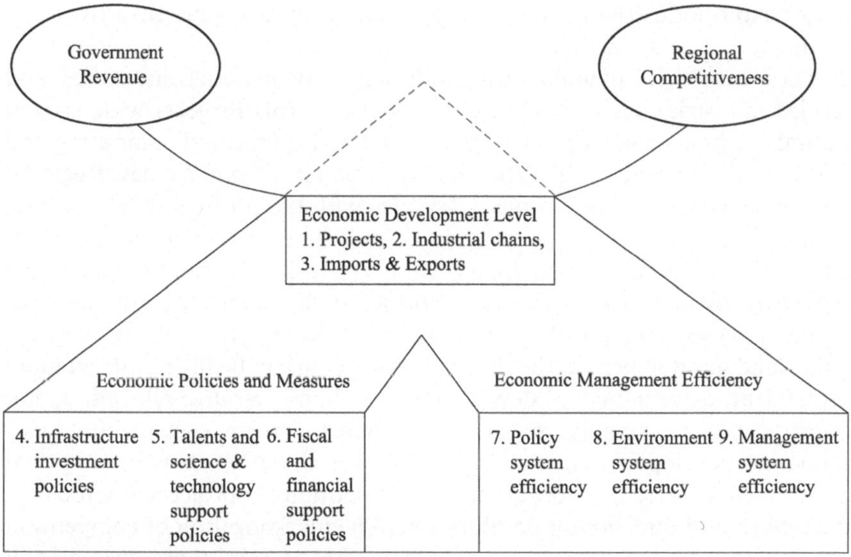

Figure 5.1 Diagram of "9-in-3" competition.

I name the above classification the "9-in-3" Competition Theory of regional governments, or "Sheep's Horns Competition Theory" (for the diagram looks like a sheep's horns). The left horn represents the objective function of regional government competition, that is, the determination mechanism of fiscal revenue, and the right horn is the index function of regional government competition, that is, the determination mechanism of regional competitiveness. The most potent determinant of the objective function and index function of regional government competition is the region's economic development level, which mainly depends on three factors—projects, industrial chains, and imports and exports. The two essential contributors to economic development level are the region's economic policies and measures and economic management efficiency, the former covering policies about infrastructure investment, policies supporting talents and science and technology, and policies about fiscal and financial support, and the latter comprising policy system efficiency, environment system efficiency and management system efficiency. In the following part, we will look into the "9-in-3" Competition Theory or "Sheep's Horns Competition Theory" in detail.

The first aspect is the regional economic development level, which mainly depends on project competition, industrial chain competition and import and export competition.

First, competition in projects, which mainly includes three types: (i) Major national projects, including key national projects, major projects listed in national science and technology support programs, major national science and technology infrastructure construction projects, and major engineering projects and industrialization projects financed by the state. (ii) Private investment projects, including those in high-tech industries, emerging industries, equipment manufacturing industries, raw materials industries, and service industries such as finance and logistics. (iii) Projects with foreign capital, such as projects in intelligent manufacturing, cloud computing and big data, the Internet of Things, and construction of smart cities. Regional governments vie for these projects because with the projects they can, first, directly introduce capital, personnel and industries to their region, second, effectively raise funds, obtain finance and expropriate the land needed in the region by virtue of the legitimacy of project policies and the rationality of public services, and thirdly, through the implementation of the projects, guide land development in the region, construct urban facilities, attract more investment, drive industrial development, optimize resource allocation, and improve policy capacity, so as to ultimately ensure sustainable socio-economic development in the region. It's for these benefits that regional governments across the world take the competition for projects as a focus of their work and direction of development. The marketization of competition requires regional governments across the world to raise their awareness in terms of projects, development, efficiency, advantages, conditions, policies and risks.

Second, competition in supporting industrial chains. In general, every region has its own industrial foundation and characteristics, which mostly depend on its natural resource endowments. The natural course of action would be to maintain and optimize the region's endowed resources and in addition to attract and gather high-end resources from outside the region. To do this, the key is optimizing the industrial structure and effectively deploying the industrial chain, and efforts should be concentrated on moving towards the high end of industries, forming industrial agglomeration, and guiding industrial clustering. Regional governments' competition in supporting industrial chain is carried out in two aspects, production factors and industrial clustering. In terms of production factors, low-end or primary factors of production cannot form stable and long-lasting competitiveness, and strong industries with competitive advantages can be established only by introducing and investing in high-end factors of production such as industrial technologies, information technology, network resources, transportation facilities, professionals, and R&D think tanks. In terms of industrial clustering, the theory of regional competitiveness holds that establishing effective supporting industries primarily with existing industrial base within the region can reduce enterprises' transaction costs and raise their profitability, and the smile curve suggests that the two ends of the industrial value chain, namely, R&D and the market, produce the most value. These reveal that an important path to sustainable regional development is to cultivate advantageous industries, establish complete industrial chains, and attract investment with clear targets according to the region's industrial structure.

Third, competition in imports and exports. In an open international economic system, the performance of global regions in imports and exports has become an important contributor to regional competitiveness. Such competition is mainly in four aspects. First, in processing trade and general trade, regional governments endeavor to reduce the proportion of processing trade and increase that of general trade so as to give impetus to the region's commodity trade and service trade. Second, in investment abroad, regional governments push for enterprises' development in foreign countries and compete for overseas projects to extend their region's interests and market value chains to overseas areas. Third, in terms of capital export, regional governments promote capital account convertibility, in other words, they take various measures to promote the circulation of monetary capital and facilitate free currency exchange under the circumstances of facilitated international current account investment. Fourth, in terms of import, regional governments across the world take all sorts of preferential policies and measures to attract and support the introduction of high-tech products, industries and projects, and even spend heavily to assist their investment, construction and production. Performance in import and export competition is one important factor affecting regional economic growth across the world.

The second aspect is the region's economic policies and measures, including infrastructure investment policies, talents and science and technology support policies, and fiscal and financial support policies.

First, competition in infrastructure, that is, competition in a series of sectors including hard and soft urban infrastructure construction and the development and operation of modern smart cities. Hard infrastructure includes transport facilities such as expressways, railways, ports and aviation, energy facilities such as electricity and natural gas, information platform facilities such as optical cable and network, and engineering infrastructure such as science and technology parks, industrial parks, business incubation parks and creative industry parks. Soft infrastructure is public infrastructure for education, science and technology, health care, sports, culture, social welfare, etc. Smart city development involves intelligent technology platforms such as big data, cloud computing and the Internet of Things. A region's infrastructure system provides support for its socio-economic development and could be classified into three types based on its maturity relative to the region's development level: advanced, adaptive and lagging. Reasonably advanced provision of regional infrastructure will not only bring immediate benefits to the region itself but also raise the region's competitiveness, and, by creating sound urban structure, building facilities of appropriate sizes, establishing reasonable spatial layout and providing high-quality services, reduce the costs of enterprises in the market competition so as to lift their production efficiency, hence accelerating the development of industries. Across the world, the completeness and soundness of a region's infrastructure will directly affect the current and future state of its economic development.

Second, competition in talents and science and technology. To do well in this field of competition, the most fundamental is to establish the notion that human resources are the primary resources and that science and technology are the primary productive forces, the most rudimentary is to perfect local personnel training system and increase input in local personnel training and science and technology innovation, and the most essential is to create conditions to attract, bring in, cultivate and utilize talented personnel. Main indicators to measure a region's competitiveness in science, technology and personnel include the scientific and technological personnel resource index of the region, the number of people engaged in scientific and technological activities per 10,000 people, the number of scientists and engineers per 10,000 people, the number of students enrolled in higher education per 10,000 people, the total expenditure on scientific and technological activities, the proportion of expenditure on science and technology in regional GDP, per capita scientific research fund, the percentage of scientific and technological appropriations in local fiscal expenditure, per capita fiscal expenditure on education, the total amount of local fiscal expenditure on education and the number of full-time teachers employed in higher education. Regional governments in countries across the world endeavor to elevate their competitiveness in talents and science and technology through improving and raising their performance in these indicators.

Third, fiscal and financial competition. Regional fiscal competition is composed of competition in fiscal revenue and that in fiscal expenditure. As aforementioned, an increase of a region's fiscal revenue mainly relies on economic growth and the rise in tax revenue and fee income. Nevertheless, the key to competition actually lies in fiscal expenditure, which could be classified into social consumption expenditure, transfer expenditure and investment expenditure, and it is in investment expenditure that the majority of competition takes place. Investment expenditure includes the government's investment in infrastructure, in scientific and technological research and development, and in policy-based financing to support industries in urgent need of development. Fiscal investment expenditure is an important driving force of economic growth. Despite the usually limited total scale of fiscal revenue and expenditure, regional governments build various platforms for investment and financing and mobilize and attract financial resources including capital, talents and information from regional, domestic and international financial institutions to serve the industrial development, urban construction and social welfare in the region. Regional governments also compete in terms of preferential policies, for instance, by giving more weight to certain items in fiscal expenditure and adopting particular financial measures to attract capital.

The last aspect is the region's economic management efficiency, which is comprised of policy system competition, environment system competition and management system competition.

First, competition in the policy system. A regional government's policy system could be divided into policies directed beyond the region and policies for within the region, which is also the case between countries. As policies themselves are public goods characterized by being non-exclusive and easy to imitate, a policy system must possess the following characteristics to be good and competitive: (1) Practicality, that is, being realistic and in line with the requirements of economic and social development; (2) Advancement, namely, being visionary, ahead of its time and innovative; (3) Operability, that is, being clear, well-targeted and implementable; (4) Good organization, that is, having dedicated agencies, posts and personnel responsible for its implementation; and (5) Being result-oriented, that is, having mechanisms for inspection, supervision, assessment and evaluation, including resorting to a third party to realize policy objectives. The level of completeness and soundness of the policy system also has a great impact on regional competitiveness.

Second, competition in the environment system. Here environment refers to a synthesis of ecological environment, human environment, policy environment and social credit system. A sound development environment is indispensable for regional government competition, and it should be one where encouraging investment is in harmony with ecosystem protection, attracting investment is coupled with policy services, pursuing wealth is balanced with repaying the society, legal supervision is complemented by social credit, etc. Build a good environment system is a secret weapon to enable regional governments to attract investment, develop projects and sustain economic development, which has been proven true by the experience of successful regions at home and abroad.

Third, competition in management efficiency. A regional government's management efficiency is the overall reflection of the speed, quality and effectiveness of its administrative management activities, and could be classified into four categories, namely, macro-efficiency, micro-efficiency, organizational efficiency and individual efficiency. As far as compliance is concerned, the administration of regional governments should meet the standards of legitimacy, interests and quality. As far as efficiency is concerned, the administration should meet the standards in terms of quantity, time, speed and budget. Regional governments' competition in management efficiency is in essence the competition in their organizational system, responsibilities assumed, service consciousness, work skills and technological platforms. Developed regional governments have already pioneered the competition in management efficiency in practice by adopting parallel and integrated modes of service.

Regional government competition could be examined further from the perspective of the three types of resources discussed previously. Regional resources are urban resources, which, as mentioned in Chapter 3, could be understood in a broad sense or a narrow sense. Urban resources in the broad sense include industrial resources, livelihood resources and urban infrastructure resources, and in the narrow sense refer only to urban infrastructure resources, which themselves cover hard and soft urban infrastructure and even modern smart cities. Along this line of thinking urban economy in a broad sense could be said to include industrial economy, livelihood economy and urban economy, which mainly involves infrastructure construction, while in a narrow sense urban economy specifically refers to the investment in and development and construction of urban infrastructure. This means regional government competition could also be understood in a broad sense or in a narrow sense.

According to the "9-in-3" Competition Theory or the "Sheep's Horns Competition Theory," regional government competition in a broad sense includes the competition for urban operative resources (industrial economy), non-operative resources (livelihood economy) and quasi-operative resources (urban economy). The competition in livelihood economy mainly involves regional governments providing non-operative resources, namely public goods and services, by formulating and implementing certain policies, so as to ensure social security with the principles of "guaranteeing basic needs, ensuring fairness and justice, raising effectiveness and efficiency." The goal of such competition is to maintain social stability and create a good environment for regional investment and development. It is related to the third aspect, namely, economic management efficiency, in the "9-in-3" Competition Theory. The competition in the industrial economy mainly involves regional governments playing the role of "planning and guiding, support and coordination, supervision and management" by formulating and implementing policies related to operative resources, namely the three major industries. The goal of such competition is to maintain the openness, fairness and justice of the market, promote the coordinated development of the industrial economy, and lift the overall production efficiency of the region. It is related to, in the "9-in-3" Competition Theory, the first category, namely, economic development level, and the talents and science and technology support policies and fiscal and financial support policies in the second category, economic policies and measures. Regional government competition in the narrow sense refers to the competition in the urban economy, which mainly involves regional governments formulating and implementing policies related to quasi-operative resources or urban infrastructure. Regional governments' participation in and allocation and management of the urban economy can not only prevent urban resources from laying idle or being wasted and avoid poor-quality and disorderly urban construction, but also promote the comprehensive and sustainable development of urban construction and social economy. It is related to, in the "9-in-3" Competition Theory, the first category, economic development level, the infrastructure investment policies of the second category, economic policies and measures, and the third category, economic management efficiency.

According to the "9-in-3" Competition Theory, regional government competition in the broad sense is competition in a large market system, one that's manifested as regional governments' efforts to optimize the distribution of the three types of resources that they have the authority to distribute through formulating policies accordingly. Specifically, it is the competition in the three aspects of economic development, economic policy and economic efficiency, and more specifically, in the nine factors. In its essence, the competition is about how regional governments, when distributing regional resources, adopt what policies for the industrial economy to enhance the vitality of enterprises, adopt what policies for the livelihood economy to create a good environment, and adopt what policies for the urban economy to promote the sustainable development of the region. The regional government's distribution of the three kinds of resources and the strength of its policy measures in the "9-in-3" competition directly determine the region's fiscal revenue in a certain period of time. Therefore, regional government competition in the broad sense is essentially the competition of regional government's objective function in industrial development, urban construction and social welfare, that is, the competition of regional fiscal revenue determination mechanism (see Chapter 4 for details).

According to the "9-in-3" Competition Theory, regional government competition in the narrow sense is manifested mainly in the competition in the investment into and development and construction of urban infrastructure, that is, the competition of governments' performance in formulating supporting policies and optimizing allocation in the field of urban infrastructure. Of the "9-in-3," such competition lies primarily in optimizing regional fiscal expenditure structure and giving play to the functions of fiscal investment expenditure. In the investment into and development and construction of hard and soft urban infrastructure and modern smart cities, the way regional governments participate, the rules they follow in their behaviors and the supporting policies they formulate are all embodied in their fiscal expenditure structure. Regional government competition in the narrow sense is the competition in urban infrastructure, or, the competition of the determination mechanism of regional fiscal investment expenditure (see Chapter 4 for details).

To sum up, regional governments compete in "9-in-3." In the broad sense, the competition is essentially in the effective distribution of the three kinds of regional resources (at this time government behaviors focus on the determination mechanism of regional fiscal revenue), yet with particular emphasis on the urban economy, which is embodied in the investment into and development and construction of urban infrastructure, that is, the quasi-operative resources in the field of resource generation (at this time government behaviors focus on regional fiscal expenditure structure, mainly the proportion of investment expenditure). This is the central idea of the "9-in-3" Competition Theory.

5.4 Determination mechanism of regional government competitiveness—the DRP model

DRP is short for District Resource Planning and the DRP model is one for optimizing regional resource allocation. With this model, the regional government is able to appropriately distribute resources under its authority and adjust resource structure to the better, so as to improve the efficiency of resource utilization in the region. The core of DRP model design is to study how regional government could maximize the objective function of regional economic efficiency.

We will discuss the construction of the DRP model still from the standpoint of fiscal revenue and expenditure, and then establish a performance evaluation system of regional government from the perspective of urban development.

5.4.1 Fiscal surplus and the determination mechanism of "9-in-3"

In a given period of time, in addition to tuning the total amount of its fiscal expenditure (FE), the regional government can also arrange the structure of its expenditure, that is, the proportions of expenditure spent in different fields, in order to obtain maximum benefits. As aforementioned, regional government's FE could be put into three categories: (1) Consumption expenditure (CE), which is mainly used to improve the level of environment support, management support and policy support in the region and whose impact is primarily on regional government's management efficiency; (2) Investment expenditure (IE), which is mainly used to improve the construction level of regional infrastructure such as roads, bridges and power grids and whose impact is primarily on the quality of regional government's economic policies; and (3) Transfer expenditure (TE), which is mainly used to improve the level of support in terms of talents, science and technology, and treasury and finance in the region and whose impact is primarily also on the quality of regional government's economic policies.

As mentioned in Chapter 4, the three expenditure types always fit in the following formula:

$$CE + IE + TE = FE \tag{5.1}$$

When variable coefficientφ_i is introduced, we could get the following relationship:

$$Y = \varphi_1(Y_1, Y_0) * CE + \varphi_2(Y_2, Y_0) * IE + \varphi_3(Y_3, Y_0) * TE + Const1 \tag{5.2}$$

Let's further introduce variable λ ($0<\lambda<1$), which was mentioned in Chapter 3, to represent the proportion of quasi-operative resources in the region allocated in the public sector. The proportion, that is, the value of λ, has an impact on the number of infrastructure goods that could actually be leveraged by fiscal expenditure and thus influences the actual effect of investment expenditures. So multiplier λ is introduced to get formula (5.4). As discussed in Chapter 3, λ is influenced by the development level of the market economy (Y), fiscal revenue and expenditure conditions (including fiscal budget B and fiscal expenditure (FE) and resident awareness (γ). Following the assumptions and conclusions in Chapter 3, we can get the following expression of λ:

$$\lambda = e^{-\left(aY+b\frac{FE}{B}\right)}\left(\frac{Y}{Y^*}\right)^{-c\gamma} \tag{5.3}$$

When multiplier λ is used to adjust formula (5.2), the following formula could be got:

$$Y = \varphi_1(Y_1, Y_0) * CE + \varphi_2(Y_2, Y_0) * \frac{IE}{\lambda} + \varphi_3(Y_3, Y_0) * TE + Const1 \tag{5.4}$$

As discussed in Chapter 4, the government's Fiscal Income (FInc) has the following relationship with tax revenue ωY and fee income from infrastructure projects $\tau CumP(IE)$:

$$FInc = \tau CumP(IE) + \omega Y + Const2 \tag{5.5}$$

In the above formula, ω is the tax rate, τ is the fee rate, and $\tau CumP(IE)$ represents the fee income government obtains from infrastructure projects and is a function of IE. Const2 represents other incomes.

Then fiscal surplus FS could be calculated with the following expression:

$$FS = FInc - FE = \tau CumP(IE) + \omega Y + Const2 - FE \tag{5.6}$$

Based on the above formulas, the function expression of the "9-in-3" Competition Theory could be discussed.

First, regional output level DEV could be represented by regional economic development level Y:

$$DEV = Y = \varphi_1(Y_1, Y_0) * CE + \varphi_2(Y_2, Y_0) * \frac{IE}{\lambda} + \varphi_3(Y_3, Y_0) * TE + Const1 \tag{5.7}$$

Second, regional economic management efficiency (EME), mainly involving the policy system, environment system and management system established by the regional government and determined by the proportion of investment expenditure in the government's fiscal revenue, could be defined as:

$$EME = \omega\varphi_1(Y_1, Y_0) * CE/FInc \tag{5.8}$$

Third, regional economic policy level POL, mainly referring to the region's infrastructure construction, talents level, science and technology level and the level of fiscal and financial support, and determined by the proportion of investment expenditure and transfer expenditure in the government's fiscal revenue, could be defined as:

$$POL = \omega\varphi_2(Y_2, Y_0)\frac{IE}{\lambda}/FInc + \omega\varphi_3(Y_3, Y_0)TE/FInc \quad (5.9)$$

5.4.2 Comprehensive measurement and objective function

From the above discussions it could be summarized that in a relatively short period of a region's development, regional economic efficiency mainly depends on the following five indicators: Fiscal expenditure elasticity (ELA) and fiscal surplus (FS) in the quantity dimension, and regional economic development level (DEV), regional EME and regional economic policy level (POL) in the structural dimension. Regional governments raise annual fiscal revenue mainly by improving the level of fiscal expenditure of the year and optimizing its structure. The regulatory variables are mainly government FE and its three components, CE, IE and TE, and the relationship among the four is expressed by formula (5.1).

The next questions would be how to construct a comprehensive measure SYN, that is, regional economic efficiency, on the basis of the above-mentioned five measures, and how to adjust the four major dependent variables (FE, CE, IE and TE) to achieve a maximum comprehensive measure SYN.

The key to answering the above questions is to find the appropriate weights and function forms that would enable us to reflect the information in different dimensions with one general index. We have noticed that the measure of regional economic efficiency is embodied in two dimensions: the quantity dimension and the structure dimension.

The indicator of quantity measures the input of policies and focuses on assessing whether the policies can play an effective and sustainable role, while the indicator of the structure measures the output of policies and focuses on assessing whether the policies can bring about real economic improvement. Since the two indicators do not overlap in the information they measure, their comprehensive measure is the weighted sum of the two:

$$SYN = \omega_1 Q(ELA, FS) + \omega_2 G(DEV, EME, POL) \quad (5.10)$$

The weights $\omega_1 + \omega_2 = 1$. In specific scenarios, if we need to simplify the assumptions of the model, we can also assume that the comprehensive measure depends only on the structural dimension and not the quantity dimension, in which case $\omega_1 = 0$, $\omega_2 = 1$. It should be noted that ELA is not determined by the four dependent variables, but by the economic environment at the time, which means that regional governments in most times regard it as an external condition and make decisions depending on the circumstances. To facilitate our discussion, we can propose the following simplified assumptions and use ELA as the basis for setting the values of ω_1 and ω_2.

$$\text{SYN} = (\text{ELA}/ELA + \overline{\text{ELA}}) * \text{FS} + (\overline{\text{ELA}}/ELA + \overline{\text{ELA}})\text{G}(\text{DEV, EME, POL}) \tag{5.11}$$

$\overline{\text{ELA}}$ represents the mean value of ELA in each historical time interval.

The meaning of formula (5.11) is that under the condition of the government making rational decisions according to the circumstances when the elasticity of FE is higher than the historical average, the regional government should attach more weight to the effect of FE, and when the elasticity of FE is lower than the historical average, the regional government should keep the fiscal surplus to maintain the sustainability of expenditure and prevent the economy from overheating.

As aforementioned, DEV is the outcome of EME and POL in combination, and they in essence also constitute a relationship of quantity and structure. To simplify the further discussion, we assume that the two are parallel, namely:

$$\text{G}(\text{DEV, EME, POL}) = \text{DEV} * (\omega_3\text{EME} + \omega_4\text{POL}) \tag{5.12}$$

In the formula, ω_3 and ω_4, respectively, represent the preference the comprehensive measure outcome demonstrates for economic management efficiency and economic policy level, and $\omega_3 + \omega_4 = 1$. The value of ω_3 and ω_4 depends on the decision maker's preference for specific fields.

If the decision-maker takes the efficiency of fiscal expenditure as the only principle, we can use the variable coefficient φ_i in formula (5.2) to give weights, that is:

$$\omega_3 = \frac{\varphi_1}{\varphi_1 + \varphi_2 + \varphi_3}, \ \omega_4 = \frac{\varphi_2 + \varphi_3}{\varphi_1 + \varphi_2 + \varphi_3} \tag{5.13}$$

When the above formulas are put into formula (5.12), we can get:

$$\text{G}(\text{DEV, EME, POL}) = \text{DEV} * \left(\frac{\varphi_1}{\varphi_1 + \varphi_2 + \varphi_3}\text{EME} + \frac{\varphi_2 + \varphi_3}{\varphi_1 + \varphi_2 + \varphi_3}\text{POL}\right) \tag{5.14}$$

Then we can get the expression of comprehensive measure SYN:

$$\text{SYN} = (\text{ELA}/(ELA + \overline{\text{ELA}})) * \text{FS} + (\overline{\text{ELA}}/ELA + \overline{\text{ELA}})\text{DEV} \\ * \left(\frac{\varphi_1}{\varphi_1 + \varphi_2 + \varphi_3}\text{EME} + \frac{\varphi_2 + \varphi_3}{\varphi_1 + \varphi_2 + \varphi_3}\text{POL}\right) \quad (5.15)$$

Within the limit of the budget, the regional government strives to reach the maximum possible value of the comprehensive measure through adjusting the proportions of the three types of fiscal expenditure. So the DRP model could be defined as:

$$\max_{\{\text{CE,IE,TE}\}} (\text{ELA}/(ELA + \overline{\text{ELA}})) * \text{FS} + (\overline{\text{ELA}}/ELA + \overline{\text{ELA}})\text{DEV} \\ * \left(\frac{\varphi_1}{\varphi_1 + \varphi_2 + \varphi_3}\text{EME} + \frac{\varphi_2 + \varphi_3}{\varphi_1 + \varphi_2 + \varphi_3}\text{POL}\right) \quad (5.16)$$

$$\text{s. t. } \text{CE} + \text{IE} + \text{TE} = \text{FE},$$

$$\text{FS} > 0,$$

$$\varphi_1 + \varphi_2 + \varphi_3 \neq 0.$$

The DRP model indicates that the regional government could, by adjusting the three types of fiscal expenditure, reach a fiscal expenditure structure that's the most favorable for the region's competitive advantage and thus achieve the optimal economic efficiency for the region in a particular development period.

5.4.3 Government performance assessment system

In short-term regional government competition, as shown by the DRP model discussed above, the objective of the regional government is to achieve an optimized expenditure structure and optimal regional economic efficiency. Yet from a long-term point of view, government performance should not be assessed simply based on how it does in fulfilling economic development goals in a short period but should be evaluated with multiple dimensions including urban economic construction and development. A sound performance assessment system should be able to evaluate the overall performance of the region in a comprehensive manner so as to detect the region's weaknesses and strengths in industrial development, urban construction and social welfare.

Following the structure and content of the "9-in-3" Competition Theory, the following indicators and weights could be set to constitute a regional government performance assessment and appraisal system (Table 5.1).

Table 5.1 Assessment and Appraisal System for Regional Government Performance

Aspect	*Factor*	*S.N.*	*Indicator*	*Positive/ Negative*	*Weight*	
Economic Development Level	Projects	1	Number of major national science & technology projects	Positive	7	17
		2	Number of projects with private investment	Positive	6	
		3	Number of projects with foreign capital cooperation	Positive	4	
	Industrial Chains	4	Completeness of industries with resource advantages	Positive	6	13
		5	Development level of industrial clustering	Positive	4	
		6	Introduction and development of high-tech industries	Positive	3	
	Imports and Exports	7	Proportion of foreign capital in local enterprise input	Positive	4	12
		8	Year on year growth rate of total import and export volume	Positive	5	
		9	Structure of foreign enterprise investment	Positive	3	
Economic Policies and Measures	Infrastructure Investment Policies	10	City intelligence	Positive	5	15
		11	Convenience of public transportation	Positive	3	
		12	Perfection of basic education facilities	Positive	3	
		13	Development level and coverage of medical facilities	Positive	4	
	Talents and Science and Technology Support Policies	14	Local employment rate of higher education graduates (including the number of high-end personnel introduced)	Positive	5	10
		15	Patent index	Positive	3	
		16	Proportion of R&D investment of enterprises	Positive	2	
	Fiscal and Financial Support Polices	17	Growth rate of circulation market value of local listed companies	Positive	4	9

(*Continued*)

Table 5.1 (Continued)

Aspect	*Factor*	*S.N.*	*Indicator*	*Positive/ Negative*	*Weight*	
		18	Preferential financing subsidies for small and medium-sized micro enterprises	Positive	3	
		19	Perfection of industrial structure	Positive	2	
Economic Manageme-nt Efficiency	Policy System Efficiency	20	Social welfare system	Positive	4	8
		21	Popularization of legal education	Positive	2	
		22	Satisfaction of urban and rural residents	Positive	2	
	Environment System Efficiency	23	Resident happiness index	Positive	4	9
		24	Green environmental protection index	Positive	2	
		25	Frequency of resident complaints	Negative	3	
	Management System Efficiency	26	Residents' satisfaction with administrative services	Positive	3	7
		27	Complicatedness of government administrative services	Negative	3	
		28	Social evaluation of response to emergencies	Positive	1	

In actual evaluation, it cannot always be made sure that all the data needed are available without abnormal values. So we use the following methods to process the data:

If the data for the evaluated year are not complete, the data of the region in the previous year or the data of all regions in the evaluated year will be used as a reference. Specifically, if the indicator of the region in the previous year is available, it shall be used as a replacement, and if it's not available, the median of the same indicator of all regions in the evaluated year shall be used as a replacement.

If the value of an indicator is obviously abnormal, in order to prevent erroneous data from undermining the appraisal, we adopt the following methods: If the index value is less than the median of its historical data and is beyond the double standard deviation of the median, it shall be replaced by the median minus the double standard deviation, and if the index value is greater than the median and is beyond the double standard deviation of the median, it shall be replaced by the median plus the double standard deviation.

To better use this regional government performance evaluation system, we can assess government performance on each indicator with a basic score, a quality score and a leverage score. The full basic score is 50, the full quality score is 30 and the full leverage score is 20.

As different regions are in different stages and levels of economic development (see Chapter 6 for details), the target standards set for their evaluation can be different. The difference can be made up by the basic score of the region. Based on the region's level of target completion a basic score B_i could be obtained.

For example, for an indicator, we can set four levels as follows: A basic score of 20 will be given if the region completed none of the preset objectives, 30 will be given if the region completed some of the preset objectives, 40 will be given if the region completed all the preset objectives, and a full score of 50 will be given if the region exceeded the objectives.

To measure the quality score, we distinguish indicators into positive ones and negative ones, for each of which a relative quality score can be calculated:

$$\text{For positive indicators: } Q_i = \frac{X_i - X_{min}}{X_{max} - X_{min}} \times 30$$

$$\text{For negative indicators: } Q_i = \frac{X_{max} - X_i}{X_{max} - X_{min}} \times 30$$

Q_i represents the quality score of indicator i, X_i is the value of indicator i, X_{max} is the maximum value of the indicator in all comparable regions, and X_{min} is the minimum value of the indicator in all comparable regions.

It can be seen from the above formulas that the quality score measures the comparative advantage of the region in the competition with other regions. In the formula for positive indicators, the more the value of indicator i exceeds the minimum value and is close to the maximum value, the higher the score will be. In the best case, indicator i is equal to the maximum value and the region gets the highest possible score of 30. On the contrary, the worse the region's comparative advantage, the farther away from the maximum value index i will be, and the higher the score of the negative indicator will be. In the worst case, the value of index i is equal to the minimum value and the negative indicator score will reach the maximum 30.

To measure the leverage score, we also introduce two types of indicators, positive and negative:

$$\text{For positive indicators: } L_i = 20 * I_{\{S_i > S_{med}\}}$$

$$\text{For negative indicators: } L_i = 20 * I_{\{S_i < S_{med}\}}$$

L_i is the region's leverage score in indicator i, S_i is the region's indicator i value, and S_{med} is the median of the region's historical values on the indicator (the value of the evaluated period included in the calculation of the median, the same below). $I_{\{Si>Smed\}}$ is an indicative function, that is, I is taken as 1 when the region's performance in the evaluated period exceeds the median of the historical values and will be taken as 0 otherwise. In the formula for negative indicators, $I_{\{Si<Smed\}}$ is also an indicative function. When the region's performance in the evaluated period is lower than the median of the historical values, I is 1, and otherwise it is 0.

It can be seen from the above formulas that the leverage score measures the advantage of the region's performance in the evaluated period comparative to its historical performance. For positive indicators, when the region's performance in the evaluated period exceeds its historical performance, the region gets a full leverage score of 20, and when the performance in the evaluated period is poorer than its historical performance, the region does not get any leverage score on the indicator, that is, the leverage score is 0. It's the opposite for negative indicators—the region's leverage score is 20 if its performance in the evaluated period is poor, that is, lower than the historical performance, otherwise the leverage score is 0. We can choose which formula to use to calculate the leverage score according to specific needs, that is, whether the indicator is positive or negative.

Putting the three scores together, we can get the region's score on indicator i:

$$V_i = B_i + Q_i + L_i$$

Therefore, to evaluate the region's performance on a factor, the score can be calculated with the following formula:

$$Factor_k = \sum_{i=1}^{n} [V_i \times (w_i / \sum_{j=1}^{n} w_j)]$$

$Factor_k$ represents the region's total score on factor k, which contains n indicators, and W_i represents the weight of indicator i in factor k.

Combing the region's scores on all the factors, we can get its total performance evaluation score:

$$Score_p = \sum_{k=1}^{l} [Factor_k \times (w_k / \sum_{j=1}^{l} w_j)]$$

$Score_p$ represents the total performance evaluation score of region p, where there is l factor, and W_k represents the weight of factor k in region p.

This evaluation system is similar to the "9-in-3" competition structure. Economic development level (projects, industrial chain, and import and export) is still where the main competitive advantage of the region lies at this stage, which is the reason for its relatively high overall weight.

As urban construction, urban economy and residents' living standards gradually improve, although economic development level remains an important aspect of regional competitive advantage, the other two aspects—economic policies and measures (policies on infrastructure construction, on talents and science and technology, and on treasury and finance) and economic management efficiency (policy system efficiency, environment system efficiency and management system efficiency)—will play a growing role in urban construction and economic development. The latter two aspects will not only improve residents' life satisfaction but also contribute to regional economic development and achieve a more far-reaching impact.

It is worth noting that when this performance evaluation system is put into use, the weights of different indicators and factors can be adjusted according to the particular development stage the evaluated region is in and its particular resource advantages and development priorities. The weight setting could be more flexible for research purposes.

Comparing the evaluation system with the DRP model, we can see that with the DRP model we focus on studying regional resource allocation from the standpoint of regional government's optimizing its fiscal expenditure structure in a certain period, while with the regional government performance evaluation system, we focus on the regional government's efforts in promoting industrial development, urban construction and social welfare. First, an evaluation system for each factor is built with individual indicators, and then the factors are grouped into categories to eventually form an evaluation system structured after the "9-in-3" competition, that is, an evaluation system focusing on the appraisal of the region's economic development level, economic policies and measures and economic management efficiency.

The DRP model and the regional government performance evaluation system complement each other, offering two different approaches to discussing regional government competition and regional economic development, which is helpful for economic researchers to learn about and understand the theories on regional government competition and regional economic development from different levels and perspectives.

5.5 "Voting with Feet" to select regional government

In a modern market system, enterprises are the main player in industrial resource allocation and regional governments are the main player in urban resource allocation. In practice the two are blended together, following market rules in relatively independent operation mechanisms and optimizing resource allocation through market competition. Market rules, supply and demand competition and the operation of the modern market economy are three key points of market economy that both enterprises and regional governments have to follow.

Here the government in government competition refers mainly to regional governments, and the government in government regulation refers mainly to the national government within one country and the United Nations internationally. "Government" could refer to multiple entities, including regional government as a single entity, and the national government or the United Nations as a joint entity. (The strength of the UN's functions in international affairs will not be discussed here. The subject is under the topic of international economic system reform. Yet, the importance of intergovernmental economic alliances' role in international economic affairs should not be denied.) Due to their dual (micro and macro) attributes, regional governments will participate in economic competition, which gives importance to the role of the national government and the United Nations in regulating and coordinating such competition by legal means.

Regional government competition helps form the scale effect, cluster effect and neighborhood effect of urban economic development.

The scale effect of the urban economy refers to the "1 + 1 > 2" effect of the organic combination of various factors of production after the total economic volume of the region reaches a certain scale. In other words, the growth of the urban economy scale elevates its overall economic benefits and social benefits. On the part of the regional government, the factors determining the scale of the regional economy lie mainly in its policies and measures on the development and utilization of the three types of resources in the city, specifically, what policies it adopts to plan, guide, coordinate, support, supervise and manage operative resources (industrial economy) to invigorate enterprises, what policies it adopts on non-operative resources (livelihood economy) to ensure fairness and justice, guarantee basic needs, and raise effectiveness and efficiency so as to optimize the investment environment, and what policies it adopts on quasi-operative resources (urban economy) to promote sustainable development. These policies and measures are manifested in the regional government's "9-in-3" competition. Put in other words, the regional government's performance in "9-in-3" competition ultimately determines the scale effect of the region, specifically, the scale effect of the region's urban infrastructure, the scale effect of its population and the scale effect of entrepreneurship and employment brought by population, the scale effect of science and technology, the scale effect of capital, the scale effect of industry, the scale effect of market openness and trade, as well as the scale effect of policies and organizational management. Regional government competition can form and strengthen the positive scale effect of an urban economy.

The cluster effect of the urban economy refers to the comprehensive economic and social effect produced by the spatial concentration of various economic resources and activities in the region, as well as the centripetal force resulted from that concentration, a force that pulls various surrounding economic resources and activities towards the region. The cluster effect is the basic drive for the continual expansion and development of an urban economy. It covers the effects of the clustering of economy, culture, talents, science and technology, capital, transportation infrastructure, organizational management and policy measures. For example, the effects of industrial clustering include the following: First, the formation of vertical industrial clusters that stimulate scientific and technological innovation; second, the extension of industrial chains to form a virtuous cycle of "resources → products → wastes → resources → products," and the comprehensive use of the resources; and third, the attainment of energy conservation and emission reduction, ecological and environmental protection, as well as the organic combination of economic benefits and comprehensive social benefits. Industrial clustering brings cost advantages and fosters division of labor and cooperation. That all enterprises in the region share the advantages of the same industrial brands allows enterprise investment scale to constantly expand, the quality of strategic management to continuously improve, and the social service system to become increasingly complete. Further, industrial clustering advances the transformation of regional economic growth mode because the advantages of the clustering of talents, land, capital, technology, management, and services exert impact on a wider scope and as a result accelerate industrialization, urbanization and informatization, push for effective utilization of various resources in the region, and promote sustainable development of the economy. To enhance the cluster effect of the urban economy, regional governments should strive to perform better in the "9-in-3" competition.

The neighborhood effect of the urban economy refers to the influence of regional environment characteristics on the mind and actions of people. When the vast majority of the people expect to build a harmonious, comfortable and convenient environment and strive to attain the greatest rewards at the lowest cost in economic activities, the influence of the regional environment will promote the spread and exchange of such mentality and economic behavior. Such influence is what we call the neighborhood effect. Needless to say, neighborhood effect can be beneficial or detrimental, benign or malignant, positive or negative. Also contributing directly to the neighborhood effect are the regional environment and the region's comprehensive social development level, which specifically includes the region's economy, culture, talents, science and technology, capital and transportation infrastructure and the regional government's organizational efficiency and policy effectiveness. Regional government's voluntarily taking part in the "9-in-3" competition is conducive to guiding beneficial, benign and positive neighborhood effect into play.

In an open social and economic system, the scale effect, cluster effect and neighborhood effect of talents, capital, technology and other factors lead to investors to choose where their factors of production should flow, that is, leading investors to "vote with their feet." Investors' choices in the flow direction of their talents, money and materials prompt regional governments to provide better public services and a better public environment. On the surface "voting with feet" is to choose cities and regions, yet, in essence, it is to choose a regional government, regional environment and regional services. Regional governments can effectively raise the attractiveness of their regional brand by fully taking part in regional "9-in-3" competition, specifically, by planning, guiding, supporting, coordinating, supervising and managing the industrial economy, by ensuring the fairness and justice of, guaranteeing basic needs of and encouraging the effective improvement of livelihood economy, and by investing in, developing and advising on hard and soft urban infrastructure and smart cities.

6 Competitive economic growth

6.1 Growth stage dominated by industrial economy competition

For regional governments, the competition in the industrial economy is mainly manifested in the development level of the region's industrial chain and industrial cluster and in the competition of regional industrial policies. For countries around the world, industrial economy competition takes place mainly in the initial stage of regional economic growth, that is, the factor-driven stage.

The first point I want to discuss is regional industrial chain and industrial cluster development. The essence of the issue is the competition in distributing the production factors in the region and regional governments' distributing and competing for primordial resources.

Regional production factors include natural resources, human resources and capital resources. In the initial stage of regional economic development, almost all successful enterprises and industries depend on the region's basic production factors. In most cases, local enterprises at this stage compete with each other in the form of price war. They provide few products and have a low technology level. Moreover, they have no ability of their own to create technology yet and so must rely on foreign enterprises for experience and technology. Their technologies mainly come from imitation or are introduced from foreign enterprises that invest in the region. More specifically, most of the advanced product designs and technologies owned by local enterprises are provided by factories built by foreign investors who choose the region as a production site or are learned by local manufacturing enterprises while conducting semi-finished products processing. Local enterprises at this stage rarely have direct contact with the final customers of the products, and most of the trade opportunities in domestic and foreign markets are in the hands of foreign agents. Therefore, at this stage, the regional government should take effective measures to attract investment, carry out project competition, improve industrial chain, form industrial clusters, encourage imports and exports, give full play to the region's

DOI: 10.4324/9781003244837-6

production factor advantages and push resource allocation, so as to constantly promote regional economic growth.

In a certain period of time, with production technologies in the region fixed, the functional relationship between the input and combination of various production factors and the output of products can be expressed as follows:

$$Q = f(L, K, E, N)$$

Q stands for output, *L* stands for labor, *K* capital, *E* various natural resources led by land and *N* entrepreneurial talent and the management ability of the regional government.

In the initial stage of economic development, the technical level is relatively low and will not significantly improve in a fairly long period of time, and the capital lacks effective accumulation and is often insufficient. So the region relies more on the simple quantitative expansion of production factors such as labor force and natural resources to obtain and maintain the power that drives economic growth. This mode of economic growth is relatively simple and easy, and the short-term effect is significant. Therefore, in this stage, regional governments of all countries can play a great role in promoting economic growth simply by creating conditions to attract investment and competing effectively in optimizing the allocation of production factors in the region.

The stage dominated by industrial economy competition is essentially the factor-driven stage of regional economic growth. This stage could be roughly divided into three periods. In the first period, the region relies on local resources for development, and areas that first achieved relatively advanced economy are often those with abundant land, labor and natural resources. In the period, the launching of economic development and the short-term rise of industries all depend on large quantities of production factor input and then on extensive expansion of the scale of such input. But such factor-driven growth solely relying on local resources could only be a primary and short-term mode of expansion and will, in the long run, lose its momentum and eventually transit to the mode of competing for resources from outside the region, which is the second period, during which the region sets out to attract investment, talents and knowledge. During this period the industrial development in the region relies not merely on the competition for projects, improving the industrial chain, forming industrial clusters, expanding imports and exports, and occupying domestic and foreign markets, but also, and more heavily, on the competition in scientific and technological talents and the supporting environment. This is the period where industrial parks, science and technology parks, industry incubation parks, and even special economic zones built and developed according to the Port-Park-City (PPC) model spring out one after another. These competition activities will soon push regional economic development into the third period dominated by the competition in supportive policies and environment optimization. Regional governments' supporting policies contribute substantially to the outcome of investment and talents influx. Thus, it's natural that each region will compete in project policies, land policies, industry subsidy policies, preferential policies for high-end personnel, science and technology investment policies, guarantee and discount policies, and even policies related to children's schooling and parents' medical treatment.

The second point I want to discuss is another facet of industrial economy competition—supportive industrial policies, which is a bone of contention in the discussions about market economy. The contention is mainly on three aspects: First, whether to adopt industrial policies; second, what kinds of industrial policies are essential, that is, how to objectively evaluate the industrial policies of countries around the world and third, what should be the theoretical framework to make a case for industrial policies.

Peking University held an intellectual forum on industrial policies at the end of 2016, which opened the debates on whether to retain or scrap industrial policies. Two economists, whom please excuse me for using A and B instead of their real names to refer to, exchanged sharply opposing views, which could be summarized into the following ten points.

First, what are they debating about? The contention is in short a dispute between free market and industrial policy. A believes that industrial policies refer to the government's favorable policies in the form of subsidies or administrative interventions to help certain industries develop, while B believes that industrial policies include not only government subsidies to enterprises but also the government's allocation of limited scientific research resources based on possible returns.

Second, are industrial policies a gamble? B thinks that the existing industries could be classified into five types, each of which calls for different industrial policies. A holds that all industrial policies should be abolished on the grounds that innovation can't be foreseen and thus the government is in no place to make any plans for new industries or innovations. A believes that the only way to achieve innovation is to carry out free economic experiments rather than locking oneself in a preset path through industrial policies.

Third, does efficient market exist? B believes that the economic development of a country takes the joint forces of an efficient market and an effective government. A stresses that the central function of the government is to protect intellectual property rights and maintain the fairness of market rules with the law, and that any government behavior going beyond this range will render it impossible for an efficient market to take shape.

Fourth, who is the leading player of the market? B believes that continuous economic development needs both the market and the government because an effective government is needed to steer entrepreneurs towards their own benefits according to circumstances and help them solve technical problems. A believes that the leading player of the market are entrepreneurs, whose basic function is to find and create trading opportunities, and that comparative advantages are created by entrepreneurs, which makes the combination of free market and entrepreneurs sufficient for the utilization of comparative advantages and renders any national strategy unnecessary.

Fifth, should we reward the first person to eat crabs? B holds that the government should subsidize the first people to eat crabs in some industries, while A believes that the government should neither prevent anyone from eating crabs nor pay for those who eat crabs because such reward will tempt many people to pretend to eat crabs, that is, eating bread with the posture of eating crab.

Sixth, will industrial policies lead to rent-seeking of those with political power? B holds that the government may use its power to help entrepreneurs solve problems and it's not that entrepreneurs do not need the protection of the government. A believes that it's very difficult to design sound incentive policies, that the formulation of a specific industrial policy is often the result of a game of interests, and that both the formulation and implementation of industrial policies are full of rent-seeking activities.

Seventh, who drives technological innovation? B points out that revolutions of basic sciences are not affected by entrepreneurship and are instead driven by scientists supported by the government, and that the innovations of entrepreneurs are also based on breakthroughs of basic scientific research and public technologies backed by the government. A believes that the essence of social progress is the improvement of labor productivity, which depends on technological innovation and progress, the source of which are entrepreneurs and entrepreneurship.

Eighth, how to give play to comparative advantages? B thinks that the role of the government should be fully tapped in making use of comparative advantages to promote economic development. A believes that the market is the most effective system to fully tap comparative advantages, that all market transactions are based on comparative advantages, and that entrepreneurs are the geniuses in finding comparative advantages.

Ninth, is entrepreneurship exclusively for entrepreneurs? B agrees that it takes entrepreneurship to discover new opportunities, but points out that those who discover new opportunities could be entrepreneurs as well as intellectuals or government officials. He holds that entrepreneurship should not be understood as something only entrepreneurs can possess because that would narrow the scope of the application of entrepreneurship. A believes that every entrepreneur decides what to do or not to do with his vigilance, imagination and judgment and then successful innovations will be copied and failed businesses will be stopped and that it's tens of thousands of entrepreneurs that are coordinating supply and demand and the effect of such coordination determines their ability to make money.

Tenth, does "corner overtaking" really exist? B points out that there have been 13 successful economies after World War II and their governments have all supported industrial development and argues that industrial policies are necessary for a developing country to catch up with developed countries. A, on the contrary, believes that only market competition can achieve such overtake, that what industries a country pursues should depend on the judgment of entrepreneurs, and that there would be disastrous consequences if the government insists on using industrial policies to lead economic development.

In this debate on whether to keep or abolish industrial policies that took place in the ivory tower, both sides gave strong arguments, public opinions vary and there's no definite conclusion.

Professor Michael Porter of Harvard University made the following statements on industrial policies in his *The Competitive Advantage of Nations*. First of all, since the primary goal of government formulating industrial policies is to raise productivity and to encourage and stimulate industrial development, the government should promote the development of human resources and related capital and create a good environment for industrial development. The long-term goal of a country's economic policies should include improving productivity for otherwise the policies themselves are prone to being ill-directed. While establishing an appropriate goal is the first prerequisite for designing sound industrial policies, the second condition is establishing an appropriate model to support regional economic competition. Every policy with an impact on a country's comparative advantage is designed with its own specific considerations. In this regard the main or general policies the government might adopt include currency devaluation, liberalization, privatization, relaxation of product and environmental standards, encouraging various forms of cooperation between enterprises, encouraging merger, tax reform, promoting development, setting restrictions on imported products, maintaining business order, targeted investment in R&D, improving the education system, setting up venture funds, and willingly doing more national defense procurement or other forms of government procurement. Second, the following fundamentals must be kept in mind because each industrial policy, be it local, regional or national, will affect the competitive advantage of the industry: (1) It is enterprises and not governments that engage in industrial competition. (2) The competitive advantage of an industry at the national level is relative and not absolute. (3) Competitive advantage comes from long-term vitality rather than short-term cost advantage. (4) The country needs industrial development to bring economic prosperity. (5) Industries that demonstrate national competitive advantage usually feature geographical concentration. (6) While it takes a new company only three or four years after setup to get on the right track, it will take a decade or even longer for an industry to form national competitive advantage. (7) The competitive advantage of a country lies in its difference from rather than commonality with other countries. (8) Which industries would form a national competitive advantage is not associated with how industries are classified. (9) The process of maintaining a competitive advantage is not easy for enterprises and employees. Third, when formulating industrial policies the government faces many challenges, common ones including often having multiple departments in charge of one issue and policy incoherence caused by the change of government. Last, industrial policies have a strong impact on production factors. Indicators of economic development are usually set based on the quantitative and qualitative improvement rates of production factors. To upgrade productivity enterprises must constantly take possession of high-quality human resources, scientific and technological knowledge, economic information and other factors of production, and on this basis enhance their competitive advantage. The government's industrial policies have a significant impact on this process.[1]

In my opinion, Professor Michael Porter's views on industrial policies convey the following valuable messages: First, he basically affirms support for industrial policies; second, he sets forth the basic contents of industrial policies; third, he puts forward the prerequisites and possible challenges of formulating industrial policies; fourth, he points out that the goal of formulating industrial policies is to improve productivity; fifth, he confirms that the positive effect of tax reduction on promoting industrial development is greater than that of subsidy policy, and that indirect subsidy behaviors will achieve better outcome than direct subsidy.[2]

After the above analysis we can now answer the debate about "whether market economy needs industrial policies." First, the theoretical framework justifying industrial policies comes from the actual economic growth needs dominated by industrial economy competition. Second, development, in reality, needs the government to mend market failures using the following three levels of industrial policies: (1) To remedy *deficiencies in the market mechanism* through planning and guiding. (2) To fill *gaps in the market mechanism* through support and coordination. (3) To overcome *barriers to the market mechanism* through supervision and management (see Chapter 9 for details). Third, industrial policies are not confined to industrial subsidies, and the government must abandon interventional behaviors divorced from market rules. Industrial policies should be designed in a manner that lets the market decide the allocation of industrial resources and gives better play to the role of the government in planning and guiding, support and coordination, supervision and management. In this growth stage dominated by industrial economy competition, the regional government will focus its fiscal expenditure on transfer payment items and its role will be the most pronounced in the competition of the three factors in the first category of the "9-in-3" Competition Theory.

6.2 Growth stage dominated by urban economy competition

For regional governments, urban economy competition is mainly the competition in hard and soft urban infrastructure, in the development and construction of smart cities, as well as in supportive policies and measures related to them. For all countries in the world, urban economy competition takes place mainly in the second stage of regional economic growth, a primarily investment-driven stage.

The first aspect I want to discuss about urban economy competition is the investment into and the development and construction of hard and soft urban infrastructure and smart cities, which are in essence the process of the region transcending the limitation of factor-driven economic growth and starting investment-driven growth, a process characterized by the regional government competing for and developing derivative resources.

Here I'd like to explicate two points. The first is that the "investment-driven" I am talking about is different from the "investment-driven stage" as defined by Professor Michael Porter in his *The Competitive Advantage of Nations*. Professor Porter's "investment" mainly refers to the investments conducted by enterprises in broader industries on the basis of profiting from the basic production factors they already possess. These are large-scale investments whose nature is production capacity expansion, not the urban infrastructure investments under discussion in this book. The second point is that of the three major categories of fixed asset investment in a region defined by economic statistics, namely, infrastructure investment, real estate investment and enterprises' technology transformation investment, this book mainly focuses on regional infrastructure investment.

As mentioned in Chapter 3, urban infrastructure includes hard urban infrastructure, that is, the six major engineering systems—energy supply system, water supply and drainage system, transportation system, post and telecommunications system, environmental protection and sanitation system, and defense, disaster prevention and safety system; soft urban infrastructure, that is, social infrastructure including administrative management, culture and education, medical and health care, commercial services, finance and insurance, and social welfare; the four types of infrastructure related to urban-rural integration—rural production, rural life, rural ecological environment construction and rural social development; and the development and construction of smart city projects, a new addition to urban infrastructure that comes along with urban modernization. In the following part Chicago's urban planning program in the early 20th century will be taken as a case to further clarify the contents of urban infrastructure and its role in promoting regional economic development.

To study the case of Chicago one cannot overlook the 1909 *Plan of Chicago*, a landmark work and the origin of American modern urban planning and construction that set off a wave of urban construction in the USA in the early 20th century. The Plan was adopted by the city and basically laid out the following development plan for Chicago, especially for its lakefront areas. As the most prominent document on urban investment, development and beautification, the Plan provides objective, rigorous, practical and feasible solutions for modern urban construction, including detailed planning and design of traffic network, station facilities, municipal buildings and landscaping.

The Plan of Chicago covers the origination of the Plan, ancient and modern urban planning, Chicago's status as a metropolis in the Midwest, Chicago's heart, and Chicago's park system, transportation and urban street system. It can be said that the regional economic achievements brought by Chicago's urban planning and construction still have a profound impact till this day on urban planning and construction in the USA and even the world.

In 1994, in an analysis of the formation and growth of public investment in the USA, Holtz Eakin classified the public investment in the country into four categories according to its end use: Education investment, road and highway investment, sewage treatment facility investment and public utility investment. According to Holtz Eakin's estimation, in 1988, the proportion of the four categories in the total government investment in the USA was 20.2% in education, 34.5% in roads and highways, 7.5% in sewage treatment and 13.2% in public utilities.[3] In a 2001 study, Shioji Etsuro included Holtz Eakin's last three categories into one entity termed public investment in infrastructure to distinguish them from the first category, public investment in education. The Japanese definition of public investment is relatively broad, comprising 14 items in total, which Shioji Etsuro put into four categories: first, education; second, infrastructure, including public housing, sewage treatment, garbage treatment, water supply, parks, roads, ports, airports and industrial water; third, state-owned protected land, including mountains, rivers and coasts; and fourth, agriculture and fisheries. In 1990, the proportion of the above four categories in public investment in Japan was respectively 12.2%, 60.6%, 13.5% and 13.7%.[4]

For regional governments, urban economy competition is primarily the competition in the investment into urban infrastructure as well as its development and constructioninfrastructure. As described in Chapter 5, according to the analysis of Richard Abel Musgrave and Walt Whitman Rostow about the stages of economic growth, in the early stage of a region's economic development, government investment accounts for a fairly high percentage as the government constantly provides infrastructure for regional economic development by investing in the transportation system, the environmental safety system, the education, science, culture and health system, the legal and order system, etc., which are essential for the region to enter the "take-off" stage and then the middle development stage. When economic development in a region enters the middle stage, government investment will continue to exist but will gradually become a supplement to private investment. Throughout the entire process of regional economic development, the absolute value of total investment in the region and the absolute value of government investment will both keep going up, but the proportion of total regional investment in regional GDP and the proportion of government investment in fiscal expenditure will both decline. Once the economy reaches the mature stage, regional fiscal expenditure will be devoted less to infrastructure construction and more to education, science, culture, health and welfare, and the growth rate of expenditure spent on the latter will greatly exceed the growth rate of other expenditures, and also become higher than the growth rate of the regional GDP.

The total amount and structure of investments in a region constantly change as the region progresses from one economic development stage to another. Once a region's per capita income level achieves a substantial rise, people will start pursuing a higher quality of life and set out higher requirements for regional development, which will force the regional government to provide a better environment, more advanced transportation, faster communication, education, sanitation, health services of higher quality, etc. As a result, the regional government's fiscal investment expenditure and social consumption expenditure will both experience considerable growth. It can be seen that how the total amount and structure of regional government's investment change depends on the structure and elasticity of investors' and the public's demand for regional public goods, and such structure and elasticity of demand change as regional economic development enters different stages. The improvement of hard and soft urban infrastructure and the development of smart cities can not only upgrade the region's investment environment but also help the region break the bottleneck of factor-driven economic growth, turn to an investment-driven mode, and enter the growth stage dominated by urban economy competition.

The second aspect concerning urban economy competition I want to discuss is regional governments' supportive policies. In this aspect regional governments serve three functions, namely, "formulating overall plans, participating in construction and conducting orderly management."

The overall planning of the urban economy involves three levels of regional resource allocation. The first level is the conceptual planning of regional economic development. The conceptual planning defines the region's main economic and social functions and the goal is to build the region into one that is suitable for living, business and tourism and to realize inclusive, coordinated, green, open and shared development. The second level is the urban-rural planning of regional economic development, which focuses on the layout, development, investment and construction about hard and soft infrastructure involving urban-rural integration and will have direct impact on the competitiveness of urban economy. The third level is the land planning of regional economic development, regarding which the government should, in strict accordance with the nature of land use, distinguish different investment projects, formulate stringent access system and build a reasonable and knowledge-based layout of urban resource allocation. Conceptual planning, urban-rural planning and land planning—the three form an organic whole that demarcates the policy scope of urban economy competition and enables the regional government to formulate detailed regulations and play its role in the strategic planning, implementation standards, project evaluation, market access, legal guarantee and other aspects of urban economy, so as to promote urban economic development.

Here it is imperative to review the discussion on regional government's urban infrastructure investment, development and construction in Chapter 4. In order to profit from its urban infrastructure investment and construction, regional government will reform the equity structure of its existing assets as well as optimize the equity structure of incremental assets so that the assets conform to market competition rules, and, through various financing methods of the capital market and making use of its charging power, pricing power, and other means, uses Design-Build-Operate (DBO), Build-Operate-Transfer (BOT), Build-Operate-Own (BOO), Build-Operate-Own-Transfer (BOOT), Build-Lease-Transfer (BLT), Build-Transfer-Operate (BTO) and Transfer-Operate-Transfer (TOT), amongst others, to implement capital operation of franchise rights. Regional government also, according to the specific characteristics and conditions of different urban infrastructure projects, selects and sometimes combines different capital operation modes, for instance, adopting Public-Private Partnership (PPP) or Port-Park-City (PPC) model, using franchise operation modes such as BOT or TOT, reorganizing project companies to be listed when conditions are mature, and further strengthening and expanding urban infrastructure projects through issuing stocks or bonds. Such measures enable the regional government to prevail over the constraints of fund bottleneck, improve its investment, development, operation and management abilities to achieve science-based and sustainable development of urban infrastructure, and achieve multiplied effects with limited regional public finance to more effectively meet the growing demand of the region's people for public goods and public welfare. In the investment-driven stage, the size and depth of regional government's participation in urban economy, the scale and structure of fiscal investment expenditure and social consumption expenditure, the degree of market openness, and relevant policies and measures all have direct impact on regional economic growth.

According to Justman and others, by encouraging diversified infrastructure construction, the regional government can reduce fiscal expenditure waste, and more importantly, can form differentiated competitive advantages compared with other regions, meet the requirements of regional diversified development, and form a virtuous circle.[5] Bucovetsky believes that the government's infrastructure investment can produce labor agglomeration effect, that is, sound infrastructure and public environment can help the region attract more labor with strong mobility and good skills. Yet the infrastructure investment competition among regions may also be harmful because governments' competition to attract liquidity factors may increase the cost of infrastructure investment and construction.[6] Wilson believes that regional government officials are very motivated to invest in infrastructure because such an investment has a positive effect on the efficiency of labor and capital in the region and can bring regional government a larger tax base, which would strengthen the positive correlation between infrastructure investment and tax revenue.[7] Chinese scholars Zhang Jun, Gao Yuan, Fu Yong and Zhang Hong concluded from their study on infrastructure investment and construction in China that the yardstick competition among regional governments in attracting investment and the transformation of government governance are important factors to explain China's infrastructure investment and construction, and that regional governments' supportive policies and measures to attract investment are essential for creating incentives for infrastructure investment.[8]

Just as there are different types of market failures, the government failures a country or region might suffer from could also be classified into three types: *Inadequate support for livelihood economy*, *lack of industrial polices* and *gaps in urban construction* (see Chapter 9 for details). Of the three types, government failures associated with *gaps in urban construction* might take any of the following forms: First, there is practically no policy or measure to promote urban infrastructure construction; second, the government neither participates in urban construction as a competitor nor plays its role in planning, supervising and regulating urban construction; and third, the government does participate in urban construction, but does not adhere to market rules—for instance, investing without profiting, constructing without operating, or focusing on social benefits only but ignoring economic benefits—which results in huge wastes of urban resources, poor quality and low efficiency of urban infrastructure investment and construction, and disorderliness of urban planning and management. These problems hinder the sustainable growth of the regional economy in the investment-driven stage.

The growth dominated by urban economy competition is competitive growth. Here competition refers to the competition among regions in investing in and constructing urban infrastructure and in improving supportive policies and measures. To gain advantages in such competition, regional governments should not only do a good job in infrastructure planning but also follow market rules and serve the functions of macro guidance, effective regulation and adequate supervision in the investment, development, operation and management of the field. The essential task of regional government in the investment-driven stage is to, through policies and measures, achieve an organic, seamless and effective combination of government promotion, enterprise participation and market-based operation. How regional government performs in this regard will affect the scale and quality of regional economic growth. In this growth stage dominated by urban economy competition, the regional government will focus its fiscal expenditure on fiscal investment expenditure items and social consumption expenditure items, and its role will be the most pronounced in the competition of the three factors in the second category of the "9-in-3" Competition Theory.

6.3 Growth stage dominated by innovative economy competition

For regional governments, innovative economy competition is mainly the competition in their policies and measures designed to promote innovations in concept, technology, organization and institution. For all countries in the world, innovative economy competition takes place mainly in the third stage of regional economic growth, a primarily innovation-driven stage.

Of the four kinds of innovation of concept, technology, organization and institution, regional governments' conceptual innovation is the focus of regional competition. As mentioned before, when the regional economy is in the factor-driven or investment-driven stage, economic growth mainly relies on simple quantitative expansion of production factors such as land, labor, capital and other natural resources. Such growth, fueled by the vying for more resources and lower costs and often involving overusing, will easily lead to industrial and urban resource exhaustion, low production efficiency, lagging technologies, brain drain, intensification of social conflicts and other problems, and therefore call for the soonest transformation of the growth mode. At this juncture, the region's approach, direction and means for the next development stage become vital and need to be led by advanced concepts. The conceptual innovation of regional government not only involves how to grasp and coordinate the region's resources in an overall manner, work out the region's future development strategy and devise a comprehensive planning for the region's development mode but also entails drawing up development methods and development motivations in top-level design. After the factor-driven stage and the investment-driven stage, the regional government should lead, guide and promote the sustainable development of regional economy with the ideas of innovative, coordinated, green, open and shared development.

In the innovation-driven stage, the regional government's technological innovation is the winning point in regional competition. Technological innovations have an exponential driving effect on economic development. They enable the regional economy to make the leap from quantitative change to qualitative change, bring creation breakthroughs to the entire production process and all the factors, and achieve an optimized allocation of resources. Technological innovations, being the source of new products, new industries and new models, are the core driving force in this stage of economic growth. When combined with financial and industrial innovations, technological innovations will create sustained impetus of innovation. All these make technological innovation an important means of regional competition in this stage.

In the innovation-driven stage, the regional government's organizational innovation is the key to regional competition. When the economy progresses from the factor-driven stage to the investment-driven stage, the primary means of regional competition is expanding the investment scale to stimulate economic growth. The multiplier effect of investment on economic growth has been proved in the effective demand theory of Keynes, that is, investment plays an important role in boosting effective demand and raising Gross Domestic Product (GDP), especially when the regional economy experiences low growth speed, during which the government can reverse the economic downturn and drag the economy out of the recession by increasing investment. Nevertheless, the one-sided pursuit of the short-term incentives of investment could easily cause "thirst for investment" and "dependence on investment," which could further bring a series of symptoms such as economic ups and downs and backward technological and innovative capacity. This makes the regional government's innovation ability in the organization the key for this stage of economic growth. The government should strengthen its quick-response ability, get close to the market, serve the enterprises, develop network structure and matrix structure, and simplify the administrative structure, in one word, manage in a more standardized, efficient and flexible manner, so as to promote stable and orderly economic development and contribute more to regional competition.

In the innovation-driven stage, regional government's institutional innovation is indispensable for regional competition. Institutional innovation is a fundamental condition for conceptual innovation, technological innovation and organizational innovation and can promote the integrated advancement of the three. If we assume that the regional economic development of all countries in the world basically follows the same path of going from factor-driven stage to investment-driven, innovation-driven and sharing-driven stages, we could see that the innovation-driven stage is featured by rapid development of the three major industries, growing environmental awareness of the public, and constant emergence of new economic development modes and personal growth modes. In such a period the regional government needs not only innovations in concept, technology and organization but also institutional innovation to ensure the competitive advantage of the region, because the flexibility, rapidity and diversity characterizing economic development in the innovation-driven stage calls for matching institutions and policies from the government. Only by this can the government keep up with the pace of the innovation-driven era, lead the way of economic development and maintain sustained vitality of the economy. Innovations of concept, technology, organization and institution in all aspects, all processes and all factors—none of these is dispensable for regional competition in this stage.

To further illustrate the importance of innovation, we will take carbon emissions trading resources—a type of inverse resource mentioned in Chapter 5 that is relatively unfamiliar to people—as a case, and analyze how China deals with carbon emissions. China is one of the largest emitters of greenhouse gases in the world. The 2015 China Carbon Pricing Survey conducted jointly by China Carbon Forum (CCF) and ICF International indicates that China's carbon emission peak will appear in 2030. Facing the problem of carbon emissions, China has two paths to choose from: One is to deal with it passively, treating it as a burden and pay high costs to reduce emissions; and the other is to, accepting it as an inevitable phenomenon that occurs when the economy progresses from the factor-driven stage to the investment-driven stage, boldly innovate concepts, technologies, organization and institution according to the characteristics of inverse resources and curb emissions by emissions trading. With the second path, China can not only curb carbon emissions but also explore new ways to realize the internationalization of the Chinese RMB by formulating national and even international trading standards, using the RMB to settle payments, and, taking advantage of the "One Belt, One Road" initiative, pushing the RMB to grow from a payment settlement currency to an international reserve currency or anchor currency.

The coming decade will be a critical period for China's emission reduction. It is reported that the developed world such as the USA and Europe are pressing for carbon taxes and tariffs to be imposed around 2020, just when China's carbon emissions are to peak. Once carbon tariffs are imposed with the tax amount being determined according to US and European standards, China's exports, due to the high carbon emissions, will face high tariffs which will constitute a trade barrier. This is why the next five to ten years will be a critical period for the transformation and development of Chinese enterprises. If they fail to make good use of this period to transform and upgrade, they will not only face high emission quota costs but also face export setbacks caused by high emissions. Therefore, we should set out to look into the issue to establish as soon as possible an Asian or global carbon trading market dominated by China, a market that's a complete carbon trading system comprising both spot trading and future trading. The system should form a deterrence mechanism to spur on enterprises to accelerate their green transformation. At the same time, the government should formulate relevant industrial policies and tax policies to guide and encourage enterprises to voluntarily adopt low-carbon technologies, provide services with environmental protection in mind and produce low-carbon products. These measures would substantially elevate the position of Chinese enterprises in the global industrial chain and enable China's foreign trade to complete the green upgrading.

A good response to the issue of carbon emissions has the following significance for China's economic development:

First, carbon emissions trading offers an opportunity for institutional innovation to optimize China's industrial allocation across regions.

Practice at home and abroad has shown that, compared with imposing carbon taxes or simply coercing to reduce emissions by administrative means, carbon emissions trading is the most efficient way to solve the interrelated problems of climate and energy in the framework of the market economy. The nature of carbon trading is to deal with the negative externality of carbon emissions through the market mechanism, specifically, an institutional arrangement that internalizes the external cost of emissions into the internal cost of the emitters so as to realize emission reduction and optimize the global allocation of carbon resources. Carbon trading can transform emission reduction cost to carbon income through market means and encourage financial resources to tilt in favor of low-carbon economic sectors, so as to minimize the total emission reduction cost of the society. This would also help countries to speed up the transformation and upgrading of industrial structure and the transformation of economic development mode.

China has a vast territory and unbalanced economic development across regions. Some local governments have the ill mindset of blindly pursuing regional GDP growth as the single indicator of development, when in fact many underdeveloped areas in central and western China are not suitable for developing high-intensity manufacturing industry due to the limitation of the natural environment and the need of ecological protection. In such circumstances, to build a carbon trading market system the soonest will encourage less developed areas to reduce carbon emissions by protecting the ecological environment and developing forest carbon sinks, and in the meanwhile will enable high energy-consuming developed areas to support the development of the less developed areas by purchasing emission quotas from them. This will transform the existing unbalanced development into a market-based mode featuring coordinated development of ecology and economy, which will eventually promote the coordinated development of different regions and optimize industrial allocation among regions.

Second, building a standardized carbon trading market system is an important ground for organizational innovation concerning China's 21st Century Maritime Silk Road.

So far a carbon trading market based on compulsory emission reduction mechanism has just budded in Asia because only Japan, India and some other countries have carried out small-scale carbon trading activities and the ten ASEAN countries have not made efforts in carbon trading. This offers China a chance for organizational innovation with respect to its construction of the 21st Century Maritime Silk Road. Building China's carbon trading market as soon as possible and then establishing a regional carbon trading system covering Southeast Asia and other countries and regions would help exhibit China's sincerity and determination to "share opportunities, meet challenges, develop and prosper together" with neighboring countries and regions, help build a financial system serving low-carbon economic development between China and Southeast Asian countries and regions, and help enlarge the scope and enhance the strength of the impact of China's financial market.

Last but not least, the technological innovation of "carbon emissions trading tied to the RMB for settlement," that is, the "carbon-RMB," opens up a new path for the RMB to "corner overtake" towards internationalization. Specific analysis is as follows:

First, the international currency should have three basic functions. First, acting as settlement and payment currency in international trade; second, becoming the reserve currency of the monetary authorities of other countries or regions and third, becoming the anchor currency of the monetary authorities of other countries or regions to adjust the foreign exchange market. To become an international currency or even a key currency, a country's currency usually follows the basic path of "settlement and payment currency to reserve currency and then to anchor currency," eventually becoming a currency that can be accepted by most countries in the international monetary system and that's capable of convenient cross-border circulation. Under the existing international monetary system, international currencies mainly include the US dollar, the euro, the Japanese yen, and the British pound, of which the US dollar is the key currency.

Second, tying a currency to energy for settlement is often the booster for the rise of the currency to become an international currency due to the very high percentage of energy trade in total trade volume. Around World War I, the trade volume of energy, primarily coal, jumped from the third place after cotton and wheat to the second place, and after World War II, in the Goldman Sachs Commodity Index system (covering 24 commodities), energy (including WTI Crude Oil, Brent Crude Oil, RBOB Gasoline, Heating Oil, Gas Oil and Natural Gas) accounts for 64.51% of the US dollar weight of all the commodities in the index system.[9] As international trade and finance develop, how deep a country's economic activities and energy trade are intertwined becomes an important determinant of the status of the country's currency, and the rise of a country's currency is often directly affected by whether it is tied with the settlement and payment of international commodities, especially energy.

Third, before the First Industrial Revolution, the binding between energy and currencies was not clear. In the 16th century, the center of international trade moved from the Mediterranean region, notably Italy, to Belgium and the Netherlands in the northwest corner of Europe. In the following century, the Netherlands established a hegemonic position in world trade and the Dutch Guilder became a key currency in international trade. Yet at that time there had not emerged any binding relationship between energy and currency because, as human production at that time was mainly by manual workshops, there was little demand for energy and international trade was mainly of commodities that fulfill basic necessities of life, specifically, wood, fish, grain, fur, spices, cotton textiles, silk, porcelain, etc.

Fourth, the First Industrial Revolution gave birth to the binding relationship between coal and the British pound. In the last 25 years of the 18th century, the UK replaced the Netherlands to become the world's leading trading power and London replaced Amsterdam as the most important financial center. The advent of the steam engine brought a series of technological revolutions that helped humans realize the leap from hand production to powered machine manufacturing, and along with this coal became the primary "food" of modern industry. The advent and development of the First Industrial Revolution and large-scale machine-based industries led to a sharp increase in the demand for energy. In 1840, the UK became the first country to undergo the First Industrial Revolution and also the first country that used coal as the main source of energy. By the middle of the 19th century, the UK's coal production accounted for about two-thirds of the world's total, not only making it the major coal supplier in the world but also putting it at a position to completely control the world coal market. The pound being tied to coal trading for settlement made it the key currency in international trade. It came to occupy a prominent position in the gold standard system as the central banks of many countries chose the pound instead of gold as the reserve currency. At that time, 90% of international settlements were conducted in pounds.[10]

The fifth point is the binding between oil and the US dollar. The replacement of the US dollar of the pound as the key currency is by virtue of the change of the world's primary source of energy during the two world wars, that is, oil replacing coal. In the second half of the 19th century, the emergence of the internal combustion engine made oil the "blood" of the Second Industrial Revolution. With the popularization of internal combustion engines in the 1920s, the demand for oil grew and oil trade expanded rapidly. The USA became the main energy (oil) supplier for the Allies during World War II, and came to control almost two-thirds of the world's crude oil production after World War II.[11] It was during this period, specifically, in the 1970s, that the USA and Saudi Arabia reached an agreement to establish the US dollar as the only pricing currency for oil. The world's top two oil futures markets, the Chicago Board of Trade and the London-based International Petroleum Exchange, all adopted the US dollar for pricing, settlement and payment. These granted the US international pricing power over oil as a commodity, thus establishing the dollar standard in the international monetary system.

Sixth, in 2001, the famous American international financial scientist and Nobel Prize winner in economics Robert Mundell put forward the bold idea of "three islands of stability," that is, the US dollar, the euro and the RMB standing side by side to form a stable global monetary system. Mundell suggests that the exchange rate between the euro and the US dollar should be maintained stable and fixed within a certain range such as 1.2 to 1.4 dollars per euro, that the RMB, as its convertibility grows, be integrated into the fixed exchange rate mechanism of the dollar and the euro to create a tripolar currency area involving the dollar, the euro and the RMB, and that then other currencies in the world form floating exchange rates with this currency area, which Mundell believes would be conducive to not only the formation of a stable international monetary system but also more flexible development of the settlement and payment relations among countries. Mundell's idea reflects that, on the one hand, the current international monetary system featuring the dollar standard urgently needs reformation, and on the other hand, it has become an important research topic at home and abroad how other currencies represented by the RMB could "corner overtake" to become international currencies and even key currencies.

The seventh and the last point is the binding of carbon emissions trading and the RMB. The tying of coal to the pound and that of oil to the dollar led to the rise of the two currencies, showing a simple and clear path of currency status evolution, which suggests that China should promote the binding of carbon emissions trading and the RMB. First, innovation-based development and low-carbon economy will be the future economic growth mode of all countries, and with the emergence of new breakthroughs, new utilizations and new combinations of clean energy technologies, new energy trade characterized by low carbon, such as the trading of carbon credits, carbon commodities and carbon emission quotas, will flourish. Second, China is one of the largest emitters of greenhouse gases in the world, is considered to be the most potential emission market and has more and more enterprises participating in carbon emissions trading. Last, the calculation of the World Bank indicates that global carbon trading volume is expected to reach 3.5 trillion US dollars in 2020 and by then the carbon emissions trading market will surpass the oil market to become the world's largest trading market. With all these favorable conditions, after the international monetary system experienced the "coal-pound" and the "oil-dollar" structures, now the opportunity arises for China, using the technological innovation of "carbon emissions trading tied to the RMB for settlement," that is, the "carbon-RMB," to establish a financial system serving low-carbon economic development with Southeast Asia and other countries and regions, and in this way open up a new path for the RMB to "corner overtake" towards internationalization and to rise in international energy trade.

To sum up, in the economic growth stage dominated by innovative economy competition, regional governments around the world should not only lead economic development with technological innovations but also thoroughly and creatively deal with the harmful elements brought by economic development to the regional society. In this stage, regional governments should innovate in terms of concept, technology, organization and institution in a scientific manner and according to the real conditions of the economy, which will promote science-based and sustainable development of the regional economy and achieve gratifying results in the innovation-driven stage, that is, to achieve growth backed by the increase of "total-factor productivity."

The so-called increase of total-factor productivity is a concept put forward by the winner of the Nobel Prize in economics Robert Solow in the 1950s. Referring to the increase of productivity brought about by pure technological progress excluding all tangible production factors (labor, capital, land, etc.), it's essentially a measure of technological progress. In other words, the increase of total-factor productivity is the rise of productivity brought by changes in intangible resources when the amount of all tangible production factors used remains unchanged. It is the prime-mover of long-term economic growth. Pure technological progress includes the improvement of knowledge, education, technical training, scale economy, organization and management, and policies and institutions. It refers to disembodied technological changes that bring about rises of production efficiency. Innovating concepts, technologies, organization and institution is an important way to improve a region's total-factor productivity. Such extended innovations will drive regional economic growth based on rising total-factor productivity, and it is such growth that is truly high-quality and sustainable. In this stage, the inclining and pooling of the region's talents, capital, technologies, management, policies and other resources towards innovations in concept, technology, organization and institution will form a new economic growth point and transfer the regional finance from one dominated by expenditure to one dominated by income, which is also a main feature of this economic growth stage.

6.4 Growth stage dominated by competitive and cooperative economy

After the three development stages respectively dominated by industrial economy competition, urban economy competition and innovative economy competition, regional economic growth will enter the stage dominated by competitive and cooperative economy, a stage where the regional economy undergoes more profound transformations—from relying on resources within the region to exploring beyond the region, to developing all kinds of international economic resources (space resources, deep sea resources, polar resources, etc.) and to switching economic development mode; from allocating industrial resources through enterprise competition only to regional governments competing with each other and participating in the allocation of urban resources and other new generative resources and from relying solely on market mechanism to combining effective government and efficient market to build new investment engines and new innovation engines for regional economic growth. During such transformations, the competition among regions will inevitably bring about the challenge of maintaining fairness and justice in the economic governance system. While an open economic system has to be kept and expanded, the economic interests of each region have to be protected and the economic order among regions maintained. Moreover, regions will have to make new rules to deal with new problems that they meet while exploring new areas of the economy, and this will constantly create new cross-regional challenges. This will shape a cross-regional landscape featuring the coexistence of competition and cooperation. Therefore, the fourth stage of regional economic growth, that is, the sharing-driven stage, will be dominated by a competitive and cooperative economy.

At this growth stage, the regional industrial system has upgraded to a modern one with regional competitiveness. First, traditional industries have finished transformation and upgrading as the internet, big data and artificial intelligence get deeply integrated with the real economy and as the manufacturing industry extends from processing and production to R&D, design, brand, marketing, remanufacturing and other links featuring more intelligent development. Second, strategic emerging industries continue to grow as the new generation of information technologies and new industries such as biotechnology, new energies, new materials, high-end equipment, energy-saving and environmental protection equipment, 3D printing, intelligent robot and new energy vehicle develop vigorously, gradually forming new industrial clusters and agglomeration belts with regional competitiveness. Third, the development of modern service industries picks up speed as sectors serving either production or living, such as finance, logistics, shipping, tourism, culture and exhibition, are transforming towards specialization and high quality. Regional industrial economy competition promotes the mutual complementing, close cooperation and synchronized development of industries among regions.

At this growth stage, a complete and fully functional network of regional infrastructure has taken shape, one that features interconnection within the region and smooth channels outside the region. First, there's already in place a modern comprehensive transportation system with a strong service capacity of ports, waterways, port railways, highways and other basic transport facilities with main coastal ports as the focus, high utilization efficiency of airspace resources with aviation hubs as the core, and unimpeded comprehensive transportation channels with expressways, high-speed railways and fast railways as the backbone. Second, an intelligent transportation system with a focus on integrated application of information technologies such as the internet of things, cloud computing and big data is becoming increasingly perfect. Third, smart city infrastructure, soft urban infrastructure and the energy infrastructure and water conservancy infrastructure for urban-rural integration are constantly being improved. Regional urban economy competition promotes the smooth interconnection and reasonable layout of infrastructure among regions.

At this stage, the region has formed an open community for collaborative technological innovation that gathers all sorts of innovation resources. First, the region's highlands for technological innovations and important breeding grounds of new industries have gradually formed as more technological innovation corridors are built, the regional flow of innovation elements such as talents, capital, information and technologies is expanded, the construction of big data centers and innovation platforms are accelerated, more technological innovation activities are carried out by universities, scientific research groups and enterprises, basic abilities for innovation are elevated, and the innovation alliance of industries, universities and research communities are constantly developing, expanding and deepening. Moreover, various institutional and policy environments dedicated to raising the transformation ability of scientific and technological achievements are being optimized. Specifically, regional innovation systems and mechanisms are constantly reformed for the better, regional cooperation in science and technology, academia, talents, projects, etc. are facilitated, transformation of scientific and technological achievements, technology transfer, cooperation in science and technology service industry, and the protection and application of intellectual property rights are promoted, science and technology, finance and industries are combined with innovation policies, and concepts, technologies, organization and institution are deeply joint with innovation measures. Regional innovative economy competition promotes innovative cooperation, collaborative innovation and integrated development among regions.

Further analysis on the basis of the above discussions would reveal that competition as the driver of regional economy or the competitive economic growth of the region leads to the emergence of the four kinds of shared products or public products of human society. The first kind is ideas as public goods. Such ideas include the new understandings about the operation of the market mechanism, that is, market competition is not only limited to enterprise competition in the industrial economy, but also includes regional government competition in the urban economy, and that a mature market economy should be one that combines effective government and efficient market. The second type is material public goods. The combination of informatization with industrialization, urbanization, agricultural modernization and internationalization is one example. The construction of relevant hard and soft infrastructure improves the region's material conditions such as public transport, urban management, education, medical treatment, culture, commerce, energy and environmental protection. The third is organizational public goods. For instance, the traditional urban construction mode described as "urban sprawl" should give way to grouped layouts required by modern urban development, and the reform and innovation of organization and management take place when the structure of regional economic order upgraded upgrades from "urban sprawl" to grouped layouts. The fourth is institutional public goods. For example, institutional arrangements under the guidance of following the principles of "let the region bring more development opportunities" and "let the fruits of economic growth be shared" will further improve the region's labor, employment, security and social policies, with the fruits of such undertakings shared by all. It can be seen that in the growth stage dominated by competitive and cooperative economy, that is, the sharing-driven stage, regional governments should follow the following basic principles: First, innovative development led by reforms; second, coordinated development with overall consideration; third, green development with ecological protection; fourth, open development with win-win cooperation; fifth, shared development with benefits to people's life. In a word, the sustainable mode of economic growth at this stage is to build an innovative, open, linked, inclusive and shared regional economic system that blends competition and cooperation.

6.5 Gradient transference model of regional economic competition

Regional economic competition down the history of the economic development of countries around the globe could be described by a gradient transference model (see Figure 6.1).

In Figure 6.1, A to I represent different regions and 1 to 4 represent the four stages of regional economic development, that is, (1) the growth stage

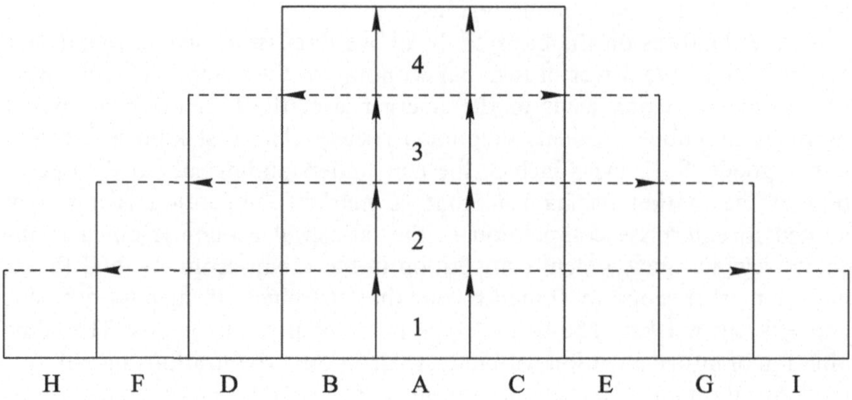

Figure 6.1 The gradient transference model of regional economic competition.

dominated by industrial economy competition, (2) the growth stage dominated by urban economy competition, (3) the growth stage dominated by innovative economy competition and (4) the growth stage dominated by competitive and cooperative economy. As aforementioned, stage 1, the initial stage of regional economic development, features a relatively low technical level, low capital accumulation, and a regional growth momentum formed by the simple quantitative expansion of production factors such as labor force and natural resources. Therefore, the growth at this stage is primarily driven by factors of production and the growth mode features fundamentality and universality. This stage represents the first level of government competition. Stage 2, the expansion stage of regional economic development, starts with large amounts of investment in hard urban infrastructure, proceeds to large amounts of investment in soft urban infrastructure and hard and soft urban-rural integration infrastructure, and ends with the development and perfection of smart cities. During the process regional economic growth experiences, one climax after another and is primarily driven by investments. This stage of economic growth has obvious traces of government participation and represents the second level of regional government competition. Stage 3, a high-quality stage of regional economic development, is featured by technological innovation leading wide-ranging innovations of concept, organization and institution, innovations that continuously bring forth new economic growth modes and raise the quality of economic development in an all-round way. This stage is primarily driven by innovations and elevates regional government's economic competition to higher altitudes. It represents the third level of government competition. Eventually, regional government competition will move to stage 4, the advanced stage featuring a combination of competition and cooperation. In this stage, regional economy, primarily driven by sharing, will follow the trajectory of "competition dominance → competition and cooperation coexistence → win-win cooperation dominance." During this stage, the ideological, material, organizational and institutional public products formed in the regional economic competition will become economic growth achievements shared among and enjoyed by different regions and promote the coordinated economic and social progress of all regions.

Corresponding to the above four stages of economic development are four kinds of economic theories. The first is the theory of industrial effect, which describes the economic growth stage dominated by industrial economy competition. In this stage, regional economic development is not synchronized in terms of space. Often regions with internal factors and external conditions favorable for industrial development take the lead. As industries in these regions gather and the economy keeps growing, the regions interact with those lagging behind so that various production factors needed for industrial development constantly converge from underdeveloped regions to developed ones, forming regional competitive advantages and industrial effects. Therefore, to stand out in competition in this stage, regional governments should attract investments, introduce projects, improve the industrial chain, encourage imports and exports, expand domestic and foreign markets, and strengthen policy support for the industrial economy in terms of planning and guiding, support and coordination, supervision and management.

The second is the theory of urban expansion, which describes the stage of economic growth dominated by urban economic competition. During this stage, the main driving force of regional economic growth comes from investments into multi-level urban infrastructure and the advancement of urban-rural integration, specifically including the investments into hard and soft urban infrastructure, the construction of urban-rural integration infrastructure and the development and utilization of smart cities. Regional governments in multi-level urban systems should follow the principles of "government promotion, enterprise participation and market-based operation" when designing policies for investment and construction of urban infrastructure, for only in this way can regional governments extend and expand urban functions, improve and optimize regional economic development environment, build a perfect urban economy system and establish regional competitive advantages, so as to achieve sustainable growth of the regional economy.

The third is the theory of innovation as the driver, which describes the economic growth stage dominated by innovative economy competition. Regions experiencing such innovation-driven stage (mostly more developed regions) are characterized by a series of innovation activities in their industrial sectors, products, technologies, production mode and marketing mode, and on the basis of these innovations, a series of innovation activities in organizational and management mode, institutional and policy measures, etc. With the passage of time, such innovations of economically developed regions will gradually transfer to economically backward ones. In this stage of regional economic competition, regional governments should timely and effectively promote policies and measures conducive to innovation so as to promote regional economic growth and establish regional economic advantages.

The fourth is the theory of coordinated development, which describes the economic growth stage dominated by a competitive and cooperative economy. In this stage, competition keeps pooling industrial resources and urban resources to economically developed regions, but the growth of these regions will still be naturally constrained by their internal factors and external conditions. So various shared public products will form among regions to guarantee continuous economic and social progress of all regions. Therefore, in this stage, regional governments should formulate all kinds of economic policies and measures following the trajectory of "competition → competition and cooperation → win-win cooperation" to promote the coordinated development of all regions.

On the basis of the above analysis, we will elaborate on the theory of regional economic gradient transference. As shown in Figure 6.1, the regional economic gradient transference model has four characteristics. First, regional economic competition is initiated by economically developed regions that take the lead in developing industrial economy, urban economy and innovative economy, and then, with the passage of time and the change of each region's internal factors and external conditions, gradually moves from developed regions to underdeveloped regions, that is, progresses horizontally from A, B, C regions in Figure 6.1 to D, E, F, G, H, I regions. Second, with the continuous upgrading of economic development level and economic growth stage, regional economic competition gradually expands from the industrial economy to urban economy, innovation economy and other fields, that is, progressing vertically from stage 1 in the figure to stages 2, 3 and 4. Third, regions that launch effective policies and measures early in the stages dominated by industrial economy, urban economy and innovation economy will have a leading advantage in economic development, and the differences between regions in terms of the strength and effectiveness of their policies and measures will place the regions in different positions in the inter-regional gradient economic structure. For instance, regions A, B and C are superior to other regions as shown in Figure 6.1. Fourth, the upgrading of the economic growth stage, specifically, from the stage dominated by industrial economy competition, to one dominated by urban economy competition, to one dominated by innovative economy competition, and eventually to one dominated by the competitive and cooperative economy, is a long historical process, and over that course all types of public products jointly created by human economic society will, in the long run, drive the popularization of sharing economy and promote the coordinated development of inter-regional economy. As shown in Figure 6.1, competition and cooperation interact to jointly promote economic growth. Although regions differ in economic development, the trend of orderly horizontal progression and coordinated vertical development always exist to ultimately result in win-win cooperation as the mainstream.

In the end, there are still two points calling for explication. The first is the connections and differences between the theory of four stages of competitive economic growth elaborated in this chapter and the theory of "four stages of economic development" defined in Professor Michael Porter's *The Competitive Advantage of Nations*. The connection is that I agree with and draw upon Professor Porter's methodology of dividing national economic development into four stages, namely, factor-driven, investment-driven, innovation-driven and wealth-driven stages. The difference is that the competitors in Professor Porter's four-stage economic development theory are enterprises, while the competitors in the four-stage theory elaborated in this book are regional governments. From this point of view, I have defined four stages of regional economic growth in countries around the world, namely, the growth stage dominated by industrial economy competition (mainly driven by factors), the stage dominated by urban economy competition (mainly driven by investment), the stage dominated by innovation economy competition (mainly driven by innovation), and the stage dominated by competitive and cooperative economy (mainly driven by sharing), and on this basis, I have analyzed the policy measures taken by regional governments, the characteristics of fiscal expenditure, and its effects in different stages of competition.

The second point worthy of attention is that though it is theoretically workable to divide regional economic growth into four stages, in reality, it is difficult to clearly split between the stages, which is already proved by history. I emphasize the periodicity of regional economic growth to lay stress on the dominant characteristics and particular paths of regional economic growth in different stages so as to press home that regional governments should take appropriate policy measures suited to each stage. But we should also be aware that the four stages of regional economic growth are mutually penetrating and arrive one after another with considerable overlapping. Therefore, though I believe regional governments should give more weight to certain aspects when designing policy measures for each particular stage, I'll never deny the importance of regional governments making efforts to do policy preparation, cultivation and guidance for the next development stage.

Notes

1 Porter, M. E. (2019, February). *The competitive advantage of nations* (Second Half). China Citic Press, pp.131–140.
2 Porter, M. E. (2019, February). *The competitive advantage of nations* (Second Half). China Citic Press, pp.152–153.
3 Holtz-Eakin, D. (1994). Public-sector capital and the productivity puzzle. *Review of Economics and Statistics*, *76*(1), 12–21.
4 Shioji, E. (2001). Public capital and economic growth: A convergence approach. *Journal of Economic Growth, 6*(3), 205–227.
5 Justman, M., Thisse, J. F., & Ypersele, T. V. (2002). Taking the bite out of fiscal competition.' *Journal of Urban Economics*, *52*(2), 294–315.

6 Sam, B. (1982). Inequality in the local public sector. *Journal of Political Economy, 90* (1), 128–145.
7 Wilson, J. D. (1999). Theories of tax competition. *National Tax Journal, 52*, 269–304.
8 Zhang, J., Gao, Y., Fu, Y., & Zhang, H. (2007). Why does China have good infrastructure. *Economic Research Journal*, (3),4–19.
9 Wang, Y., & Guan, Q. (2009). Carbon trading valuation and settlement currency: Theory, reality and choice. *Journal of Contemporary Asia-Pacific Studies, 109*(1), 110–128.
10 Wang, Y., & Guan, Q. (2009). Carbon trading valuation and settlement currency: Theory, reality and choice. *Journal of Contemporary Asia-Pacific Studies,109*(1), 110–128.
11 Wang, Y., & Guan, Q. (2009). Carbon trading valuation and settlement currency: Theory, reality and choice. *Journal of Contemporary Asia-Pacific Studies,109*(1), 110–128.

7 Government foresighted leading (GFL)

7.1 Competition policies of regional government

In Chapter 5 "Regional Government Competition," I have discussed in detail the types, ways and resources involved in regional government competition. The competition policies of regional government refer to the series of guiding principles and corresponding measures the regional government formulates on the basis of the understandings mentioned in Chapter 5 to establish leading economic advantages and promote the sustainable development of the region. Such competition policies are incorporated in the entire process of regional government work. Policy means mainly focus on adjusting regional fiscal expenditure structure, specifically, the proportions and amounts of social consumption expenditure, investment expenditure and transfer expenditure. The effect is mainly reflected in the attainment of the objective function of regional fiscal revenue, and the ultimate goal is social stability, sustainable economic growth, and residents of the region living and working in peace and contentment.

When further broken down, regional government competition policies could be described in the following aspects:

First, the maker and executor of regional policies is regional government. Whether the behaviors of regional government conform to relevant standards has great impact on the effect of the competition policies. If attention is paid only to policy goals and policy tools with little concern for the behavioral preferences of regional government, the regional government will often go against the policy objectives, abuse policy tools and cause adverse consequences when implementing the policies. Therefore, the study on regional government competition should attach weight to the analysis of the behavioral standards of the government, which will help prepare for, prevent and overcome deviations in the implementation of policies so as to achieve better policy execution.

The second is the contents of competition policies. In a broad sense competition policies encompass regional government's policies for the

DOI: 10.4324/9781003244837-7

planning, guidance, support, coordination, supervision and management of operative resources (industrial economy), the policies to guarantee the basic needs, ensure fairness and justice and raise the effectiveness and efficiency of non-operative resources (livelihood economy), and the polices for allocating, participating in and maintaining the order of quasi-operative resources (urban economy). In a narrow sense, competition policies are the region's policies for planning, participating in and managing the urban economy with a focus on urban infrastructure construction. It should be noted that regional competition-related laws, such as the law against impediment to competition and the law against unfair competition, refer to a set of market control laws established by regional governments to prevent market competitors (such as enterprises) from abusing their dominant position or power in the market, while regional competition policies are a series of guiding principles and corresponding measures formulated by regional governments to protect and promote market competition in their own regions, encompassing not only measures for advancing effective regional competition but also those for restraining unfair competition. In this sense, competition-related laws are a part of regional competition policies, with the scope of the latter being much broader than the former. The two complement each other to establish regional competitive advantages as well as to maintain regional competition order, so as to effectively allocate the three types of resources in the region and maximize economic and social benefits.

The third aspect is the goal of competition policies. The goal of the regional government's guiding, regulating and monitoring industrial economy is to maintain the fairness and efficiency of the market mechanism. The goal of allocating, participating in and safeguarding the urban economy is to boost economic growth and improve regional environment. The goal of guaranteeing, supporting and elevating livelihood economy to is to maintain social stability and promote harmonious development. The ultimate goal of these three kinds of competition policies is to make the regional environment suitable for living, business and tourism and to realize sustainable growth and leading advantages of the regional economy. It can be seen that the policies and measures of the regional government are vital for industrial development, urban construction and social welfare in the region.

The fourth aspect is the means of competition policies. The first is fiscal means, which cover, in addition to conventional tax means, various other supportive means such as regional government's fiscal policies, expenditure structure, public debt issuance and fiscal subsidies, especially the proportions and amounts of fiscal investment expenditure, social consumption expenditure and transfer payment expenditure, which will be the primary fiscal means of regional government competition. The second is financial means. In addition to national-level monetary means such as interest rate and exchange rate, financial means available for regional government competition primarily include setting up project funds, offering guarantee and re-guarantee, building financial, technological and industrial integration platforms, and promoting inclusive finance. The third is environmental means, which comprises at least three levels: (1) The construction and upgrading of infrastructure. (2) The improvement and elevation of education, science, culture, health and social security conditions. (3) The building and optimizing of social credit system and institution. The fourth is efficiency means, which are mainly reflected in two aspects: (1) Functional efficiency brought by supportive policy systems and (2) time efficiency brought by innovations in the management mechanism. The fifth and also the last is legal means, of which the most essential are laws and regulations related to property rights protection, such as the intellectual property rights protection law. Of course, legal means also include the aforementioned market control laws. The five types are closely linked and mutually restricting and are all important policy means of regional government competition. It is worth mentioning that many regional governments emphasize fiscal means and financial means while overlooking environmental means and efficiency means, when in reality environment and efficiency have a direct impact on the success or failure of regional government competition and hence should not be ignored.

The fifth aspect is the effect of competition policies. The effect depends on the competition policy means used by the regional government and different means have a different effect. In reality, different policy means overlap and influence each other. To simplify the matter for research purpose, I work under the assumptions that legal means plays its role through the four other means and that the effects of the four other means are independent of each other. In this way, we can get the formula of competition policy effect as follows:

$$Y = f(T) + f(E) + f(P) + f(L) \tag{7.1}$$

Y represents the overall effect of competition policies, f(T) represents the competition policy effect brought by fiscal means, f(E) represents the effect brought by financial means, f(P) represents the effect of environmental means and f(L) represents the effect of efficiency means. When the contribution of one particular means to the overall effect reaches a certain degree, the effect of this means will weaken while the impact of the other means will relatively strengthen.

To analyze further, we could assume that fiscal means focus on adjusting investment expenditure, financial means focus on adjusting consumption expenditure, and environmental means and efficiency means to focus on adjusting transfer expenditure. Meanwhile, similar to the study on the objective function of fiscal revenue, the contribution of different means to the overall effect is significantly different in different development stages. Therefore, formula (7.1) is extended as follows:

$$Y = \varphi_1(Y_1, Y_0) * T + \varphi_2(Y_2, Y_0) * E + \varphi_3(Y_3, Y_0) * P + \varphi_4(Y_4, Y_0) * L \quad (7.2)$$

Under a specific fiscal expenditure structure, the multipliers of fiscal means, financial means, environmental means and efficiency means are $\varphi_1(Y_1, Y_0)$, $\varphi_2(Y_2, Y_0)$, $\varphi_3(Y_3, Y_0)$ and $\varphi_4(Y_4, Y_0)$, respectively. These multipliers are changeable and can take different forms. Their values depend on the initial economic level and the threshold value or target value (Y_i) in different stages of economic development. In different stages fiscal expenditure structure differs markedly, calling for different policy means.

For example, when the economy is in the factor-driven stage, the multipliers of environmental means and efficiency means are bigger and the effect of competition policies depends more on the role of environmental means and efficiency means. Similarly, when the economy is in the investment-driven stage, investment expenditure contributes more to economic development, infrastructure construction has a greater impact on the economic development level and, accordingly, the multiplier of fiscal means is relatively larger. At this time the effect of competition policies is attributable more to policies related to fiscal expenditure structure.

In one word, what means should be used to establish regional competitive advantages depends closely on the region's economic development level and other factors. Regional government should not simply take fiscal means as the only approach of competition but should use a variety of means based on the actual situation to achieve its competition goal.

The sixth aspect is the "lag" of competition policies. When bridging between the policy system and the economic environment is attempted, a certain element stood between the two. It is an important responsibility of the regional government to recognize and transform this element so as to achieve the goal (expectation) of competition policies through means (tools). The working of regional government's competition policies involves a complex transmission mechanism, and it is here that lies the "lag" problem of competition policies.

There are two kinds of the so-called "lag," inside lag, that is, the time to initiate the policy, and outside lag, that is, the time for the policy to work on the economy. Inside lag can be further broken down to recognition lag, the time taken to see the problem, decision lag, the time taken to decide to act, and action lag, the time taken to undertake the action. Outside lag is mainly caused by environmental factors (see Figure 7.1). In the process of transforming competition policy means (tools) to goals, it is important for the

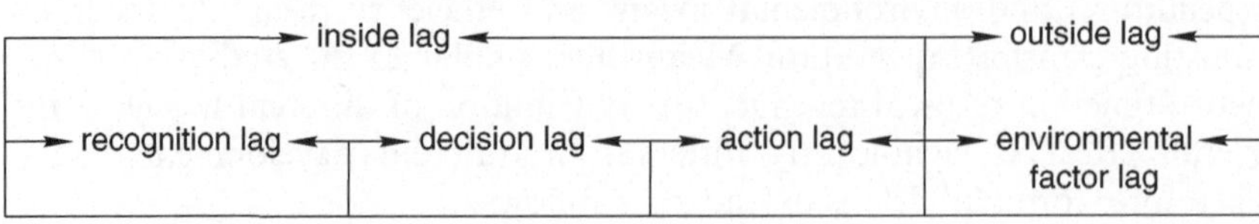

Figure 7.1 Lag of spontaneous competition policy.

regional government to "spontaneously" take response measures to counteract different types of lag, so as to achieve the desired policy goal and raise competitiveness.

Countries around the world have all seen regional governments making various competition policy explorations in the three fields of industrial development, urban construction and social welfare. China as a developing country has also made genuine efforts during reform and opening up. The following is a detailed examination of regional governments' policy initiatives in the three fields with Guangdong Province in China where I worked as a case and also with comparisons to the situation in the USA, the UK, Germany, the Republic of Korea, etc.

First, let's look at the field of industrial development. As early as in 2005 the GDP of Shunde District of Foshan City, Guangdong Province reached 60.1 billion *yuan*, with the secondary industry accounting for 61%. Of the total industrial output, household appliances and electronics accounted for 70%, and the household appliances sector was dominated by three giants, Midea, Kelon and Galanz. In such a situation, the poor performance of the single dominant industry or poor management of individual enterprises could bring region-wide economic crisis. To prevent the risk, Shunde Government devised and put into practice the reality-based and science-based "three-three-three" industrial development strategy: Guiding and supporting the coordinated development of the primary, secondary and tertiary industries; guiding and supporting at least three-pillar sectors in each industry; guiding and supporting at least three leading enterprises in each sector; perfecting the industrial chain, forming industrial clusters, and promoting sustainable development.[1] In response to the weak foundation, shortage of funds and other problems faced by a large number of small and medium-sized enterprises in their endeavor to grow, Shunde Government innovatively set up a credit guarantee fund for small- and medium-sized enterprises. With the fund, the government arranged special fiscal funds of fixed amounts and worked with professional guarantee institutions and commercial banks to provide guarantees and loans to growing small- and medium-sized enterprises that found it difficult to obtain loans from banks due to lack of collateral.[2] Results show that Shunde Government's guidance, regulation and monitoring in the economic field have promoted high-quality development of the primary industry, optimized development of the secondary industry and accelerated development of the tertiary industry, have advanced the transformation and upgrading of traditional industries, the breeding and expansion of emerging industries and the rapid growth of high-tech industries, and have led to the formation of the desirable industrial landscape of gradient development of large-, medium- and small-sized enterprises and complementary advantages of industrial clusters. Till now Shunde still keeps its leading position among the more than 2,800 county-level economies in China.

Western developed countries are also stepping up efforts to guide, promote and coordinate the development of the industrial economy. The National

Network for Manufacturing Innovation (NNMI) program of the USA is one of the country's important measures to implement its "reindustrialization" strategy. After the international financial crisis, the USA issued the Framework for Revitalizing American Manufacturing, passed the Manufacturing Enhancement Act of 2010, launched the Advanced Manufacturing Partnership (AMP) program in June 2011 and then launched the NNMI in March 2012. The NNMI consists of linked Institutes for Manufacturing Innovation (IMIs)[3] with common goals but unique concentrations. The USA first established 15 IMIs across the country with an investment of one billion dollars, further proposed to increase the number of IMIs to 45 within 10 years in July 2013, and implemented the proposal in its 2015 fiscal year budget. The NNMI program has the following characteristics. First, it is guided by national strategic objectives and organizes R & D projects in a relatively independent manner according to specific regional and industrial needs. Second, the program, centered on resource optimization and redistribution, realizes the integration of existing innovative resources through a combination of "top-down" approach and "bottom-up" approach. Third, it is backed by public-private cooperation with the federal government providing relatively stable support in the early stage and universities and private organizations following up the projects. Fourth, the program is supported by network governance realized by each IMI linking regional, federal and international innovation resources and the NNMI establishing a leadership council to promote coordination and cooperation among the IMIs. With the program, the government plays a potent role in bridging government and market, in optimizing government investments, and in coordinating multi-party interests, guiding investments, realizing leverage effect, leading industrial research and development, laying out high-end manufacturing industry and accelerating innovation and commercialization.

Besides the USA, the Knowledge Transfer Partnerships (KTP) scheme of the UK also deserves attention. Launched in 2003, the scheme serves to help businesses innovate by linking them to academic institutions and, taking personnel with certain knowledge and skills as the medium, transferring knowledge, technologies and skills from research institutions to enterprises. Funding for the scheme includes public funds of the government and public institutions as well as supportive funds of enterprises. There are fund application standards, fund approval procedures and a system for project implementation, acceptance and evaluation. The scheme expands the services provided to enterprises, pushes up enterprise input in innovation, and helps upgrade industrial structure by pooling the innovation resources of talents, enterprises and institutions.

Then let us turn to the field of urban construction. With the favorable conditions of the reform and opening up, by 2006 Foshan City in Guangdong Province achieved an economic growth of 30 times with a construction land increase of only three times. Yet the city was also faced with the grim reality that the increasing land supply-demand imbalance had become a major bottleneck impeding future urban development. Foshan Government has been exploring methods to tackle the problem in governance practice. It issued the Decisions on Accelerating the Transformation of Old Towns, Old Factories and Old Inside-city Villages (shortened as Transformation of the Three Olds) in 2007 and issued the Special "Three Olds" Transformation Plan of Foshan City (2009—2020) in 2009 and officially offered 253,000 *mu*[4] of the city's land occupied by "three olds" for transformation in a market-based mode of "policy from government, land from owner (user) and fund from developer." In the first three years after the launch of the Plan, 35.7 billion *yuan* worth of private funds were invested in 730 "three olds" transformation projects covering an area of about 30,000 *mu* with 23.99 million square meters of new construction area. Foshan's urban-rural transformation program followed the mechanism of "government promotion, enterprise participation and market-based operation." It quickly improved regional construction conditions, greatly improved land-use efficiency, and contributed to the adjustment and optimization of land use structure and industrial structure. The program was titled "Foshan Experience"[5] by Guangdong Provincial Government and the central government to be promoted across China. Then in 2010, Foshan Government put forward the "smart Foshan" development plan, a plan intended to drive industrialization with informatization, promote urbanization with informatization and accelerate internationalization with informatization, so as to comprehensively raise the competitiveness of Foshan. Foshan Government energetically developed smart transportation, smart environmental protection, smart land monitoring, smart public security, smart urban management, smart education, smart health care, smart culture, smart business, smart government, etc., and in this way has fully realized the goal of building a city that's safe, efficient, convenient, green and harmonious, promoted the region's transition to industrialization, accelerated urbanization and deepened internationalization.[6]

The government plays an important role during the modernization of urban governance. This is also true of western developed countries. One example is the remarkable transformation of the Ruhrgebiet, once Germany's "poisonous industrial capital." While making great contributions to German economy, the Ruhrgebiet brought serious pollution. To deal with the pollution, the Nordrhein-Westfalen state government and the German government formulated a three-step outline—adjusting the industrial structure, developing new industries and ecological restoration, transformation, and improvement of industrial heritage—an outline covering a long time range from 1968 to 1979 and then to 1989. Following the outline, the Ruhrgebiet eventually achieved a unity of cultural heritage, industrial transformation, infrastructure upgrading and urban development, and turned itself from an old industrial zone into a new type of urban industrial zone suitable for living, business and development.

The last is the field of social welfare. In 2016, the government of Guangdong Province set for itself ten tasks to tangibly improve people's life quality: First, ensuring and elevating people's bottom-line livelihood; second, increasing assistance to disadvantaged groups; third, doing better in making sure low-income groups have basic housing; fourth, improving production and living conditions in rural areas; fifth, improving grass-roots medical and health services; sixth, promoting fair and balanced allocation of educational resources; seventh, encouraging entrepreneurship and employment; eighth, strengthening pollution control and ecological construction; ninth, devoting more to public security and tenth, doing well in disaster prevention and mitigation.[7] Each task is specific and carried out.

Another classic example is the "new countryside campaign" of the Republic of Korea that began in the 1970s. Facing the then precarious situation of about 70% of the population engaged in farming coupled with the agricultural industry on the verge of collapse, the government of the Republic of Korea initiated the new countryside campaign, which was aimed at reviving the country's agriculture. Favorable policies were made and material support was given to help launch rural construction projects and agricultural associations were encouraged to run their own cooperative finances to give full support to the building of a new countryside. This was how the "Miracle on the Han River" was created and how the country's economic takeoff was achieved. This experience of the Republic of Korea holds typical significance for other countries in their attempts to improve people's life, especially to solve the serious imbalance between urban and rural areas.

7.2 Spillover effects of competition policies

In theory, regional government competition policies can be classified into five types. The first type is to adopt extremely loose and laissez-faire competition policies in markets both within and beyond the region. The second is to adopt extremely strict competition policies in markets both within and beyond the region. The competition policies of most regions are between the two. In fact, regional governments often use the so-called "rule of reason," that is, weighing the gains and efficiency of other regions' anti-competitive practices and then after comparison making a policy choice. The third type is to use the "rule of reason" in the regional market and to adopt loose competition policies in markets outside the region. The fourth type is to formulate competition policies following the "rule of reason" in markets both within and outside the region. The fifth kind is to adopt strict competition policies within the region and lose ones beyond or the other way around.

From the economics point of view, the competition policies a regional government adopts will always, whichever type they belong to, have two kinds of influence on the markets within and beyond the region, influences that resemble internal economy, internal diseconomy, external economy and external diseconomy.

The external influence of an economy is termed the externality or spillover effect of the economy. Such externality originally refers to the favorable or unfavorable influence on other enterprises or consumers caused by the behaviors and decisions of enterprises or consumers as micro units in the industrial economy. It can be classified into positive externality (when the behavior or activity of a microeconomic unit brings benefits to other people or the society without incurring cost on the beneficiary) and negative externality (when the behavior or activity of an enterprise or individual as a microeconomic unit causes damage to other people or the society without having to bear the cost for the damage). An external economy refers to a positive externality and an external diseconomy refers to a negative externality. In one word, the externality of an economy is the "non-market" impact of one economic force on another.

Here it is necessary to review the relevant research of Alfred Marshall, Arthur Pigou and Ronald Coase. In 1890, Alfred Marshall, the founder of the Cambridge school and a representative neoclassical economist, published *Principles of Economics*, in which he put forward the concept of "external economy." In Marshall's view, what an enterprise possesses is more than the three production factors of land, labor and capital. There's still another factor—"industrial organization," a concept that Marshall used to refer to a wide range of contents including division of labor, the relative concentration of certain industries, large-scale production and enterprise cooperation and management. Marshall used a pair of concepts—"internal economy" and "external economy"—to explain how the change of this fourth production factor led to the increase of production.

According to Marshall, internal economies refer to the saving of production cost brought by various factors inside the enterprise, including the working enthusiasm of workers, the improvement of working skills, the improvement of internal division of labor and cooperation, the adoption of advanced equipment, the improvement of management level, and the reduction of management cost, and external economies refer to the reduction of production cost brought by various factors outside the enterprise, factors including the distance between the enterprise and raw material supplier, the distance between the enterprise and the product sales market, the size of the market, how convenient transportation and communication are, and the development level of other related enterprises. That is to say, Marshall used internal economies to refer to the efficiency improvement brought about by the division of labor within enterprises and used external economies to refer to the efficiency improvement brought about by the division of labor amongst enterprises.

The second economist worth mentioning is Arthur Pigou, author of the 1912 work *Wealth and Welfare*, which was published again under the new title *The Economics of Welfare* in 1920. Pigou was the first who, using the method of modern economics and from the standpoint of welfare economics, brought up the concept of "external diseconomy" on the basis of Marshall's "external economy," shifted the research on externality from external factors' influence on enterprises to the influence of enterprises or individuals on other enterprises or individuals. The shift corresponds to the two types of externality, positive ones and negative ones.

Pigou explained externality with the difference between marginal private net output value and marginal social net output value. He pointed out that marginal private net output value refers to the output value obtained by an individual enterprise by adding one unit of production factor during production, and marginal social net output value is the additional output value brought by the addition of one unit of production factor in production of the whole society, and that the two had the following relationship: The marginal social net output value is greater than the marginal private net output value if apart from the marginal private net output value there are other people benefitting from the addition of the production factor, and otherwise, if other people suffer losses, the marginal social net output value is less than the marginal private net output value. Pigou termed the beneficial effect of a producer's production activity on society "marginal social benefit" and the adverse effect of a producer's production activity on society "marginal social cost." Based on this, he encapsulated externality as the disparity between marginal private cost and marginal social cost and that between marginal private benefit and marginal social benefit. When there is a negative externality, there will be external costs, such as the additional cost one manufacturer has to bear for installing pollution control facilities in order to maintain its original production when affected by another manufacturer's environmental pollution. In this scenario, the sum of marginal private cost and the marginal external cost is a marginal social cost. Contrarily, when there is a positive externality, there will be external benefits, such as the benefits created by an enterprise's decision-making that are shared by the society rather than being owned by the enterprise itself. In this scenario, the sum of marginal private benefit and marginal external benefit is marginal social income. In practice, the government should adopt economic policies to eliminate the disparity between the marginal private benefit and the marginal social benefit and that between the marginal private cost and the marginal social cost, specifically, by taxing entities incurring more marginal social cost than marginal private cost, that is, taxing enterprises when there is an external diseconomy, and by rewarding and paying allowances to entities creating higher marginal social benefit than marginal private benefit, namely, subsidizing enterprises when there is an external economy. Pigou believed that such taxations and subsidies could internalize externalities and these measures he proposed were later called "Pigouvian taxes."

Ronald Coase, the winner of 1991 Nobel Memorial Prize in Economic Sciences and founder of new institutional economics, criticized Pigouvian taxes on the grounds of the following three reasons. First, in many cases, externalities are mutual instead of a one-way problem that one party infringes on the other. The typical environmental dispute between the chemical plant and the residential area could serve as an example. It is actually not appropriate to levy pollution tax on the chemical plant as long as it discharges wastewater without making clear whether the chemical plant has the right to discharge pollution because there's the chance that the chemical plant is built prior to the residential area, in which case the chemical plant may have the right to discharge pollution. Perhaps the right way to limit wastewater discharge from chemical plants is not for the government to tax the plants but for affected residential areas to "buy back" pollution discharge from them. Second, Pigouvian tax would be utterly unnecessary when transaction cost is zero, that is, when property rights are clearly defined and trade is possible, optimal resource allocation could be achieved through voluntary bargaining of the parties involved. There would be no need for the government to meddle in since bargaining can achieve the same effect as Pigouvian taxes. Third, even when transaction costs are not zero, the best approach to internalize an externality should be pinpointed by weighing and comparing the cost-benefit of various policy means. In other words, Pigouvian taxes as institutional arrangements may be effective or inefficient. These criticisms constitute the Coase theorem: If transaction costs are zero, market transaction and voluntary bargaining will lead to an optimal allocation of resources regardless of the initial definition of rights; and when transaction costs are not zero, institutional arrangement and selection would be of importance. That is to say, to solve an externality, we can either make institutional arrangements according to the overall cost-benefit comparison, or adopt market transaction, or voluntary bargaining, as a replacement for Pigouvian tax.

Following the footsteps of Alfred Marshall, Arthur Pigou and Ronald Coase and on the basis of their research, many later economists made important contributions to the development of theories on externalities. There have formed seven classifications of externalities, each from a different angle. The first way of classification is by the impact of the externality. In this way, an externality can be external economy (or positive external economic effect, or positive externality) or external diseconomy (or negative external economic effect, or negative externality). Second, by production field, externalities could be classified into four types: External economy of production, external economy of consumption, external diseconomy of production and external diseconomy of consumption. Third, by the time and space of origination, externalities can be classified into intragenerational externalities and intergenerational externalities. The externality we normally refer to is more of a spatial concept mainly considering whether resources are allocated reasonably for the time being, that is, externality within the time of a single generation. In comparison, intergenerational externality involves the influence of human behaviors on later generations, especially the adverse effects of a previous generation on later generations and those of the contemporary generation on future generations. Such intergenerational externalities can be understood as "present externalities extending to the future" and could be classified into intergenerational external economy and intergenerational external diseconomy. This way of classification arose from the concept of sustainable development. The fourth way is to classify externalities by the conditions under which they emerge, into those in a competition-dominated situation and those in a monopoly. The fifth is to classify externalities into stable ones and unstable ones. Stable externalities are ones that can be curbed, or, be internalized through various coordinative means, and unstable externalities are those whose uncertainties and side effects take time to be exposed and people would be likely to be deceived by this incubation period. Sixth, by direction, externalities can be classified into one-way externality (the external economy or external diseconomy brought by one party to the other) and reciprocal externality (when all parties have the right to approach a certain resource and incur costs on each other). Seventh, by root, externalities can be classified into institutional externalities (essentially the asymmetry between social responsibilities and rights) and technological externalities (such as the externalities of network economy caused by the innate feature of the network itself of being systematic, the mutuality of the information flow and logistics within the network, and the long-term monopoly of network infrastructure).

It can be seen that with the efforts of many economists the study of externality theory has become a new hot spot in modern economics research. Nevertheless, there are also doubts about the concept of externality with some believing that the concept is vague and repetitive. Here I have no intention to comment on the right or wrong of externality theory. Nor would I use it the way it's originally intended in this chapter, that is, to analyze the impact of the behavior of a micro unit such as an enterprise or an individual on other micro units in the industrial economy. What I am intending is to apply the meaning and method of externality or spillover effect to the field of a regional government competition to answer the following questions: whether regional governments' competition policies will produce spillover effects, what the spillover effects are, what the basic approaches and means would be to solve these spillover effects, etc.

The maker and executor, contents, goal, means (tools), effects and time lag of regional governments' competition policies are interconnecting aspects that complement each other to form a complete system. Among the above aspects, it is mainly the tools of regional government competition policies that can produce externality or spillover effect. The spillover effect of competition policies could be classified based on the type of competition policy tool into the spillover effect of fiscal means, that of financial means, that of environmental means, that of efficiency means and that of legal means.

Fiscal means include making fiscal budget, changing expenditure structure, issuing public debt, giving fiscal subsidies and adjusting taxes. When money supply stays unchanged, the government's increasing investment in urban infrastructure will pull up the demand for money, leading to a rise of interest rate, which will directly bring two spillover effects. First, the financing cost of the private sector in the region will go up, resulting in shrinkage of private investment as at such times private investors in the region will make choices after weighing the financing cost and possible future return on the investment. The second spillover effect is a faster influx of large amounts of private capital from outside the region drawn by the double temptations of high interest rate and investment return in the region to participate in its urban infrastructure construction and other projects.

In terms of financial means, in addition to national-level monetary means such as interest rate and exchange rate, other tools available to most regional governments include setting up project funds, offering guarantee and re-guarantee, building platforms and promoting inclusive finance. Financial means produce two spillover effects. First, they can help turn potential production factors in the region into real ones, change industrial development and industrial structure for the better, and raise the region's total economic volume. Second, it will affect the region's consumption demand and investment demand, not only by indirectly influencing the consumption expenditure of individuals in the region but also by directly stimulating the private investment demand within the region as well as attracting more private investment from outside the region. From these points of view, the externalities created by regional governments' financial means are similar to those created by fiscal means.

Environmental means include upgrading hard and soft urban infrastructure and optimizing the social credit system of the region, efficiency means mainly involve improving functional efficiency and time efficiency by building a sound policy system and innovating the management mechanism of the region, and legal means comprise the protection of property rights as well as the maintenance of the fairness and justice of the regional market. Their common spillover effect is the attraction of large amounts of people, capital, materials and information from outside the region, forming a regional landscape of "four influxes as one," which optimizes the region's investment environment and promotes the sustainable growth of regional economy. During the transformation of cross-regional economy from unbalance to balance, if a region's government uses competition policy tools in a timely and effective manner, it will be able to surpass the other regions to be the first to achieve regional economic aggregate growth and economic quality improvement.

From another angle, the spillover effects of regional government competition policies could be put into three categories, the first of which is the effects of regional supply side and demand side. The various policy tools of regional government firstly produce supply-side effects, notably the increase of total supply and the improvement of supply structure, which then drive the generation of demand-side effects. In most cases, regional governments first invest in urban infrastructure, and then start investing in high and new technologies, venture capital and urban-rural integration. These investments will, in addition to increasing effective supply and improving supply structure, create expansion effect with the investment multiplier mechanism and hence increase the total demand, which will then bring about demand-side effects, first, the demand for commodity supply and second, the demand for industrial development. The combination of the two demands then creates the demand for people, capital, materials and information, which jointly promote economic growth. In summary, the externalities (effects) of regional supply side and demand side are primarily demonstrated in the region's attraction and concentration of people, capital, materials and information from outside the region as well as in the formation and functioning of such a "four influxes as one" mechanism.

The second category is the effects of regional economic stock and increment. As I have discussed in Chapter 4, regional government competition first takes place during the transformation of urban quasi-operative resources. In order to give play to the decisive role of the market in allocating resources and at the same time achieve multiplied effects with limited fiscal funds, the regional government will not only transform the region's existing assets so that they meet the requirements of market economy competition mechanism, but also, at the very beginning of the acquisition of new assets, build for them property right structure carriers such as equity system and public-private joint venture, in addition to using diverse and flexible financing and cooperation methods such as Build-Operate-Transfer (BOT), Transfer-Operate-Transfer (TOT), Public-Private Partnership (PPP) and Port-Park-City (PPC) as well as other means including issuing bonds, helping enterprises to go public, and encouraging mergers and acquisitions, to support project companies to become bigger and stronger, and ultimately to promote regional economic growth. It could be said that the externalities of regional economic stock and increment mainly depend on the region's innovation mechanisms in terms of concept, technology, organization and institution being more advanced than those of other regions.

The third category of externalities is the effects of the region moving from imbalance to balance. The impact of regional government's competition behaviors on the regional economy, which is exhibited in the relationship between government subsidies and industrial development, that between fiscal expenditure and urban construction, and that between social security and people's rights and interests, all unfold while regional economy transitions from unbalanced to balanced development. This type of externality finds reflection in two aspects, the first being the gradual alleviation of the contradiction between people's growing demand for a better life and the unbalanced and inadequate development of the region as well as the gradual maturing of the region into one with environmental advantages suitable for living, business and travel, and the second being interregional economic growth forming a pattern in line with the 80/20 rule.

The 80/20 pattern of interregional economic development is a subject worthy of further study concerning the externalities of regional government competition. The 80/20 rule was discovered by the Italian economist Vilfredo Pareto, who believes that in any group of things, the most important accounts for only a small percentage, about 20%, and the other 80%, though being the majority, is only secondary in importance. Now the theory,

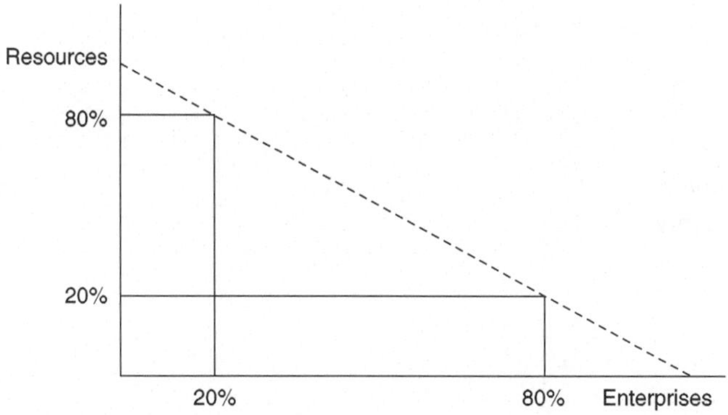

Figure 7.2 The 80/20 rule.

termed the 80/20 rule, has become a common axiom in sociology, business management and other disciplines and practices.

In management studies, the 80/20 rule usually means that 80% of a company's profits come from 20% of its projects. Taken a step further, it is used by many economists to refer to the belief that 20% of the people own 80% of the wealth, and the remaining 80% possess 20% of the wealth. And we could take it one step further to believe that 20% of the enterprises hold 80% of the resources and the remaining 80% of enterprises have 20% of the resources (see Figure 7.2).

The externalities of regional government competition bring regional economic development into a pattern that conforms to the 80/20 rule. Therefore, attention should be paid to the relationship and interaction between the 20% and the 80% to promote coordinated and sustainable development of the regional economy.

7.3 Innovation is the key to regional government competition

The goals of regional government competition are at bottom economic growth, regional prosperity and people's happiness, which from the standpoint of economics is to realize concrete progress in the industrial development, urban construction and social welfare of the region. If a coordinate system is built with the vertical axis indicating the year and the horizontal axis representing the regional modernization progress (covering industrial development, urban construction, social welfare, etc.), each region, based on its own progress in terms of industrial development, urban construction and social welfare, will be able to identify its own position in this coordinate system as well as to locate which stage of regional economic growth described in Chapter 6 its own modernization is in (see Figure 7.3).

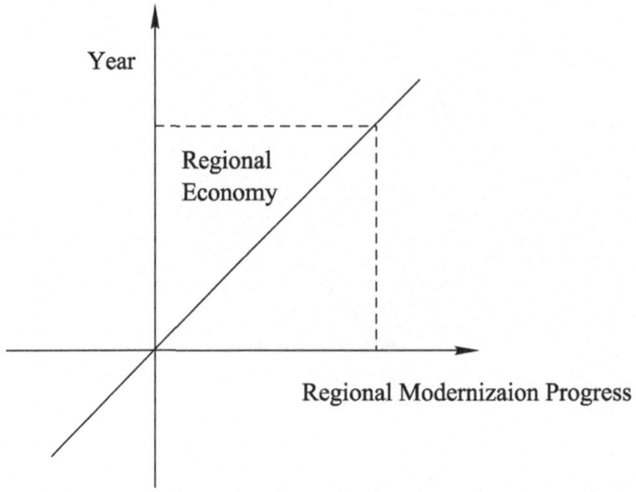

Figure 7.3 Regional modernization progress and regional economic development.

Foresighted leading of regional government will enable the region to stand out in regional government competition and regional economic competition, to become part of the important minority, that is, the key 20% in the 80/20 rule. And the most essential part of foresighted leading, also the key to regional government competition, is innovation in terms of concept, technology, organization and institution.

To innovate concepts, the regional government has to, while exercising public power and managing the region, conduct forward-looking theoretical analysis and thinking on new situations and problems that constantly occur during industrial development, urban construction and social welfare progress, make forward-looking judgments on regional economic and social phenomena, and obtain new theoretical nourishment from past experience and present practice, so as to guide the innovation and development of the region's economic institution, organizational form and technical means. For example, in every stage of economic growth, the regional government should constantly innovate concepts in effective governance, government affairs openness, management efficiency, etc. to give full play to its role in foresighted leading, promote innovations of the management system, management behaviors, management methods and management technologies, and ultimately to provide correct guidance and huge power for regional development.

Technological innovation requires the regional government to play an active role in concentrating regional resources, specifically, by directly or indirectly participating in major scientific and technological research projects, helping the building of regional technological innovation capacity, promoting technological progress and encouraging regional technological inventions. Specific measures include two aspects. One is to create a favorable external environment for enterprises in the region to improve technological innovation ability, such as by strengthening the region's patent system and product standardization system. The other is to take direct policy measures to encourage technological innovation, such as by setting up science and technology foundations, funding the research and development of key scientific and technological fields, building integrated platforms of production, learning and research, and setting up science and technology incubators, parks and corridors, all of which are means to promote the region's scientific and technological development.

Organizational innovation entails the innovation in organizational structure, mode and management, which will elevate the organization-based guarantee mechanisms for the region's industrial development, urban construction and social welfare, and promote the region's economic development and social progress. Management innovation is an especially important part of organizational innovation. It not only requires the regional government to choose the best direction and make reliable predictions about the feasibility and results of the course of action before actually taking action, but also requires the regional government to make reasonable macro planning and regulation on the strategic objectives and realization paths of regional economic development as well as the needed methods for resource distribution and measures for safeguard and supervision.

Institutional innovation entails creating new and more incentive institutions and normative systems to raise resource allocation efficiency and thus realize sustained development of regional economy and society. The regional government should innovate the institutions for social and economic management in a way suited to the stage the region is in industrial development, urban construction and social welfare and also in a way that works well with the region's innovations in concept, technology and organization. The essence of institutional innovation is changing the rules governing people's economic and social behaviors and interaction, and changing the relationship between economic entities and the external environment. Its goal is to better stimulate people's enthusiasm and creativity, help optimize the allocation of regional resources, promote the continuous growth of social wealth, and eventually advance the progress of regional economy and society. At the same time, institutional innovation is conducive to the building of an innovative regional government, which will, in turn, enable the regional government to do better in foresighted leading.

In practice, both regional government's foresighted leading and its competition find their focal point in the formation, application and improvement of regional government's competition policy tools. Regional governments' innovation in concept, technology, organization and institution needs a carrier. Serving as such a carrier is primarily the policy tools used by regional governments in competition, specifically, the aforementioned fiscal, financial, environmental, efficiency and legal means. The innovation of these policy tools is the materialization and substantiation of the conceptual, technological, organizational and institutional innovation of regional governments. How far and how fast competition policy tool innovation is promoted will directly affect the process of regional economic modernization.

To have a deeper understanding of the essential role played by innovation in regional government competition, let's take the EU's and China's innovations in greenhouse gas emission reduction as an example to examine the issue in more detail. First, let's look at the exploration and efforts of the EU. Faced with the severe situation after the USA announced its withdrawal from the Kyoto Protocol in 2001, the EU took effective measures to convert carbon emissions as a burden into entitlements for trading, which essentially was a policy tool innovation. Emissions trading as a new financial instrument enabled effective disposal of inverse resources and at the same time made the EU a leader in international climate action. Carbon emissions trading quickly became an indispensable policy tool of the EU to deal with climate change and the most important means for its member countries to fulfill their emission reduction commitments.

The EU builds its competitiveness in the global carbon market through the following measures: First, establishing a unified carbon trading market within the EU to raise the liquidity of emission reduction quotas within the EU and second, through the clean development mechanism (CDM), achieving compatibility with the carbon trading system in developing countries to reduce its own emission reduction costs. In January 2005, the EU Emissions Trading System (EU ETS) was officially put into operation and with it the EU became the largest carbon trading market in the world. From 2005 to 2012, the annual trade volume of the EU carbon market rocketed from 10 billion dollars to 150 billion dollars, with an average annual growth rate of 47%. By 2012, the carbon trade volume of the EU accounted for 99.3% of the global quota trading market, meaning that the EU had the main pricing power on the international carbon market. The EU ETS was to be implemented in four phases and is now in Phase 3 (2013–2020). It's required that the total carbon emissions of the EU should decrease at a rate of no less than 1.74% every year, which must be achieved so as to ensure that the greenhouse gas emission in 2020 would be at least 20% lower than that in 1990. At the current phase more than 50% of the allowances are allocated by auction, and the target is to realize allocation of all allowances through paid auction by 2027.

At present, the spot products listed and traded on the European Climate Exchange include the European Union Allowance (EUA) and the Certified Emission Reduction (CER). The derivative products mainly include CER futures contract, EUA futures contract, CER options contract and EUA options contract.

From innovating policy tools to realizing tangible progress and from spot trading to futures trading, the EU emissions trading market has come to occupy a leading position in the world and formed strong regional competitiveness. Moreover, the EU carbon emissions trading market has encouraged the development of the European carbon finance industry—as carbon emission rights take on more and more commodity attributes and as the trading market continues to mature, many financial institutions such as investment banks, hedge funds and securities companies and even private investors are vying to join the market, making carbon emission management one of the fastest-growing businesses in the European financial service industry. The joining of these financial institutions and private investors constantly expands the capacity of the carbon market, further raises its liquidity, and makes the market more transparent, all of which are attracting more enterprises to enter the market. It could be said that the EU's regional policy tool innovations have greatly elevated the competitiveness of the European financial industry and even the economy of Europe at large.

Then let's look at the explorations of China, one of the world's largest greenhouse gas emitters and regarded by many countries as the emission reduction market with the greatest potential. In 2011, the National Development and Reform Commission of China made the following municipalities and provinces pilot places for carbon emissions trading: Beijing, Tianjin, Shanghai, Guangdong, Shenzhen, Hubei and Chongqing. In 2012, the seven pilot places studied and formulated pilot plans and carried out basic preparations. Shenzhen started carbon emissions trading on June 18, 2013, Shanghai started on November 26, 2013, Beijing on November 28, 2013, Guangdong on December 20, 2013, and Tianjin on December 26, 2013, followed closely by Hubei and Chongqing. The 2015 China Carbon Pricing Survey conducted jointly by China Carbon Forum (CCF) and ICF International was released on September 8, 2015. The survey indicates that China's carbon emission peak will appear in 2030 and that as time passes carbon price will gradually go up from the current low level.

With such prospects in mind, China is speeding up its efforts to establish a nationwide emissions trading market and has set forth a three-stage plan. The first stage, the preparation stage, is from 2014 to 2016, the key period for China's carbon market building. The second stage, the stage for official launching, is from 2016 to 2019, during which China comprehensively started work related to all carbon market elements and put the carbon market "machine" to operation and test. By the end of 2017, a nationwide carbon trading system framework had been set up. The third stage starts after 2019. By then China's carbon market will enter the "high-speed operation mode" and play the most essential role in the field of greenhouse gas emission reduction.

The goal of China's efforts is to, through a combination of voluntary international reduction and compulsory domestic reduction, force carbon trading into a unified nationwide market, establish and improve a carbon market system covering both spot trading and futures trading, build a national trading platform and a worldwide trading platform, strengthen exchanges and cooperation with the international carbon market, and ultimately, obtain pricing power or energy-related discourse power in the international carbon market, especially in the Asian carbon market. Possible innovative policy tools are in three aspects. The first is about standardization, that is, specific carbon emission standards and basic trading mechanisms should be set forth. In other words, while mechanisms for emission licensing and for initial emission quota allocation should be specified to curb overall emission intensity and cap the total emission amount within target, mechanisms for emission and trading registration and those for monitoring and certification should also be specified to improve the standardization of emission control. The second is to design appropriate trading standards and mechanisms of carbon futures, including establishing sound transaction and settlement mechanisms and effective risk management mechanisms. The third is to strengthen the legal system, which entails establishing a sound national law on carbon asset property rights protection and formulating sound national and international regulatory codes for the carbon spot and futures market. The next decade will be a critical period for China's carbon reduction and continuous innovation and optimization of policy tools at this juncture will place China at an advantageous position in regional economic development.

7.4 Essential differences between foresighted leading and keynesianism

In practice at least three conditions have to be met for the government of any country to lead the economy with foresight. The first is to keep pace with the times, which mainly requires regional government innovation to keep abreast with and even surpass new technologies. The rapid development of science and technology is giving birth to new resources, new tools, new industries and new business forms, which will deliver a blow to the old government management system. While creating new demands and high efficiency of production and life, new technologies also bring new issues (such as the application of big data) that regional governments aren't readily able to deal with and render it difficult for governments to make decisions based on instinct as they often did before. Faced with such challenges, governments should take the initiative to make achievements in the three major aspects of their function, namely, industrial development, urban construction and social welfare, or, in the distribution of non-operative resources, operative resources and quasi-operative resources. Their ideas, policies and measures should all keep pace with the times. The second condition is all-encompassing competition, that is, to realize foresighted leading, regional governments should innovate their concepts, technologies, organization and institution and to take part in the competition in all factors and throughout the entire process in an all-round and systematic manner in the fields of social welfare (optimizing public goods allocation and improving economic development environment), industrial development (guiding, supporting, regulating and supervising market players to raise production efficiency) and urban construction (following market rules and participating in projects). Such competition, though still with enterprise competition as the basis, goes beyond the traditional concept of commodity production competition and covers the entire process towards realizing comprehensive and sustainable development of regional economy and society, from setting the objectives to choosing the paths and methods, carrying out the policies and measures and obtaining the final results. The third condition is open government, that is, regional governments should make transparent the decision-making, implementation, management, services and results of their proceedings and disclose information about key issues (areas). Openness and transparency of government affairs guarantee the right to know, to participate, to express and to oversee of all parties in the society, which will help better distribute resources in the industrial development, urban construction and social welfare of the region. In addition, a transparent, innovative and clean regional government that rules by law and endeavors to serve the people will in itself stimulate market vitality and people's creativity, which will then promote regional economic growth, prosperity and public happiness.

The prerequisite of government foresighted leading is that it relies on market rules and the market mechanism. The principles of government foresighted leading are for the market to determine resources allocation and for the government to guide, regulate and monitor the industrial economy, allocate, participate in and safeguard the urban economy, and guarantee, support and elevate livelihood economy. The means of government foresighted leading is to use planning, investment, consumption, price, tax, interest rate, exchange rate, law and other policies to carry out innovation in concept, technology, organization and institution. The purpose of government foresighted leading is to advance supply-side or demand-side structural reform, establish leading advantages of economic growth, and make sure that the development is on a science-based and sustainable path.

The key to government foresighted leading is innovation. While participating in the investment, construction and management of the region, regional government has to lead with foresight in terms of concept, technology, organization and institution in order to give full play to its dual (quasi-macro and quasi-micro) role and truly drive regional economic development and social progress. As aforementioned, foresighted leading in concept establishes regional government's substantial competitiveness in the factor-driven stage, foresighted leading in organization is the key to the competition in the investment-driven stage, foresighted leading in technology and institution is the winning point in the innovation-driven stage, and foresighted leading in all aspects is the only course of action in the wealth-driven stage.

There are the following essential differences between the GFL and Keynesianism. The first difference is in terms of the time action is taken. Government foresighted leading takes place mainly before a problem occurs, setting it apart from Keynesian interventions which are taken during and after the problem. The effect of the policies is not the same, either. The second difference lies in the focus and policy instruments of the intervention. Keynesianism focuses on the demand side while foresighted leading focuses on government's guidance, coordination and supervision of industrial resources, urban resources and livelihood resources. Keynesianism mainly uses fiscal policy means to intervene in the economy, while foresighted leading requires governments to take all sorts of policy means throughout entire economic processes and to constantly innovate the policy means. The third and more important difference concerns the role of the government. The GFL posits the dual attributes of the government, the role of regional government as one of the players in market competition, and a mature market economy as one that integrates government foresighted leading with market development with the government playing an indispensable part. Keynesianism, in contrast, theoretically places the government outside the market, resulting in an incomplete market theory with a narrow definition of government economy behavior, which imposes limitations on Keynesian theory and practice. The fourth difference is in the operational mode. Classical economics and neoclassical economics focus on market (the invisible hand) with an emphasis on supply (commodity, price and supply regulation). Keynesian economics focuses on government intervention with an emphasis on demand (created by investment, consumption and export). The GFL shares similarities with and also differs from classical economics, neoclassical economics and Keynesian economics. Its operational mode is a combination of government leading (intervention) and a focus on supply. It adheres to the economic principle that market determines resource allocation and in the meanwhile requires the government to play a guiding, coordinating and supervising role in such allocation process. Government foresighted leading plays an all-round role in the entire process of economic activities.

The fourth difference between Keynesianism and the GFL, namely, the difference in the two theories' operational mode, calls for more elaboration. The most typical economic operational mode of Keynesianism is "government intervention + demand-side regulation," with the predominant tool of demand-side regulation being fiscal policies. As discussed in Chapter 3, Keynes believed that the root cause of the economic crisis in the 1930s was a lack of effective demand (including the lack of consumption demand and investment demand) and that so the government should extend its "visible hand" to strengthen intervention in and regulation of the economy. The specific means is to adopt fiscal policies, especially deficit policies, to increase public expenditure, and at the same time, to adopt financial policies such as lowering interest rates stimulate consumption and boost investment as ways to pull up effective demand and achieve a balanced state featuring full employment. After taking office in 1933, President Franklin D. Roosevelt joined Keynes in opposing the liberalism idea that the government should not interfere in the economy and introduced the New Deal: on the one hand, expanding consumption demand by increasing government expenditure and reinforcing consumption tendency; and on the other hand, expanding investment demand by reducing interest rates, raising the marginal efficiency of capital and increasing money supply. This is a typical example of Keynesian economic operational mode: government intervention + demand-side regulation. If Roosevelt's New Deal measures could be regarded successful in counteracting the economic depression, I have to say that it was only the success of short-term demand-side policies focusing on adjusting aggregate demand.

One salient feature of the operational mode of the GFL in comparison with Keynesianism is "government leading (intervention) + supply-side promotion," that is, the government, on the basis of resource allocation determined by the market, playing its guiding, coordinating, and supervising role to lead the regional economy, in all aspects and throughout the whole process, to develop in a science-based and sustainable way. Specifically, the mode covers three aspects. The first is exploring the field of resource generation. It is from the GFL that the theory of resource generation derived, and generative resources comprise three categories: primordial resources, derivative resources and inverse resources. Primordial resources, such as space resources, deep-sea resources and polar resources, are naturally existing resources that human society has not been able to develop yet or is only exploring now due to historical reasons or the limitations of science & technology; derivative resources, such as hard and soft urban infrastructure and even smart cities, are resources that do not naturally exist in the first place and are instead formed by the investment and construction of human society with the development of science & technology; and inverse resources are the resources formed during the development and construction of the first two types of resources, such as the carbon emissions trading resources mentioned earlier. On the one hand, all three categories of generative resources have the four features of being dynamic, economical, productive and risky, necessitating certain conditions to be in place for their development and utilization. On the other hand, they are new engines that boost the social progress and economic growth of the region and the entire human society from the supply side, and advancing this process is a task that private enterprises are unable to undertake or cannot do well. It is a task that must be pushed forward by the visible hand of the government.

The second aspect of the operational mode of the GFL is attaching importance to the effect of competition policies. In addition to playing a part in developing the field of resource generation, regional governments should also, in response to supply-side demand, innovate and improve their policy instruments including fiscal, financial, environmental, efficiency and legal means to improve the supply effects of their fiscal expenditure, financial support, environmental support and rules and regulations. The purpose is to effectively advance structural reform with a focus on supply side, form leading advantages of regional economic growth, and promote sustainable development of the region.

The third aspect is all-round and whole-process leading, that is, government foresighted leading takes place not only in the factor-driven stage of regional economic development, but also in the investment-driven, innovation-driven and wealth-driven stages. The operational mode requires that the regional government is one with dual (quasi-macro and quasi-micro) attributes, one that participates in market competition and represents one of the dual entities of market competition, the other being enterprises, and an effective government that works with the efficient market in a mature market economy. An effective government that follows the foresighted leading theory and adopts the economic operational mode of "government leading (intervention) + supply-side promotion" will gain advantages in regional economic competition and promote the economic transition and social transformation of the region.

It should be noted that the "supply-side promotion" in the operational mode of the GFL is not the same as western supply-side economics. Supply-side economics holds a firm belief in Say's law, "supply creates its own demand," which rose to popularity in the early 19th century. Say's law holds that from the standpoint of the overall economy purchasing power is always equal to productivity and that supply is the only source of force to maintain the actual demand. Supply-side economics opposes state intervention and believes in the laissez-faire neo-conservatism. It believes that Keynesianism at best is applicable only to special situations like the great depression in the 1930s. One important characteristic of supply-side economics is the importance attached to analyzing the economic effects of government policies, such as the effects of tax reduction, of reducing social welfare expenditure, of stabilizing currency value and of streamlining rules and regulations. President Reagan of the USA based his election campaign on supply-side economics and got re-elected. Yet history shows that neither Keynesianism nor supply-side economics could solve from root the cyclical economic recession and crisis in the West.

Of course, there are commonalities between supply-side economics and the "supply-side promotion" in the GFL operational mode. The commonalities lie mainly in two aspects, one being that both theories take supply side as the starting point, and the other being that both lay emphasis on analyzing the economic effects of policies. Yet still, more essential and predominant are the differences between the two. First, they are based on different theoretical foundation. While supply-side economics assumes Say's law as true and one-sidedly emphasizes supply management with no regard for demand management at all, the supply-side promotion in the GFL focuses on optimizing the allocation of regional resources on the basis of the resource generation theory. It aims to advance the mutual reliance and coordinated operation of the two sides of regional economic activities, supply and demand, thus promoting science-based and sustainable development of industrial economy, urban economy and livelihood economy. Second, the role to be played by the government differs as believed by the two theories. While supply-side economics ignores or even denies the role of government intervention and believes in laissez-faire neo-conservatism, the supply-side promotion in the GFL recommends, and indeed, has as its prerequisite, full play of the role of government intervention on the basis of resources allocation by the market. Third, the two theories have different purposes. The policy goal of supply-side economics is to control stagflation, while the policy goal of the supply-side promotion in the GFL is to, in addition to achieving continuous development of industrial economy, urban economy and livelihood economy, build the region into one that's suitable for living, for business and for tourism, lift regional economy to an advantageous position and realize sustainable growth of the region. Fourth, the two entails different policy means. Supply-side economics blindly believes in and relies solely on tax reduction without resorting to the wide range of other policy means. The supply-side promotion in the GFL adopts fiscal and financial means as well as supportive means related to environment, efficiency and law so as to achieve all-round and whole-process progress in regional industrial development, urban construction and social welfare. The regional economic operational mode of "government leading (intervention) + supply-side promotion" could be regarded as a reform of regional production mode. Starting from the supply side, the mode utilizes generative resources to expand effective supply and adopts policy means to improve regional supply structure so that the supply system can better adapt to the change of the demand structure and total-factor productivity will be improved. It could be said that the mode represents the direction of market economy development of all countries in the world and is conducive to the gradual maturing of the relationship between government and market.

7.5 Revolutionary innovations of government foresighted leading theory

The GFL represents important innovations in the economics theory system. The theory posits that in addition to the micro economy represented by enterprises and the macro economy represented by the country there is also the mezzo economy represented by the region. This not only offers explanation to the economic miracle of many countries, especially China, but also represents an enrichment and improvement of the existing economic system. While the market economy theory lays the foundation of microeconomics and then Keynesianism divides economics into microeconomics and macroeconomics, the GFL divides economics into macroeconomics, mezzoeconomics and microeconomics. The GFL can not only fill a blank area in the economics theory system and point out a direction for the economic system reform of all countries, but also can, by accommodating regional economies and regional governments into the economics theory system, create a multi-level market system that's conducive to enhancing the economic stability of all countries in the world. In the following part the significance of the GFL is introduced in three aspects:

First of all, the GFL expands the application scope of the market. As mentioned above, from the GFL derived the theory of resource generation, and generative resources could be classified into three categories: Primordial resources, derivative resources and inverse resources. With the passage of time, the investment, development and construction of urban infrastructure in the field of derivative resources is taking on an increasingly larger scope. Now it includes not only hard public facilities such as roads, railways, airports, communications, and the supply of water, electricity and gas, but also soft public facilities such as education, science and technology, health care, sports and culture, and, along with the progress of urban modernization and urban-rural integration, is extending to the development and construction of smart cities and urban-rural infrastructure. The scope of primordial resources is also expanding. Within the solar system alone there are rich mineral resources on the moon, Mars, asteroids and other celestial bodies; rich hydrogen resources on Jovian planets and comets; vacuum resources, radiation resources and large temperature difference resources in planetary space and interplanetary space; and orbit resources and microgravity resources that could be created by spacecraft flight. This is also true of inverse resources, with the carbon emissions trading resources we have analyzed in detail being an example. By developing, utilizing and managing these three kinds of resources on the basis of following market rules, regional governments are expanding the application scope of market economy from the industrial economy field to the field of resource generation.

Second, the GFL constructed a new multi-level market system. As mentioned before, in the horizontal system of the market, in addition to the players in the industrial economy, that is, enterprises, there are also urban economy players, that is, regional governments and enterprises, as well as international economy (including space economy and marine economy) players that provide quasi-operative resources and develop new resource markets, that is, national governments and enterprises. The market exists not only in the industrial economy but also in other economic forms. It is multiple levels of competition together that constitute the modern market economy, in which the industrial economy is the basic field and the urban economy and the international economy represent the generative field. Independent but also related to each other, they are competition systems at different levels in one modern market economy. In addition to the horizontal system, there is also the vertical system of the modern market, which comprises six pillars, namely, the market factor system, the market organization system, the market legal system, the market supervision system, the market environment system and market infrastructure. The six function pillars in the vertical system of the modern market will act on the various fields in the horizontal system. That is, the vertical system of the modern market, which itself has been gradually improving as history moves on, exerts impact not only on the industrial economic field, the economic foundation of all countries in the world, but also on the urban economy of all countries, even the deep-sea economy and the space economy as various kinds of generative resources are developed and utilized. The economy in different fields and of different types produce different participants, which calls for the establishment and constant perfection of a multi-level modern market system to support economic activities and regulate economic participants. The multi-level market system outlined by the GFL, one that is different from the traditional market theory, will have theoretical significance for the economic development of countries around the world.

Lastly, the GFL illustrates the government's all-round role in the market economy. As mentioned above, the effectiveness of the government should encompass three aspects: First, appropriately distributing non-operative resources and implementing supportive policies, maintaining social harmony and stability, and improving and optimizing the economic development environment; secondly, appropriately distributing operative resources and implementing supportive policies, maintaining market openness, fairness and justice, and substantially raising the overall production efficiency of the society; and thirdly, appropriately distributing quasi-operative resources and participating in the competition, and advancing the comprehensive and sustainable development of urban construction, the economy and the society at large. In a word, the effectiveness of the government are embodied in the government's distribution of the three types of resources, the formulation of supportive polices, and the obtainment of related objectives; and the three standards of an effective government are: respecting and following market rules, maintaining economic order and stabilizing economic development, effectively distributing resources and participating in regional competition.

To sum up, the GFL offers an answer to the "Goldbach Conjecture in economics," that is, what the relationship between government and market should be, by putting forward the "strong market" mechanism and the "strong government" role, the former referring to that it should be the market to decide the resource allocation of the industrial economy and urban economy and that market rules should play the essential part in the competition of the industrial economy and urban economy, and the latter referring to that the government should, while following market rules, be the main participant of urban economy, the main implementer of industrial policies, and the main provider of people's welfare. The GFL proposes an economic operational mode that combines effective government and an efficient market. It represents revolutionary innovations to the existing economic system, especially the market economy theory, and will help countries around the world find new engines of economic growth and promote the scientific and sustainable development of the world economy.

Notes

1 Chen, Y. (2011). *Foresighted leading: Theoretical thinking and practice of China's regional economic development*. Peking University Press, pp.15–32.

2 Chen, Y., & Qiu, J. (2013). *Government foresighted leading: Theory and practice of the world's regional economic development.* Peking University Press, pp.114–116.

3 An Institute for Manufacturing Innovation (IMI) is a partnership between the industry and a university or research entity and is established with the support of the federal or local government of the United States. Each IMI focuses on a specific sector and is devoted to combining public and private resources to create a more dynamic national innovation ecosystem with the goal of transforming inventions into products faster and accelerating the development of small and medium-sized enterprises.

4 1 mu ≈ 666.7 m^2.

5 Chen, Y. (2011). *Foresighted leading: Theoretical thinking and practice of China's regional economic development.* Peking University Press, pp.128–131; People's Daily. (2016). Pearl River Delta says goodbye to old towns, factories, and villages. May 23.

6 Chen, Y. (2011). *Foresighted leading: Theoretical thinking and practice of China's regional economic development.* Peking University Press, pp.47–56.

7 *Work report of Guangdong Provincial government*, January 25, 2016.

8 New engines of economic development

8.1 Kindleberger trap and endogenous growth theory

To discuss the building of new engines for the regional economic development of countries around the globe necessitates a review of two economic theories, the Kindleberger Trap and the Endogenous Growth Theory.

The Kindleberger Trap was brought forth by Joseph S. Nye, a well-known US political scientist and professor at Harvard University, who wrote in January 2017 in his article "The Kindleberger Trap", "Charles Kindleberger, an intellectual architect of the Marshall Plan who later taught at MIT, argued that the disastrous decade of the 1930s was caused when the United States (US) replaced Britain as the largest global power but failed to take on Britain's role in providing global public goods. The result was the collapse of the global system into depression, genocide, and world war."

Nye points out, "Small countries have little incentive to pay for such global public goods. Because their small contributions make little difference to whether they benefit or not, it is rational for them to ride for free. But the largest powers can see the effect and feel the benefit of their contributions. So, it is rational for the largest countries to lead. When they do not, global public goods are under-produced."

In Nye's view, "as US President-elect Donald Trump prepares his administration's policy toward China, he should be wary of two major traps that history has set for him. The 'Thucydides Trap,' … refers to the warning … that cataclysmic war can erupt if an established power (like the USA) becomes too fearful of a rising power (like China). But Trump also has to worry about the 'Kindleberger Trap': a China that seems too weak rather than too strong."[1]

Yet a meticulous examination would show that China has actually played a fairly constructive role in the global governance system, contributing in multiple ways in different stages, from capital supply to institutional construction and then to conceptual innovation. China has been contributing more capital to global governance since 2008, injecting capital to promote multi-lateralization of the "Chiang Mai Initiative," to the International Monetary Fund, and to the World Bank. China's participation in global governance in

DOI: 10.4324/9781003244837-8

terms of institutional construction is marked by its launching the "Belt and Road" Initiative and starting the Asian Infrastructure Investment Bank in 2013, and its proposal to build the New Development Bank of BRICs in 2014. Moreover, since 2016, starting from the Hangzhou Summit of the G20 in particular, China has started contributing ideas and thoughts to global governance. From capital to institutions and then to ideas, China is gradually becoming a mature and responsible leading country.

In Kindleberger's view, global public goods encompass the international trade system, the international monetary system, capital flows, macroeconomic policies, crisis management mechanisms, etc. Joseph E. Stiglitz, Nobel laureate in economics and professor at Columbia University, classifies global public goods into five major categories, namely, international economic stability, international security, international environment, international humanitarian assistance and knowledge.

If we put aside the political and ideological disputes suggested by the Kindleberger's Trap and only examine it from an economics point of view, we will find that it entails at least three questions. First, what are global public goods, or in other words, what products count as global public goods? Second, who should provide the global public goods? Third, in what ways should such global public goods be provided or accepted?

Let's put aside the three questions for the time being and turn to the Endogenous Growth Theory. The Endogenous Growth Theory is a macroeconomic theory branch that originated in the mid-1980s. Its core idea is that the economy can grow sustainably without relying on external forces and that endogenous technological progress is the decisive factor of sustained economic growth. This theory emphasizes incomplete competition and progressive increases in returns.

Since the era of Adam Smith, the entire economics circle debated over the factors driving economic growth for more than 200 years and came to the following broad consensus: a nation's economic growth over a long period of time mainly depends on three factors, the accumulation of productive resources over time, the utilization efficiency of stock resources with the nation's technological knowledge unchanged, and technological progress. However, the neoclassical economic growth theory, which rose to popularity in the 1960s, takes technological progress as an exogenous factor to explain economic growth and concludes that long-term economic growth will eventually come to a stop as factor income diminishes. Then, the Endogenous Growth Theory newly formed in the 1990s holds that long-term growth rate should be attributed to endogenous factors and that the labor input process includes human capital arising from formal education, training, and on-the-job training and the material capital accumulation process includes technological progress arising from R&D, innovation and other activities. That is to say, the Endogenous Growth Theory internalizes technological progress and other factors to come to the conclusion that technological progress will bring a progressive increase of factor income and thereby positive long-term growth rate. This means the neoclassical economic growth theory and the Endogenous Growth Theory would go in different directions in terms of policy recommendation.

As theories develop, many economists have realized that the biggest challenge faced by the Endogenous Growth Theory is to conduct empirical analysis. In practice, such empirical research is carried out along two technical routes. One is to study a particular country to find evidence of endogenous growth, and the other is to look into factors of economic growth according to a nation's data over a long period of time or to examine the effect on the economic growth of one specific factor, such as opening up policies, taxation, equality, financial progress, education expenditure and innovation.

I have no intention to elaborate on the relevant models of the Endogenous Growth Theory and its modern development or discuss the revival of the so-called Neo-Schumpeterism. I just want to reiterate that traditional economists studying a country's economic growth factors still, even now, confine themselves to the industrial economy as described by Adam Smith, still looking for new driving forces for growth in the industrial economy and still believing that technological progress is the deciding factor of endogenous growth.

I do not mean to pass judgment on whether the Endogenous Growth Theory is right or wrong. I just want to point out the following. First, the endogenous growth of an economy should refer to the sustainable development of a nation's economy. Second, the discussion on factors of endogenous economic growth should not be confined to an industrial economy but should encompass the three economic fields of the industrial economy, livelihood economy and urban economy. Third, I do not object to traditional economists looking for endogenous growth drivers (such as technology) from the standpoint of resource scarcity in the industrial economy, but now we should spend more efforts looking for endogenous growth impetus from the resource generation in the urban economy. And fourth, new generative resources, now mainly the urban economy represented by the investment into and construction of hard and soft urban infrastructure as well as the development and operation of smart cities, and in the future also the economy in new sectors such as space, deep sea, polar areas and the internet, are not only societal quasi-public goods, but also global quasi-public goods. They are a new economic growth pole in the world, or in other words, new engines for global economic development.

Let's take foreign aid, a kind of global public good, as an example. Foreign aid is related to the three types of resources and the three types of economy and could accordingly be classified into three types, social, economic, and environmental. Foreign aid that is associated with the livelihood economy of countries around the world has public welfare nature and thus could be termed social foreign aid, that associated with the industrial economy is like commodities and could be called economic foreign aid, and that associated with the urban economy could be referred to as environmental foreign aid. Social foreign aid includes international disaster relief, assistance, poverty alleviation, medical treatment and education, and other aids with public welfare nature that are supplied to the international community for free through the United Nations and other organizations. Economic foreign aid includes products related to the three major industries that are commodity-like and are supplied to the international community through import and export and related institutional arrangements between countries in conformity with market rules. One example of environmental foreign aid is the investment into and construction of hard and soft infrastructure between countries, which in nature could be aid or commercial, or both. How environmental foreign aid is supplied is determined by many factors including the relationship between the countries involved.

Thus far we have discussed the three types of resources and the three types of economies, their characteristics and how governments should correspondingly establish supportive policies, and have extended our discussion along this line to the classification, characterization and supplying of foreign aid. This could be of great help to answering the questions entailed by the Kindleberger's Trap: What global public goods are, where they should come from, and where they should go. The field of new generative resources, primarily infrastructure investment and construction, represents quasi-public goods on a global scale, as well as new engines for national and even global economic development.

8.2 Arrival of the era of urbanization-led economic growth

The rivalry between big economies and vying among cities is a common landscape across the world, including in China. An economy participates in global competition mainly with its cities, a nation's innovative capacity is exhibited with its cities, and how the market and the government should interact with each other is to be explored with the cities. The Foshan City of Guangdong Province, where I served as Secretary of the CPC Municipal Committee and Mayor, is constantly measuring itself against other domestic cities with similar economic aggregates, such as Chengdu, Wuhan, Hangzhou, Nanjing, Qingdao, Changsha, Wuxi, Ningbo, Dalian and Zhengzhou. These cities are benchmarks for one another and together constitute a "sample pool" of urban innovation and for exploring new paths of sustainable growth of the urban economy.

Emulating the effective measures taken by other big cities, Foshan has made many plans and arrangements. First, as one of the three major manufacturing cities, the other two being Wuxi and Ningbo, Foshan should enhance its real economy, focus on intelligent manufacturing, and in particular, speed up building itself into a base of "Made in China 2025." Second, drawing upon the experience of Chengdu, Wuhan and Nanjing in cultivating new industrial clusters, Foshan will foster new economic growth poles in intelligent equipment, new energy vehicles and other fields. Third, Foshan will link itself to Guangzhou, the adjacent "mega city," and offer cross-city services. Fourth, Foshan should compete for investments and businesses and try to attract Fortune Global 500 companies. Fifth, the city should innovate financially to better serve the real economy. Sixth, Foshan should take urbanization and the integration of industries and the city as the new pivot of its competition with other cities. Seventh, as regional competition and cooperation has entered the "city agglomeration era," Foshan should learn from Wuhan's and Chengdu's experience in building hub cities, specifically, their experience in expediting the construction of major transport hubs, to build three-dimensional transportation, and make every effort to carry out a new round of infrastructure construction. Eighth, Foshan should hasten the construction of a smart city, establish a new service system desirable for living, business and tourism, and find a new "key" to tapping the potential of urban economic growth.

Foshan is only one example. The three major economic growth poles in China—Beijing-Tianjin-Hebei, the Pearl River Delta and the Yangtze River Delta—are all making urban-rural planning, advancing infrastructure construction, planning the industrial layout, protecting the environment, and improving public service quality, so as to push forward regional integration and sustainable development of the regional economy. These efforts have delivered remarkable results. Now the three economic circles are seeing their infrastructure integration progressing in order, the division of labor between and cooperation among regions improved, new-style urbanization promoted steadily, and the building of national sponge cities and national urban underground pipe galleries carried out as planned. Besides these areas, city agglomerations in other regions in China have also made unremitting efforts and taken many significant measures with remarkable attainments in promoting regional coordinated development and cultivating new economic growth poles.

In addition to regional governments' valiant efforts, the central government has also been devoted to investing in and advancing big science projects, major science and technology projects, and major science and technology platforms. The building of an interconnected rural transport network is also shaping a new infrastructure structure and promoting urban-rural integration. Infrastructure constructions of transportation, municipal administration, energy, water conservancy, information, environmental protection and others are laying solid foundations for the cultivation of new economic growth points and will continuously produce massive economic and social benefits.

The era of urbanization-led economic growth has arrived. As far as China was concerned, 2013 was an especially noteworthy turning point. That year the economic landscape of "industrialization taking the lead with urbanization lagging behind" and the growth mode primarily relying on the industrial economy begun to change. Urbanization became a new driver of economic growth and in return started pushing the gradual transformation and upgrading of the industrial economy.

Putting the whole world under examination, we could see that since before half a century ago the global population has been gathering towards big cities, and that clear positive correlations exist between city scale and economic efficiency and between city population and per capita output, that is, the larger a city is, the higher its productivity. This is true of the USA, Japan, the Republic of Korea, Singapore, Australia, Canada, etc., whose economic activities are concentrated in large metropolitan areas with far greater economic output than other areas.

Public-Private Partnership (PPP) is an effective model to unite the government and the market to promote city development. Darrin Grimsey and Mervyn K. Lewis suggested in the book *Public Private Partnerships: The Worldwide Revolution in Infrastructure Provision and Project Finance* that the greatest advantage of the PPP model lies in the introduction of market mechanism into infrastructure investment and financing. Specific effects include (1) bringing in competition mechanism to propel government integrity building; (2) alleviating the fund shortage resulting from government's lack of money and accelerating infrastructure construction and public utility development; (3) giving full play to the initiative and creativity of foreign and private enterprises to improve project operation efficiency and service quality; (4) furthering the perfection of market laws, regulations and institutions; (5) promoting technology transfer; (6) training professionals and experts; (7) promoting financial market development; (8) reducing capital expenditure of foreign and private enterprises and thus enabling them to "undertake big projects with small investments; (9) alleviating the debt burden of investors through off-balance-sheet financing and (10) making use of limited recourse to share risks, strengthen control over project income, and maintain a high investment return rate (as compared to full recourse).

In its endeavor to build the "One Belt, One Road," China is turning industrial parks along the Silk Road into large platforms that support economic interconnections and industrial development. Starting from building traffic hubs such as seaports, airports and inland waterless ports, China takes the industrial parks neighboring these ports as main carriers to systematically mend the hard and soft weaknesses of host countries restricting their industrial transfer, and has in this way summed up an effective development model, the PPC (Port-Park-City) model. At the core of this model is the development, construction and operation of ports. The goal is to, through developing supportive city functions on the basis of port management and industrial park construction, enable host countries to realize interconnected development of the region and thus form a relatively complete ecological circle integrating port, logistics and financial park. The PPC model has become a new trend in establishing trade interconnections of countries along the "One Belt, One Road," and the international economic cooperation mode characterized by "infrastructure construction + supportive industrial park" has become a new mode of international economic growth.

Infrastructure construction is playing an increasingly important role in economic development. In 2016, KPMG International envisioned ten major trends in infrastructure construction worldwide over the next five years: in the great tide of global economic development, (1) the macro risk environment has begun to shift, (2) investment competition is heating up, (3) the government will clear obstacles impeding infrastructure investment to bring economic and social benefits on a larger scale, (4) urban facility management is taking more diverse forms, (5) technological revolutions are quicker in exerting impact on infrastructure construction, (6) security is becoming an important issue in urban construction, (7) there's room for public-private partnership in infrastructure construction, (8) various institutions would bring about a rapid rise of infrastructure investment through financial innovations, (9) infrastructure construction would enter the era of debt-financed investment and operation and (10) China and India are becoming more active and are developing rapidly. KPMG's report was an observation and prediction of global infrastructure construction and revealed a possible path of world economic growth.

The Research Report on Economic Focus of G20 (2016–2017) also endorsed the importance of infrastructure construction, observing that a salient feature of the economic operation of the Group of 20 is the investment into and construction of infrastructure and that infrastructure construction is an important engine driving the recovery and sustainable growth of the world economy. The report pointed out the following. (1) The demand for infrastructure construction is huge across the world as emerging and developing economics are troubled by seriously inadequate infrastructure supply and developed economies are experiencing gradual aging of existing infrastructure. (2) During a period of global economic downturn and investment inefficiency, advancing investments in infrastructure, especially encouraging and optimizing high-quality investments, will strongly motivate economic growth, create employment and raise productivity, both in the short term and in the long run. (3) Increasing investments in infrastructure, as a part of the new growth strategy, is a common focus of the G20 and a key agendum in the G20 Summit. On the G20 Summit held in November 2014, member countries agreed to establish a Global Infrastructure Hub with a four-year mandate. The Hub was intended for providing platforms and networks of knowledge sharing to governments, the private sector, development banks and other international organizations and fostering collaboration among these groups so as to improve the financing and functioning of the infrastructure market. (4) In October 2014, the World Bank launched Global Infrastructure Facility (GIF) to specifically cater to the implementation of complex public-private infrastructure projects and encourage the private sector to play a stronger role in infrastructure investment. (5) In recent years, the BRICS club and Asian countries have also attached importance to joint construction of infrastructure as part of their economic cooperation, achieving tangible collaborations such as the New Development Bank (NDB) of the BRICS countries and the Asian Infrastructure Investment Bank. (6) A Global Infrastructure Hub estimation points to a lack of investment amounting 10 trillion dollars to 20 trillion dollars in the infrastructure market by 2030, which will adversely affect global economic development. Therefore, in 2016, the Global Infrastructure Hub called on governments across the world to re-focus on infrastructure investment, take advantage of development opportunities with high investment potential, and thus invigorate the global economy. The prospect is clear that with the continuous deepening of regional and global economic integration, the demand for infrastructure that spans and connects different regions and countries will go up constantly, bringing a new round of opportunities for global infrastructure construction. The rapid growth of infrastructure investment will be an important engine driving the recovery and sustainable growth of the world economy.[2]

Chapter 5 "Regional Government Competition" of this book analyzes the scale effect, cluster effect and neighborhood effect of urban economic development, which mainly involves the investment and construction of hard and soft infrastructure and the development and operation of smart cities. As the economic growth of countries across the world is entering the new era of urbanization and urban-rural integration, global infrastructure investment and construction are uniting all countries into one community of shared destiny. To fully tap the potential of infrastructure investment and construction as the new engine for world economic growth, all countries need to invest resources, coordinate with each other, formulate rules and advance relevant work accordingly.

8.3 Building new engines for global economic development

In 1948, Ragnar Nurkse likened trade to the growth engine of the 19th century to justify the propounded strategy of import-substituting industrialization. During the financial crisis from 2012 to 2014, the annual growth rate of global trade was lower than 4%, far below the average growth rate before the crisis, which was about 7%. This led World Bank officials to once again raise the question of how to "restart" the global trade engine. My observation is that generally the economic development of all countries around the world develops from the factor-driven stage to the investment-driven stage, and then to the innovation-driven stage. Many countries that drive economic growth with tangible factors such as land and labor, especially economies rich in natural resources such as oil, natural gas, minerals and agricultural products, have reached the ceiling of growth capacity with signs of unsustainability.

Hence, new engines are needed to realize economic growth in the new century. I believe that in the modern market system made up of "effective government plus efficient market," new structural engines on the supply side (rather than "trade engines" on the demand side) will give full play to the role of enterprises in allocating industrial resources and that of governments in allocating urban resources during competition. These new structural engines on the supply side include investment engines, innovation engines and rule engines that involve both tangible and intangible factors, and will have an important impact on global economic governance and development.

8.3.1 Building new global investment engines

Investment-driven growth depends on two aspects, both on the supply side, one being the allocation and competition of products and industrial resources, the other being the government's performance in the competition concerning urban resource distribution and infrastructure construction. Investment-driven growth is sustainable in the long run because it brings capital growth to countries, promotes technological innovation, deepens market mechanisms and increases employment. In order to build new global investment engines, the following measures should be taken.

The first is to promote supply-side structural reform, which should cover the following two aspects:

The first aspect is to advance new industrialization. New industrialization refers to industrialization that is driven by informatization and that in return advances informatization. It is industrialization that features high tech, brings good economic benefits, consumes less resources, incurs little pollution and makes full use of the region's human resource advantages. To advance new industrialization, efforts should be made in three aspects. The first is to support and steer the transformation and upgrading of traditional industries. The use of scientific and technological progress in application fields could transform old resource-consuming and environment-damaging industries into new recycling industries. By supporting and guiding enterprises to transform their technologies, countries could revitalize huge amounts of stock assets, optimize and lift industrial benefits, stimulate demand, and thus promote economic growth. The second is to support and cultivate strategic emerging industries and high-tech industries. Countries should, on the foundation of the information industry, develop incremental assets such as intelligent industry. Intelligent industry is a new industrial structure with human intelligence, computer network and physical equipment as basic elements, and it has a green growth mode. Countries should grant support to the nurturing, R&D innovation, achievement transformation and industrialization of essential and key technologies of enterprises, cultivate advantageous industries and leading industries, and build a complete and sound industrial chain and a modern service network. The third is to make use of market competition to promote mergers, acquisitions, integration and reorganization of enterprises, constantly weed out old industries, promote the development of new industries, elevate industrialization to a higher level, and enhance the core competitiveness of enterprises. This is one of the important means to realize effective investment on the supply side and shift from old growth forces to new ones.

The second aspect is to expedite the modernization of agriculture. Agriculture modernization refers to the process traditional agriculture transforms to modern agriculture. It's the process of agriculture benefiting more and more from modern industries, modern science and technology and modern economic management techniques. Countries should use modern development ideas to fuse agricultural development with ecology conservation and transform outdated traditional agriculture into eco-agriculture at a productivity level that is advanced in the contemporary world. Specifically, agricultural modernization entails not only a larger scale of cultivated land but also the "modernization of farmers." Countries should help farmers overcome ignorance and backwardness to become "educated, skilled and capable" modern farmers. For both large farms and small household-run farms, countries should support and help farmer cooperative organizations as well as individual farming households to connect to the market so that whole-process services covering pre-production, mid-production and post-production stages could be provided and whole-process operation from production material purchase to the storage, processing, transport, and sales of agricultural products could be realized. Moreover, countries should encourage scale operation and urbanization, both to appropriate degrees, and promote the professional provision of agricultural technology education. To summarize, agricultural modernization necessitates advanced production means, scientific production technologies, industrialized operation mode, agricultural service provision by the private sector, region-wide industrial layout, and the overall modernization of agricultural infrastructure, ecological environment, agricultural laborers' ability, and farmers' lives. The modernization of agriculture can create a stable social environment for industrialization and urbanization, reduce overall costs of the society, and benefit the economies across the world.

The second is to step up infrastructure investment and construction, which should cover the following three aspects:

> The first aspect is advancing new urbanization, that is, urbanization characterized by coordinated urban-rural planning, urban-rural integration, industrial interaction, conservation and concentration, ecological livability, and harmonious development, urbanization where cities of large, medium and small sizes, small towns, and new rural communities develop concurrently in a coordinated and mutually-promoting manner. In developed countries urban population generally accounts for more than 80%. As urban-rural integration picks up speed and urban patterns with cities at the center take shape in most countries, the planning and building of new human-oriented towns, the construction of basic urban-rural public service facilities such as education,

healthcare, culture and sports, and the development of recreation, tourism, business, logistics, the information industry, transportation, etc. will all offer new growth potential to countries around the world.

The second aspect is advancing the modernization of infrastructure, which includes the modernization of energy, transportation, environmental protection, information and agricultural irrigation. Specific measures include the following: building comprehensive urban transportation systems and fabricating convenient and fast regional transportation network; speeding up the construction of sponge cities and strengthening cities' disaster prevention and mitigation ability; building and improving the drainage and waterlogging prevention system to reduce urban waterlogging risks; treating black and odious water bodies and recovering urban water quality and water environment to a good state; increasing parkland in the region to allow urban residents to enjoy a green life; building urban underground pipe galleries and making sure the pipelines operate in an orderly and efficient way; building and improving urban water supply facilities and having in place a sound system to ensure water supply security; optimizing urban energy supply and vigorously promoting urban energy conservation and emission reduction; raising the efficiency and capacity of waste and sewage treatment facilities to achieve saving, recycling and reutilization of resources; and improving information infrastructure to promote the development of smart cities. Investment in infrastructure modernization, with ample room for flexibility and great potential, could be an effective driver of economic growth across the world.

The third aspect is developing and building smart cities. A smart city is a system, also known as a network city, digital city or information city. With human brain intelligence, computer network, physical equipment, etc. as the basic building elements, a smart city features smart urban management, specifically, smart infrastructure including intelligent transportation, intelligent electricity, intelligent buildings, intelligent environmental protection and intelligent security, smart life involving intelligent healthcare, intelligent education and intelligent household, as well as smart production entailing intelligent enterprises, intelligent banks, and intelligent stores. A smart city system will comprehensively modernize urban production, life, management and operation and create new economic growth points for countries across the world.

The third is to increase investment in scientific and technological projects. Examples include the National Network for Manufacturing Innovation (NNMI) of the USA, which invested one billion dollars in the first phase and set up 45 innovative manufacturing institutes in 10 years, the Knowledge Transfer Partnerships (KTP) scheme of the UK, and Industry 4.0, a German strategic initiative aimed at intelligent manufacturing upgraded by cyber-physical systems (CPSs). These measures can pool the innovative resources of talents, enterprises and social institutions, steer industrial R&D into the right direction and promote the upgrading and development of industries. The investment of countries across the world in big data, cloud computing, the Internet of Things (IoT), NBIC (nanotechnology, biotechnology, information technology and cognitive science), etc. will help achieve sustainable upgrading of economies across the world.

The fourth is to raise financial support capacities. Countries need to introduce supportive policies to direct the financial sector to better serve the real economy and also need to promote the integration of finance, science and technology and industries through policy innovations. The reform, innovation and development of the financial system are indispensable for the new investment engines.

8.3.2 Building new global innovation engines

Either it is a region, a country or the world, when its economic development mode transitions, its economy transitions from industrial resources being allocated by enterprise competition to urban resources being allocated through regional government competition, and its economic growth engine transitions from the single market mechanism to the "effective government + efficient market" mechanism. Such new economic development circumstances that are taking place around the world would inevitably lead to a series of new problems, for example, how to maintain the fairness and justice of the global economic governance system, how to protect the interests of developing countries in the global economic order, how to maintain and strengthen the openness of the economic system to fight against protectionism, and how to formulate norms to face challenges posed by new economic fields such as the internet. Rising to these challenges requires innovation and improvement of the existing public mechanisms and public goods (including ideological, material, organizational and institutional public goods) that coordinate and govern the global economic order.

First, innovation of value public goods, that is, concepts, should be advanced. To begin with, the market should be an efficient market. The vertical system of modern market is a complete system composed of six subsystems. Some countries over-emphasize the competition between market factors and market organizations and overlook the building of the legal supervision system and the perfection of the market environment system and market infrastructure, which will result in deviations from the market principles of openness, fairness and justice. Moreover, the government should be an effective government. Governments across the world should not only plan, guide, support, coordinate, supervise and manage the allocation of operative resources, that is, industrial resources, but also guarantee the basic needs, ensure fairness and justice, and raise the effectiveness and efficiency of non-operative resources, that is, public goods, and also adjust and participate in the competition of the allocation of quasi-operative resources, that is, urban resources. Furthermore, countries around the world should pursue a mature market economic mode featuring "strong form of effective government + strong form of efficient market," that is, with industrial resources allocated through enterprise competition and urban resources through government competition in the macro system of the market economy. Governments across the world should play an important role in global economic growth.

Second, the innovation of material public goods, that is, technologies, should be advanced. Currently, the most typical path of scientific and technological development is combining information technology with industrialization, urbanization and agricultural modernization to promote the modernization of infrastructure, a path that could be summarized with a term that is now popular in China, "internet +." By building smart cities that combine tangible and intangible factors, governments could provide public transport, urban management, education, healthcare, cultural services, commercial services, administrative services, environmental protection, energy services and public security services to the society in an information-based manner and therefore create a safe, efficient, convenient, green and harmonious development environment for the society's economic and welfare undertakings. These could benefit the people and in addition accelerate the industrialization, urbanization and internationalization of cities and countries, thus contributing to the rise of emerging countries.

Third, the innovation of organizational public goods, that is, management, should be advanced. Commonalities could be found in the organization and management of cities and countries across the entire world. Traditional city structuring and planning, often described as "urban sprawl," is prone to traffic light failure, road congestion, traffic jams, air pollution, low efficiency and other problems despite large-scale transport facilities already in place such as the first, second, third, fourth, and even fifth ring roads. Modern urban development requires scientifically planned grouped layout, which could solve the series of problems brought about by traditional "urban sprawl," just like how network development will reshape spatial order and how global supply chain development will "erase national boundaries." The organization and management of the world economic order, similar to urban structuring, has to transition from the "sprawl" mode towards grouped layout and constantly innovate, which nevertheless requires corresponding new rules and necessary "infrastructure" investment for a rational layout to be formed to promote harmonious and sustainable development of the world.

Fourthly, the innovation of institutional public goods, that is, rules, should be advanced. The construction of a country is under the guidance of a three-part overall planning system composed of conceptual planning, urban-rural planning and land planning. Under this framework, meticulous and minutely layered specific guidelines concerning strategic planning, self-positioning, standard making, policy evaluation and legal protection are formulated. Rules for global economic governance have the Charter of the United Nations and the regulatory mechanisms of the United Nations Conference on Trade and Development (UNCTAD), the OECD and WTO as the framework to make sure countries around the world strive towards "making globalization bring more opportunities" and "letting the fruits of economic growth benefit all and be shared by all." The importance of rules in global economic development is evident. Faced with the current new circumstances, we should innovate economic growth ideas and relevant institutional rules, push forward the fiscal and monetary structural reform in various countries, and maintain the consistency and mutual coordination among economic development, the labor force, employment and social policies. To realize healthy and sustainable growth of the global economy, equal weight must be placed on both demand management and supply-side reform, short-term policies must be combined with medium-term and long-term policies, socio-economic development must be advanced concurrently with environmental protection, and the global economic governance landscape must be discussed, established and enjoyed by all countries.

8.3.3 Building new global rule engines

A sound global economic governance system is required for the building of world economy featuring "Four I's," that is, innovation, invigoration, interconnection and inclusiveness. Corresponding to non-operative resources across the world is the international public goods supply system, corresponding to operative resources is the international industrial resources allocation system, and corresponding to quasi-operative resources is the global urban resources allocation system. These systems each operate in adherence to their respective rules that exist on their own. A sound global economic governance system requires corresponding international rules, which comprises the following:

First, the rules on international security order, peace and stability, are a common understanding of all countries and offer basic guarantee for the international public goods supply system. Countries across the world should work together to strengthen international cooperation in security-related matters, protect the purposes and principles of the Charter of the United Nations and adhere to the basic rules of international relations to create a peaceful, stable, just and reasonable international security order and establish a healthy and orderly environment for economic development.

Second, the rules regulating international economic competition, fairness and efficiency, are also basic requirements on enterprises in their competition in the industrial resources allocation system across the world. For instance, the G20 formulated the guiding principles of promoting trade and investment openness, including reducing tariffs and non-tariff barriers to trade, reducing barriers to and restrictions on foreign direct investment, adopting trade facilitation measures to reduce cross-border transaction costs, appropriately reducing border restrictions on trade and investment, promoting broader cross-border coordination, and minimizing discriminatory measures against a third party through multilateral and bilateral agreements. Another example is the guiding principles of promoting competition and improving the business environment, which specifically entails the following measures: strengthening and implementing competition laws, reducing administrative and legal barriers to starting enterprises and expanding businesses, promoting fair market competition, implementing efficient bankruptcy proceedings, reducing restrictive provisions that hinder competition, reducing unnecessary burdens in terms of regulatory compliance, having concrete supervision over the regulatory policies, strengthening the rule of law, uplifting judicial efficiency, fighting against corruption, etc. All these are the rules on fairness and efficiency that countries across the world need to adhere to when steering and regulating enterprise competition.

Thirdly, the rules on international common governance, cooperation and the pursuit for win-win situations, are basic rules that intergovernmental competition must adhere to in the urban resources allocation system. Both tangible and intangible factors exist in urban resources, among which new urbanization, smart city construction, and investments in the modernization of infrastructure for energy, transportation, environmental protection, information and water conservancy will be new engines for economic growth across the world. These engines will bring about the following positive effects: capital expansion, employment increase, technological innovation, deepening of the market, sustainable growth of the economy, social benefits, environmental improvement and growth of national strength. The effects and competitiveness of investment-driven growth differ from country to country due to their variant pace of urbanization, policy measures and institutional arrangements, but despite the differences, the competition between governments should be cooperative, conducive to sustainable development, and aimed for jointly improving the global economic governance system and innovating modes of economic growth. The basic principle of such competition should be win-win cooperation. The construction of an innovative, open, interconnected and inclusive world economic system with win-win cooperation at its core will contribute to sustained innovation in growth modes and improve global economic governance, thus benefiting all countries and the world at large.

8.4 Cases for reading and thinking

This chapter focuses on the function of generative resources as new economic engines, and in this section, several cases will be analyzed to elaborate on how infrastructure construction, rural revitalization, urban development and resource drilling, among other areas, are driving economic growth.

The first case is the USA's restarting massive investment in infrastructure.[3]

Donald Trump said the night he won the presidential race in 2016: "We are going to fix our inner cities and rebuild our highways, bridges, tunnels, airports, schools, hospitals. We're going to rebuild our infrastructure, which will become, by the way, second to none. And we will put millions of our people to work." Trump spoke highly of China's infrastructure construction and regarded China's bridges and high-speed rails as models that the USA should learn from. On April 30, 2019, the two parties of the USA agreed on a massive two-trillion-dollar investment to fund a national infrastructure upgrade. The agreement on the investment was a start for the implementation of Trump's infrastructure plan.

In fact the USA has experienced times of infrastructure frenzy before, the most typical being Roosevelt's New Deal that began in 1933 aimed at increasing employment and stimulating consumption and production through massive-scale infrastructure projects. Under the New Deal, more than 7.4 million acres of state-owned forest areas and a large number of state-owned parks were opened up through the Civilian Conservation Corps (CCC) program, and the Public Works Administration and the Civil Works Administration were created which constructed 180,000 small-scale projects nationwide. By the eve of World War II, the federal government of the USA had, with an accumulated investment of nearly 18 billion dollars, built nearly 1,000 airports, more than 12,000 sports fields, more than 800 schools and hospitals, and created a lot of jobs. Another typical period of infrastructure construction in the history of the USA was the 1950s after World War II, when the country, under the initiative of President Eisenhower, began to build the Interstate Highway System, constructed railroads across the country, erected large dams and set up a telephone network, which greatly stimulated economic development.

Yet now six decades later most infrastructure in the USA has been used for more than half a century and has reached the designed service life, and is in need of major repair or reconstruction. In its 2017 report, the American Society of Civil Engineers rated the overall state of infrastructure in the USA "D+," meaning the infrastructure conditions range from poor to okay, in most cases below standards with many facilities reaching the end of their useful life, and a considerable proportion of the facilities being obviously damaged, and that the conditions and service capacity of the infrastructure are very worrying with great risks of failure and destruction.

Where will the money for rebuilding the nation's infrastructure come from? The first source will be the gasoline tax, which has been the main source of funds for the federal government to invest in highways, bridges and public transportation since Eisenhower. But the US gasoline tax rate has not been increased for many years and now its actual value is only 40% of what it was worth 20 years ago. The US Chamber of Commerce and the American Trucking Associations have taken the initiative to suggest raising the federal gasoline tax, which has not changed since 1993, in order to finance road construction. The second source of funds is Public–Private Partnership (PPP) financing. The USA plans to let states and local and city authorities make their own decisions in fundraising and attract private investors with tolled roads, deregulation and other favorable conditions so as to build a capital pool for infrastructure construction of up to 1.8 trillion dollars made up of investments from states, local governments and the private sector. The third source would be the return of overseas capital induced by the massive tax cuts in the country. Trump's tax cut plan is estimated to reduce tax by about 1.4 trillion dollars in the next 10 years. The big cut on the corporate tax rate—from 35% to 20%—means the profits previously left overseas by a large number of US companies because of the high corporate tax will flow back to the country. The fourth source of funds would be Chinese capital. As of February 2019, China holds 1.13 trillion dollars of US Treasury bonds. Actually, for a long time a large proportion of China's foreign exchange reserves have been invested in US Treasury bonds. To instead invest in infrastructure construction in the US will bring China higher returns. Moreover, since now there are few US companies engaging in building large-scale infrastructure, a large proportion of the infrastructure construction in the country will be undertaken by Chinese infrastructure companies.

How will the USA rebuilding its infrastructure affect the world economy? As we all know, economic growth is mainly driven by investment and consumption. The large-scale infrastructure construction in the USA will bring substantial increases in investment, which will then drive consumption, and given the size of the USA as the world's biggest economy, such growth in investment and consumption will drive the global economy, especially China's economy, for one thanks to China's strongest infrastructure construction enterprises in the world, huge construction workforce, and high-quality managers and technicians, and for another because China is the biggest producer and exporter of consumer goods in the United States. Chinese construction machinery enterprises are now also globally competitive, with nine among the top 50 in the world. It could be envisioned that Chinese infrastructure enterprises and construction machinery enterprises will directly benefit from the US infrastructure investment.

The second case is China's efforts in rural revitalization.[4]

In September 2018, the Chinese Government issued the 2018–2022 Strategic

Planning for Revitalization of Rural Areas (the "Planning"). Comprising 11 parts which are then divided into 37 chapters, the Planning sets forth phased plans for the implementation of the rural revitalization strategy toward the general goal of building rural areas characterized by industrial prosperity, ecological livability, good civics, effective governance and well-off life. The third, sixth and ninth parts of the Planning are particularly worthy of attention.

The third part, titled "constructing a new framework of rural revitalization," touches upon the following aspects: Coordinating the space of urban and rural development (strengthening the control over space use, improving the structure of urban and rural layout, and conducting unified planning of urban and rural areas), optimizing the layout of rural development (coordinated use of production space, reasonable allocation of living space, and strict protection of ecological space), advancing rural development by village type (villages to be clustered and upgraded, suburban villages to be integrated, villages with special features to be preserved, and villages to be relocated, demolished or merged), well fulfilling the formidable task of targeted poverty alleviation (taking concrete measures to support the poor and lift them out of poverty, focusing on tackling entrenched poverty, and consolidating the achievements of poverty alleviation), etc.

The sixth part, titled "building ecologically livable and beautiful countryside," covers the following aspects: Promoting green development of agriculture (strengthening protection, conservation, and utilization of resources, promoting clean agricultural production, and treating outstanding problems of agricultural ecology), continuously improving living conditions in rural areas (remedy major weaknesses as soon as possible, improving the appearance of villages, and establishing and improving long-term mechanisms for countryside renovation), strengthening rural ecology protection and restoration (carrying out major projects for the conservation and restoration of important ecosystems, establishing sound systems for protecting important ecosystems, establishing sound compensation mechanism for ecological protection, bringing out the multiple benefits of natural resources), etc.

The ninth part, titled "ensuring and improving the quality of life in rural areas," involves the following aspects: Strengthening infrastructure construction in rural areas (improving the transportation and logistics facilities and conditions, constructing a sound water conservancy infrastructure network, building a modern energy system, and establishing a good foundation for informatization), improving the employment quality of rural labor (offering more channels for rural population to be employed in cities, providing more and better services for rural employment, and improving relevant institutional guarantee), increasing the supply of public services in rural areas (giving priority to education, advancing healthcare, building a sound social security system, improving the service capacity of elder care, and strengthening disaster prevention, mitigation and relief capacities), etc.

These measures of the Chinese government will not only help rise to the daunting challenge of rural poverty and improve people's lives in rural areas, but also, while speeding up agricultural modernization and advancing urban-rural integration, build better rural infrastructure, improve the urban-rural layout, promote the revitalization of villages, and therefore lead to new growth of the urban and rural economy.

The third case is about city development.

The Globalization and World Cities (GaWC) Research Network, a world-leading city research institution, ranks global cities into four levels: Alpha, Beta, Gamma and Sufficiency. In the list of world cities released by GaWC in 2018, Guangzhou was among the Alpha cities together with Los Angeles, Toronto, Madrid, Zurich and other international cities.[5]

GaWC's evaluation criteria last for 132 pages and include the following: internationality (being well-known); active engagement in international affairs and international influence; big population; important international airport (as center of international routes); advanced transportation system (such as expressway and/or large public transportation network that provides diversified transportation modes); for Asian cities, attracting foreign investment and having immigrant communities, and for western cities, having international cultural communities; hosting international financial institutions, law firms, corporate headquarters (especially of enterprise groups), and stock exchanges, and playing a key role in the world economy; having advanced communication equipment (such as optical fiber, wireless network, mobile phone services, and other high-speed telecommunication lines that are conducive to transnational cooperation); having internationally renowned cultural institutions (such as museums and universities); having strong cultural atmosphere (such as film festivals, premieres, lively music or theater venues, symphony orchestras, opera troupes, art galleries, and street performers); powerful and influential media outlets with global view; strong sports communities (such as sports facilities, local league teams, and the ability and experience of staging international sports events); and for coastal cities, having large and busy ports.

Guangzhou was ranked a Gamma city (no. 109) in 2000, rose to no. 40 in 2016, and entered the Alpha level for the first time in 2018 (ranked no. 27 among first-tier world cities). Guangzhou's success is attributable to a number of factors, of which the city's efforts to build itself into a "hub" that stimulates regional economic innovation and accelerates connections with the world have made indelible contributions. Among the "three strategic hubs" Guangzhou has planned to construct itself into a networked hub city, two are directly related to urban infrastructure and transportation, one being building itself into a strategic hub for international shipping and the other a strategic hub for international aviation. These efforts have accelerated the flow of production factors between Guangzhou and its surrounding regions and countries, driven innovation and promoted economic growth.[6]

The fourth case is the resource drilling efforts by various countries, many of whom have now started carrying out deep earth exploration, space exploration, ocean exploration, etc., and have achieved preliminary results.

China's achievements in the field of deep-earth exploration are an example. In June 2018, China's "Crust-1" 10 km drilling rig was successfully applied in the second scientific drilling well project, completing a 7,018-meter-deep hole, a new record of continental scientific drilling among Asian countries, which made China the third country after Russia and Germany with special equipment and technologies for carrying out 10 km land-based drilling programs. China plans to carry out more ultra-deep scientific drilling projects and advance efforts in deep earth exploration.[7]

In space exploration, Japan has made exemplary efforts. In 2009, Japan issued the first "Basic Space Plan" according to its Basic Space Law enacted in 2008, specifying that space development is to be addressed as part of Japan's national strategy.[8] Since then, the Plan has been continuously updated and improved to cover a wide range of activities including military aerospace, civil aerospace, aerospace industry foundation and international cooperation. It can be seen that as human beings are entering space and cyberspace after the third wave of the industrial revolution, Japan has joined space wrestling alongside the USA, Russia and other countries.

Countries have also made progress in marine exploration. A series of articles published by the *Economist* in May 2018 points to new opportunities in developing and utilizing marine resources that would present themselves to human society with the continuous development of science and technology, with seabed mining and ocean aquaculture showing particularly good prospect. For example, the six million square kilometer Clarion Clipperton Zone in the Pacific Ocean is strewn with trillions of fist-sized mineral nodules, each formed after tens of millions of years of slow condensation on the basis of a bone, a shell or a rock. The academia believes that the nickel, cobalt and manganese contained in these mineral nodules exceed the total amount that has been ascertained on land. Seabed mining will open up a new way for humans to obtain mineral resources, and ocean aquaculture will help rectify the serious pollution brought by offshore aquaculture. Now Belgium, Norway and some other countries have started experimenting and exploring new ways of developing and utilizing global marine resources to promote new global economic growth.

Notes

1 Nye, J. S. (2017, January 9). The Kindleberger trap. *Project Syndicate*. https://

www.project-syndicate.org/commentary/trump-china-kindleberger-trap-by-joseph-s--nye2017-01?barrier=accesspaylog.

2 Li, J., Li, M., Zhao, X., Zhou, T. (Eds.). (2016). *Research Report on Economic Focus of G20 (2016–2017)*. Economic Science Press, pp.39–42.

3 Yang, L. (2019, May 4). *U.S. to rebuild infrastructure with two trillion USD: Chinese economy will benefit*. http://www.sohu.com/a/311699959_114502?spm=smpc.author.fd-d.13.1568095275084OCwWeHc.

4 CPC Central Committee and State Council issued "2018–2022 Strategic Planning for Revitalization of Rural Areas." (2018, September 27). *Nanfang Daily*.

5 Guangzhou and Shenzhen both ranked first-tier world cities. (2018, November 15). *Nanfang Daily*. http://epaper.southcn.com/nfdaily/html/2018-11/23/content_7765263.html.

6 Secrets behind Guangzhou's rise to a first-tier world city. (2018, November 23). *Nanfang Daily*. http://epaper.southcn.com/nfdaily/html/2018-11/15/content_7763614.html.

7 Debut of "Crust 1" 10 km drilling rig a success, creating new depth record. (2018, June 4). *People's Daily*.

8 Japan issued first "Basic Space Plan." (2009, June 3). *Science Times*. http://news.sciencenet.cn/htmlnews/2009/6/219812.html.

Part III

9 On the dual-entity of market competition (DEMC)

9.1 Modern market economic system

9.1.1 The horizontal system of modern market

After these systematic analyses, this chapter will further clarify that in the horizontal market system, there are not only enterprises, as major players in the industrial economy, but also regional governments, which play a dominant role in the urban economy, as well as market players, including enterprises and governments that provide quasi-operative resources, or public goods, in the international economy, such as space economy and marine economy. To conclude, first, there is a market not only in industrial economy but also in other forms of economy. Second, in the horizontal market system (including industrial economy, urban economy and international economy such as space economy and marine economy), there are dual entities in market competition, enterprises and governments. At last, industrial economy is the basics of market economy, whereas urban economy and international economy (including space economy and marine economy that emerge with the progress of the times) are fields that can generate resources for market economy. Mutually independent yet interrelated, they have a competition of their own at different levels of the modern market economy. Collectively, the multi-level market competition systems constitute the modern market economy.

The traditional market theory, also known as firm equilibrium theory, specifically studies how firms determine the price and output of their products in different types of markets. As a result, there are four types of market structures that can characterize an economy: Perfect competition, monopolistic competition, oligopoly and monopoly. Therefore, the traditional market theory takes the market, firms and industries; cost, income and output; and even firm's equilibrium in perfect competition, monopolistic competition, oligopoly and monopoly as targets of research. As discussed previously, first, the traditional market theory focuses mainly on the industrial economy, or rather, the theory itself is elaborated within the framework of the industrial economy. Second, Adam Smith's *The Wealth of*

DOI: 10.4324/9781003244837-9

Nations, though undoubtedly a pioneering masterpiece in economics and market economic theory, has limitations of the times. After criticizing mercantilism and physiocracy, Adam Smith mainly concentrated on the industrial economy in his investigation into the relations of commodity, price, supply and demand, competition and market, and failed to touch on new generative resources and relevant economic fields. Third, faced with the massive unemployment of the United Kingdom (UK) in the 1920s and the Great Depression sweeping across the United States USA) and even beyond to the whole world in the early 1930s, Keynes attempted to shift to investment and construction of infrastructure to stimulate effective demand. However, he also confined himself within the framework of the industrial economy and failed to make clear the roles of governments in their participation and intervention in urban economy. Finally, as discussed earlier, contradictions between economic practice and theory, as reflected through market failure or government failure, in essence, are not due to problems of the market, but are rooted in the traditional market theory. Such contradictions have not resulted from incomplete or imperfect market theory of industrial economy, but are an inevitable outcome when the traditional market theory is applied in defining, analyzing and explaining the operation of fields of new generative resources.

Urban economic theory, in the narrow sense, mainly studies why the government provides public goods and maintains market rules on one hand and participates in the investment and competition of projects during the process of investment, construction, operation and management of the software and hardware urban infrastructure, and even in the building of a smart city on the other hand. As public goods, why do some infrastructure projects become operative in the market system and are able to drive forward the development of the regional economy? Market entities, projects, prices and supply-demand relations under urban economic theory are different from that in the industrial economy. In addition, as an important part of the horizontal market system, the urban economy, with various generative resources, is playing an increasingly important role both in practice and theory.

Apart from the urban economy, the generative economy also includes international economies such as marine economy and space economy. On one hand, these new generative resources expand the scope of the market, which requires further efforts to make exploration and optimize allocation while on the other hand, we need to enrich market theories and improve market rules in accordance with these new changes. A recent report claims that it is time to make "aerospace" a big business. According to news reports, China Rocket will develop commercial launch service, sub-orbital flight service and space resource utilization as its major business fields. For example, on commercial launch service, the company will supply space satellite networks, space lifts, space shuttles, space-tailored services to the market. For sub-orbital flights, the company will customize services such as ground zero-gravity locomotion simulation, 360-degree VR experience, sub-orbital passenger travel in accordance with ages, physical conditions and interests of customers. Backed by the vigorous Chinese aerospace industry and setting high standards as US space exploration companies, China Rocket plans to gradually inject assets, introduce strategic investors and promote the advent of commercialization era of Chinese rockets. Major powers around the globe have already begun the race in this field which rewards high investment returns. Under this circumstance, how to define "aerospace economics?" How to develop it? How effective will it be? These are questions confronted by the aerospace economy and even beyond to space economy. These new circumstances are constantly broadening the economic fields of the market on one hand and calling for interpretation over investors and relevant rules of the game for these emerging industries, on the other.

9.1.2 The vertical system of modern market

The traditional market system can be illustrated from four perspectives. First, in terms of circulation, the traditional market is composed of the commodity market and market of factors of production. Second, in terms of spatial range, it consists of regional markets of various levels in various regions. Third, in terms of institutional mechanism, it includes various market entities and intermediary organizations. Last, on the basis of the period of transaction carried out, it can be divided into spot market, forward market and futures market.

In contrast, the modern market system highlights the systematic nature of the market structure, especially the functional structure of the market, which primarily focuses on interest adjustment, and then the competition system, followed by the information exchange system. So, the vertical system of modern market covers at least the six following aspects:

i. The market factor system, which is made up of various types of markets, including the commodity market, production factor market and financial market, as well as basic elements of the various types of markets, such as price, supply and demand, and competition.
ii. The market organization system, which consists of market entities or organizations, including various types of market entities, for instance retail market, wholesale market, talent market, labor market and financial market, various market intermediaries in areas like consultation, training, information, accounting, law, property rights and asset valuation, and market management organizations, such as various chambers of commerce and industrial associations.
iii. The market legal system. Market economy features the characteristics of property rights economics, contract economics and normative economics. Therefore, laws and regulations that regulate market value

orientation, transactions, contracts and property rights, constitute the market legal system as a whole. It is composed of legislation, administration of justice, law enforcement and legal education relevant to the market operation.

iv. The market supervision system, which is based on the market legal system and complies with the implementation of economic policies in the supervision and administration of institutions, markets, business activities, and the implementation of policies, laws and regulations.

v. The market environment system, which consists of the real economy as the basis of the market, corporate governance structure and social credit system. The core of this system lies in the establishment and improvement of a market credit system by way of regulating trust relations, credit instruments and credit intermediaries through a sound legal framework as well as a social credit mechanism that is based on it.

vi. Market infrastructure, including various hardware and software market facilities. Among various market infrastructure, market service networks, supporting facilities and technologies, various market payment and settlement systems, and technology information systems are the necessary components of a mature market economy.

These six pillars of the modern market system have the following characteristics:

First, the formation of the vertical system of a modern market takes a gradual historical process. Take the USA as an example. In the early development of market economy, when the laissez-faire mode prevailed in the mainstream, the market factor and market organization systems enjoyed sound growth and government intervention in the economy was generally opposed. In 1890, Sherman Antitrust Act, the first legislation enacted by the American Congress, was introduced to curb cartel agreements and monopolistic practice. In 1914, the USA promulgated the Federal Trade Commission Act and the Clayton Antitrust Act to clarify and strengthen the Sherman Antitrust Act. Since then, the anti-monopoly and regulatory system in the USA experienced evolution and progress of nearly a century, and thus forming a pattern of dynamic coexistence of monopoly and competition, development and regulation. Since the 1990s, information communication and Internet technology in the USA have boomed, and innovation and infrastructure upgrading become the main driving forces of market competition. Meanwhile, the objective of the American government's endeavor in anti-monopoly is no longer to simply restrict market monopoly and price manipulation, as technological monopoly and network oligopoly, apart from patent protection, are incorporated into the anti-monopoly campaign. During this period, the market environment and market infrastructure of the country have been further developed and improved with progress achieved on areas such as market registration, settlement, trusteeship and backup system, capacity-building in response to major disasters and technical failures, improvements in market information system, credit system, and market supervision data sharing system, all of which have pushed forward the American market system to a modern stage, so that its market competition has leaped into a stage driven by total factors of production and systematic participation of market entities.

Second, the six pillars are integrated in the market system. On one hand, they are interconnected and interactive, organically forming a mature market economic system. During the operation of the market economy, missing any single one of them will result in market deficiencies in one field or another, leading to economic losses to the nation. Such cases are commonly seen during the economic development of nations across the world. On the other hand, among the six pillars, various factors are also interconnected, interactive and organically integrated with each other. For example, in the market factor system, apart from the interconnections and interactions of various commodity markets, factor markets and financial markets, the standardization and development of land markets, gradual establishment of unified urban and rural labor markets, development of technology markets, vigorous improvement of property rights (including technological property rights) trading markets are all important ways to improve the modern market system.

Third, the six pillars operate in an orderly manner in a modern market economy and only then can ensure efficiency. For example, to build an orderly pricing mechanism of commodities, production factors and projects (of resources or of generative resources), the market should be given full rein to play its fundamental role in resource allocation, and prices shall be adjusted according to supply-demand relations, availability of resources and resource generation as reflected by the market, thereby promoting the orderly operation of the modern market system. It is also true to the orderly competition mechanism of commodities, factors and projects. Competition is inevitable in a market economy, and also a necessary path to market economy. Only through competition can the prices of commodities, factors and projects fluctuate in the market and resources can be allocated to the most efficient enterprises, regions or industrial links, thus realizing the survival of the fittest. So market segmentation, blockade and monopoly are all barriers to be removed in the modern market system. In addition, it is necessary to build an orderly open mechanism of commodities, production factors and projects. In the open modern market system, the market of commodities, production factors and projects are open to domestic and foreign investors from different regions and industries, all of whom can have access to various resources, choose supply and demand at free will, and make investment decisions independently and such openness must be gradual, secure, steady and orderly. So it shows once again that the six pillars are mutually independent yet mutually restricted, for example, competition and supervision, freedom and the rule of law, which together constitute a complete modern market system.

Fourth, the six pillars of the modern market system are fragile in function, because of several reasons. (1) Inadequate understanding. As market participants (namely those in the commodity market, factor market and project market) have their own interests in mind, in market operation in practice, they tend to focus only on freedom, competition and demand, rather than on rule of law, supervision and balanced development, which lead to malfunctions of the role of the six pillars. (2) Delay in policies. Various investors are the main participants of the market, while market supervision primarily relies on regional governments across the world. Traditionally, during interactions between the government and the market, affected by traditional economic theory, the government is usually a bystander, lags behind the market, or tries to patch things up or close loopholes only when confronted with economic crises, which makes all the six pillars unable to fully play their part. (3) The impact of economic globalization. In the global market system where legislation, joint legal enforcement and coordinated supervision mechanism are yet to be improved, there exist various problems such as regulation gaps, regulatory arbitrages, market speculations and frictions in cross-border development, as well as counterfeiting, fraud and theft. Hence, there is still a long way to go to further improve the modern market system and the effective functioning of the six pillars.

Fifth, the influence of the six pillars is affecting or will soon spread to all fields of the horizontal system of the modern market, which means that the modern market system that comes into shape over the course of history, will not only play a role in the industrial economy, the foundation of the world economy, but also in urban economy and international economy (marine economy, space economy, etc.) with the gradual development and utilization of various generative resources. Different fields and types of commodities, production factors and projects have attracted various participants in the market, which requires the six pillars of the modern market system to constantly improve their function, which in turn demands steady progress in contemporary economic theories, in particular, modern market economic theories.

9.1.3 Rediscovering market failure

"Market failure" originates from neoclassical economics, so our analysis over market failure will also mainly concentrate on the field of the industrial economy. Through theoretical analysis of the functional structure of the six pillars of the modern market system and case study of the USA from above, we can see that first, the improvement of market rules lags far behind the realities. During the infant stage of its economic development after its founding in 1776, the laissez-faire mode prevailed in the mainstream, during which period, the USA mainly put in efforts in establishing and improving the market factor system and market organization system. In 1890, the first measure, the Sherman Antitrust Act, was passed by the US Congress to prohibit trusts. Since then, particularly after the Great Depression during 1929–1933, the market legal system and supervision mechanism of the USA gradually improved. Since the 1990s, with mixed operations and booming growth of Internet, information and communications technology, the market environment and market infrastructure of the USA gradually made headway. So it is obvious that the formation of a complete and orderly modern market system, including its six pillars, the formation of its market mechanism and market rules, has lagged far behind the actual historical process of the American economy over the past two centuries. The complete market mechanism of the six pillars, has yet to be fully recognized and utilized in both theory and practice, which inevitably leads to market failure. Among the six pillars, the lagging of the market legal and supervision system is especially prominent. It is fair to say that during the economic development of the USA, from perfect competition to monopolistic competition, to oligopoly and then to perfect monopoly, its legal and supervision system has been repeating the path of "crisis-oriented operation," "upgrading by patching up" and "closing loopholes." Until this day, as monopolistic competition is shifting towards oligopoly, it is still controversial both in theory and practice regarding how to effectively regulate oligopoly by law. Important components of the modern market system, the legal and supervision system is indispensable to a complete market mechanism while measures like patching up or closing loopholes after crises can hardly create an open, equitable and just market environment for various kinds of investors, which inevitably will lead to market failure. Second, the realization of social demands has always lagged behind the satisfaction of the interests of market entities (manufacturers or other investors). The market produces competition, and competition promotes equilibrium. However, in reality, this equilibrium is mainly firm equilibrium, which is the firm's short-term or long-term equilibrium in product and price, cost and benefit, and supply and demand relations. The balance between social demands and interests of firms is basically missing in this equilibrium and public interests are mainly guaranteed through secondary distribution of wealth of governments across the world. However, market entities, in defending their own interests, may set obstacles to this cause, thus causing market failure. Due to the above reasons, deficiencies of the modern market economic system and market failure have become quite normal.

In reality, it is still a matter of dispute regarding whether industrial economy needs the government to formulate policies to "plan, guide, support, regulate, supervise and manage." But a common consensus is that in areas where the market fails to play a due role, namely in case of market failure, the government is expected to play an active role. For example, Joseph Stiglitz, a Nobel laureate in economics in 2001, expounded on the latest discoveries on market failure in his book *Creating a Learning Society: A New Approach to Growth,*

Development, and Social Progress in 2014. He believes that first, innovation (whether through imitation or intuition), which can create strong positive externalities, can become public goods of the whole industry in some cases, and so result in limited incentives for enterprises to further innovate. Second, information search and dissemination is also public goods in nature, so it is difficult to ensure it is fully provided on the strength of market mechanism only. Finally, in the infant stages of emerging industries, there can be insufficiency or even a total lack of market, which affects not only the market of their own products, but also the market of related factors of production. Therefore, in order to fuel the development of emerging industries, non-market forces are needed to play an active role in encouraging innovation, supplying information and fostering markets, and government intervention is the most prominent and effective force in this regard. Therefore, Professor Stiglitz suggests that government intervention might make up for market deficiencies and correct market failure in ways of the following: (1) industrial and trade policies, which will help promote knowledge accumulation and dissemination within an industry; (2) fiscal and financial policies, which are necessary prerequisites for the implementation of industrial policies; (3) investment policies, with which, the government can promote production and popularization of knowledge through subsidies; (4) the building of an intellectual property rights protection system, which gives incentives to individuals who invent, produce or disseminate intellectual creations. Hence, industrial policies are indispensable in order to promote the construction of a "learning society."[1] The Professors of Peking University have also acknowledged the necessities of industrial policies and put forward five optimum conditions for the adoption and implementation of industrial policies. (1) Industrial policies must conform to market trends. (2) Competition is encouraged, which is consistent with the opinion of Philippe Aghion, a representative figure in endogenous economic growth theory, on the relations between industrial policy and competition. (3) Cautious intervention. The government is not an ideal pilot developer's dream, but should strive to be a practical servant and do a concrete job where their duties lie. (4) An exit mechanism should be put in place and political economics shall be taken into consideration. (5) An evaluation system should be built. But of course, the establishment of a rational policy evaluation system and accountability system is in itself a topic worth studying in political economics.[2] From above, we can see that scholars such as Stiglitz still hold that the government and the market are separated from each other and market failure and policy measures to remedy market failures still exist mainly in industrial economy. As a matter of fact, this view represents the mainstream opinion of the global academic community on market failure.

However, as far as I am concerned, various theoretical and practical problems in the economic development of countries across the world are not about the market or market economy, but due to the lack of a modern market economic theory and the immaturity of the modern market economy. With progress in modern economy, it calls for a new economic system fit to it. According to previous analyses, the horizontal system of modern market includes industrial resources, urban resources which are currently vigorously exploited, and international resources (such as space resources and marine resources) which are yet to be developed while the vertical system of modern market includes six pillars, the market factor system, the market organization system, the market legal system, the market supervision system, the market environment system and market infrastructure. Together, they constitute a complete modern market system, and under this framework, each can fully play their own role and contribute to a sound modern market mechanism. However, there are three kinds of market failure under such market structure. The first one is due to *deficiencies in the market mechanism* and it is mainly seen in the hot-debated industrial economy. As discussed previously, to ensure the effective functioning of the six pillars, they have to function as a whole and in an orderly manner. If defects and deficiencies occur, the modern market system will manifest fragility and once the six aspects are unbalanced, it will also lead to fragility of various kinds and levels. Such market failure can take place at various stages of economic development. The second type is caused by *gaps in the market mechanism*, which is common in the investment, development and construction of new generative resources. Traditional economic theory has no such concepts as "resource generation" and "generative resources," and hence can hardly be applied to explain the development and operation of urban economy with infrastructure construction as the key. When theories on industrial economics find no way to go in the case of urban economic development, economists turn to blame the government for intervening in the market, which results in the vacancy of guiding economic theories on investment, development and construction of new generative resources (including space economy and marine economy to be vigorously developed in the future) across the world and missing of the role of market mechanism. The third category of market failure occurs because of *barriers to the market mechanism*. From above, we know that the industrial economy and urban economy alike, are obliged to comply with the modern market mechanism, so that the six pillars of the modern market system can fully play their part. However, as market entities in both industrial economy and urban economy are driven by profits, artificial barriers that go against market rules can easily arise, thus hindering the openness, equity and justice of the market.

Various fields in the horizontal system of the modern market should follow the rules of the six pillars. In the markets of commodities, factors of production and projects, instruments such as prices, supply and demand, and competition should come into play, so that market players abide by market rules in competition and follow the principles of allocation of resources by the market, in order to realize openness, equity and justice of the market. So we have to make clear the types of market failure before prescribing the right medicine, and take targeted and effective measures to ensure the market plays a decisive role in allocation of resources while the government plays a better role.

9.2 A mature and effective government

9.2.1 Government foresighted leading

In my opinion, a mature and effective government should lead with foresight so that enterprises do what they should do while governments do what enterprises cannot do or cannot do well, and both are inevitable. Government foresighted leading means to guide, regulate and monitor industrial economy, allocate, participate in and safeguard the order of urban economy, and guarantee, support and elevate livelihood economy based on market rules and on the strength of market forces. So it requires the government to utilize measures of planning, investment, consumption, prices, taxation, interest rates, exchange rates, laws and regulations for policy, conceptual, technological, organizational and institutional innovation to effectively promote supply-side or demand-side structural reform, cultivate leading edges in economic growth, and drive forward scientific and sustainable development.

As mentioned in Chapter 7, in theory, government foresighted leading and Keynesian government intervention are fundamentally different in terms of the time action is taken, focus and policy instrument, the role of the government and operational mode. We will not go into details again here.

On the practical level, most nations are now at a critical period of economic transition, social transformation or exploration to overcome the "middle income trap." Against this backdrop, industrial transformation and urban upgrading through government foresighted leading have become one of the development paths nations across the world are exploring. I would like to take my own experience when serving as Mayor and Secretary of the Foshan Municipal Committee of the CPC in Foshan, Guangdong Province in around 2010 as an example in an attempt to explore specific measures of government foresighted leading.

With a total area of 3,797.72 km^2 and home to nearly 6.9 million permanent population in 2009, Foshan's total GDP reached nearly 500 billion yuan and its per capita GDP surpassed 72,167 yuan ($11,000), ranking eleventh among China's large and medium-sized cities. In the late stage of industrialization or the early stage of post-industrialization, it was increasingly urgent for Foshan to accelerate economic transformation and urban construction, under the new circumstances of industrial restructuring, urbanization and internationalization. Based on its actual conditions and through in-depth investigations, five major strategies were introduced to propel its industrial restructuring and urban upgrading as practices of "first trial and first execution."

First, "double transfers" and "emptying the cage for new birds." The Foshan Municipal Government actively implemented the "double transfers" (transfer of industries and labor forces) strategy by providing bank loans, discount government loans and financial guarantees to close down or relocate, upgrade, and cultivate a good number of enterprises so as to realize "emptying the cage for new birds" and accelerate industrial transformation. Specific measures are as follows:

(1) A huge number of enterprises have been closed down or relocated. Over 1,200 enterprises with backward facilities and outdated capacity have been renovated or shut down, covering ceramics, cement, dyeing, small aluminum casting and glass, among which, 649 enterprises have been closed down due to high pollution and energy consumption. Meanwhile, over the recent years, labor-intensive enterprises have been guided for relocation to late-developed regions, resulting in about 460 projects being transferred to industrial parks in mountainous regions in Guangdong, which not only clears up space for Foshan's industrial restructuring and upgrading, but also injects strong impetus to economic growth in late-developed regions.

(2) A good number of enterprises have been upgraded. Traditional industries have been transformed into heavy, high-tech and high-end ones via integration of informatization and industrialization and supporting manufacturing with matching services. Take ceramic manufacturing as an example. Only 50 enterprises, which have fully achieved clean production and clean technology for reengineering, have survived after three years' renovation and upgrading from among more than 400 manufacturers in 2007. Their original manufacturing locations have been transformed into multifunctional bases for headquarters, exhibition, R&D, logistics, information processing, etc. In three years, ceramic production in Foshan dropped by 40% while its output value and tax revenues increased by 33%, energy consumption and sulfur dioxide emissions down by 25% and 20%, respectively.

(3) A number of enterprises, from areas such as new pharmaceuticals, environmental protection and electric vehicles and especially those from fields like optoelectronics, new materials and modern services, have been nurtured through investment attraction and selection so that newly emerged industries such as new energies (solar photovoltaic) and new light sources (LCD display) have rapidly taken shape. All these measures have effectively cut the proportion of traditional industries and turned Foshan into a national demonstrative base for new industries and for optoelectronics industry. Besides, new cities, new industries and new communities have been developed through the renovation of "three olds" (old towns, old factories, and old inside-city villages), which not only improves the efficiency of land utilization but also facilitates industrial restructuring, urban transformation and environmental reconstruction.

Second, launching large projects for industrial upgrading. In promoting industrial restructuring and urban upgrading, Foshan has attached great importance to investment attraction and utilization of policy instruments to promote financial investment (such as private equity investment and venture capital) for competitive projects from strategic emerging industries, advanced manufacturing and modern service industry. Foshan has expedited the cultivation of new industrial clusters and the establishment of a strategic highland of industrial development by investing in and introducing leading projects of international level. For instance, a project of electronic display panel module of Chimei Innolux has attracted investment from upstream supporting manufacturers of chips, panels, moulds, plastics and downstream manufacturers of complete television sets, so that a complete industrial chain for LCD has taken shape, which has facilitated industrial upgrading of household appliances in Foshan. In addition, a project of Xi'an Rainbow Organic Light-Emitting Diode (OLED) has driven forward the development of the third-generation crystal display, and a FAW-Volkswagen project has motivated the transformation of the entire auto parts manufacturing industry to form industrial clusters and complete industrial chains.

During this period, 87 projects of 47 Fortune Global 500 companies and 167 projects of 99 China's Top 500 companies have been introduced to Foshan. As a number of leading enterprises set their bases in Foshan, they play an exemplary role in technology, standards and brands, which helps vigorously improve Foshan's industrial structure and urban development level.

Third, advancing scientific and technological progress and independent innovation. Foshan has more than 347,000 registered enterprises at the time, among which over 100,000 are industrial enterprises. However, only 2,200 enterprises have an output value of more than 100 million yuan and among the rest, over 99% enterprises are small and medium-sized ones. Considering the local industrial structure, the government formulated guiding and incentive policies with a view to strengthening the industrial foundation, building brands, encouraging patent registration, establishing standards and exporting brands through integrated forces of finance, science and technology and industrial growth. Enterprises are encouraged and supported to formulate industrial standards, national and even international standards, develop cutting-edge technologies, and contract production to OEMs on the basis of their own brand norms, patents and product specifications.

During this period, the Foshan Municipal Government allocated a total of one billion yuan annually as incentive funds for enterprises to intensify scientific and technological development and independent innovation, which mobilized more than 22 billion yuan from enterprises for this undertaking in 2008, up by 47% over the same period of the previous year and more than 30.8 billion yuan in 2009, up by 39%, despite the impact of the international financial crisis. Such measures boosted industrial restructuring and urban upgrading and won Foshan honorary titles such as "Top Ten National Innovative Cities," "Chinese Brand Cities" and "Metropolis of Chinese Brands." Foshan has been the only prefecture-level city in Guangdong Province that has been awarded the title of "National Demonstrative City of Well-Known Trademarks and Famous Brands." By 2010, Foshan ranked top among prefecture-level cities in China in terms of patent application and registration, with a total of more than 130,000 applications and 86,000 registrations, and ranked fourth among China's large and medium-sized cities in terms of well-known trademarks and brands, with 42 well-known trademarks and 65 brand products.

Fourth, building leading industries through financial means. Relying on the strength of capital and financial means, the Foshan Municipal Government strives to promote cooperation between enterprises and the capital market for further expansion and growth. Three financial development initiatives were put into operation. The first one was the "463" program[3] for enterprise listing, which aimed to, from 2008 on, promote the shareholding transformation or launch of public listing of at least 100 enterprises within four years, and facilitate the successful listing of 60 enterprises at home or abroad, to reach gross financing of 30 billion yuan. Through this program, 26 companies successfully went public in 2010, steadily increasing from 13 in 2007, so that Foshan boasted a fleet of 102 listed enterprises. Besides, merger and acquisitions also contributed to industrial restructuring and upgrading. The second approach was to facilitate effective matchmaking between industries and finance by nurturing equity investment funds, guarantee funds for SMEs, talent funds, etc. During this time, Foshan had a variety of 15 funds with a total size of about 1.2 billion yuan, of which 126 million yuan was invested by the municipal and district governments, which played a leverage effect and attracted 1.1 billion yuan of private capital, thus speeding up the steps of enterprises to get listed on SME board and growth enterprise market. Besides, 45 enterprises planned to apply for IPO and more than 30 were guided to or planned to be restructured. What's more, financial innovation, including developing rural banks and small-loan companies lent support to industrial transformation and upgrading.

In addition, Foshan was designated by the United Nations Industrial Development Organization (UNIDO) as the only demonstrative city for industrial clustering and effective capital market operations in China and active measures were adopted to introduce foreign banks into Guangdong High-Tech Service Zone for Financial Institutions. During the time, agreements were signed for 28 projects to settle in the service zone, with a total investment of 6.579 billion yuan. Since the implementation of the Supplement VI to the Mainland and Hong Kong Closer Economic Partnership Arrangement[4], four Hong Kong banks have set bases in Foshan, which effectively strengthened the close links between capital market and enterprises in corporate restructuring and upgrading, and helped enterprises to establish a management mechanism of international standards. Besides, it could also help private firms, which accounted for 61.8% of GDP in Foshan, to establish the modern enterprise system for more vigor and vitality.

Fifth, implementing "Intelligent Foshan via Fourization." Keeping abreast with the global revolution of information technology and the trend of building intelligent cities, Foshan advocated the strategy of "Intelligent Foshan via

Fourization," namely the integration of informatization, industrialization, urbanization and internationalization, as a major breakthrough in leading Foshan's future development and economic transformation throughout the Twelfth Five-Year Plan period (2011–2015).

(1) Foshan endeavored to integrate informatization and industrialization to vigorously nurture and develop emerging industries, such as photoelectric display, RFID, the Internet of things, industrial design, service outsourcing, and transform and upgrade traditional industries. For instance, Longjiang Town, Shunde District was home to more than 1,700 furniture enterprises, but only a few among them boasted an output value of over 100 million yuan. Wayes Group, which customized services employing three-dimensional technology, revolutionized the business mode of the furniture industry from serving "ready-made furniture only" to customization, thus turning the buyers' market into the sellers' market and creating an aggregate sales volume of over 300 million yuan within just a couple of years. Another example is the Midea Group, who upgraded traditional household appliances to intelligent ones through the Internet of things, which brought about a new revolution in home appliances industry.

(2) Foshan endeavored to integrate informatization and urbanization, actively explore to incorporate telecommunications networks, cable television networks and the Internet into a unified system, and strive to build an intelligent service and administration system for smart transportation, public security, urban administration, education, health care, culture, commerce and government administration. By doing so, an "ubiquitous" Foshan would emerge and three leapfrog transformations from city administration to services, from governance to operations and from fragmented applications to integrated services could be realized, which would turn Foshan into an intelligent city friendly for living, business and development.

(3) Foshan endeavored to integrate informatization and internationalization. At the micro level, the government guided enterprises to build an internationalized system for R&D, production, marketing and services and strengthen their capabilities in competing in international markets, by embracing technologies such as the Internet of things, the Internet and Radio Frequency Identification (RFID), like employing the Internet of things to build Foshan into an international procurement center for ceramics and home appliances. At the macro level, through the construction of an "electronic port" across sectors, industries and regions, the government could provide "one-stop" services in electronic payment, logistics and distribution, electronic declaration, and electronic inspection for enterprises to enter into the global market through such "expressway."

Foshan's GDP amounted to 265.1 billion yuan in the first half of 2010, an increase of 13.8% over the same period of the previous year. At the same time, the proportion of advanced manufacturing, high-tech and modern service industries in the total GDP were on the constant rise. A sound modern industrial system was gradually taking shape and Foshan was heading towards the path to be an advanced city. Practice shows government foresighted leading is a sound path for regional industrial transformation and urban upgrading which can effectively expedite scientific and sustainable development of regional economy.[5]

Therefore, a mature and effective government should lead with foresight in social and economic development and government foresighted leading is the key to regional competition and growth. In competition, one's competitiveness lies in innovation and constant innovation guarantees constant competitiveness. Government innovation is the core of competition among regional governments around the globe. As discussed in Chapter 7, "foresighted leading in concept" is the important competitiveness of regional economy in the factor-driven stage; "Foresighted leading in organization" is the key of regional economy in the investment-driven stage; "Foresighted leading in institution and technology" is the core of regional economy in the innovation-driven stage; "Comprehensive foresighted leading" is the necessary path of regional economy in the wealth-driven stage.

9.2.2 Rediscovering government failure

As discussed previously, "the invisible hand" and "the night-watchman state" as endorsed by Adam Smith in *The Wealth of Nations*, were further popularized by classical economics and neoclassical economics. Faced with economic recession and massive unemployment in the UK and the Great Depression in the USA and beyond to the whole world from 1929 to 1933, John Maynard Keynes put forward a series of proposals and measures on government intervention, which was further developed by Keynesian economics. Since then, government intervention has been a significant instrument for western countries to regulate the economy. By the late 1970s, western nations were trapped in stagflation with vast unemployment, economic stagnation and high inflation rates existing simultaneously, a phenomenon the Phillips curve could not explain. Hence, the concept of "government failure" started to emerge and become a hot research subject in mainstream economics.

According to traditional economics, government failure, also known as government malfunction or government defect, occurs when the government intervenes in the economy and causes inefficiencies in the public sector due to poor allocation of goods and resources so that individual's demands for public goods are not met. Such intervention can cost much for public expenditure, yet result in low efficiency. In this way, the government makes decisions of intervention that reduce economic efficiency or fail to improve economic efficiency. There are a few types of government failure in traditional economics. First, government intervention in economic activities falls short of expected targets due to limited capability or other objective reasons. Second, even if government intervention lives up to the original expectations, it is low in efficiency or high in cost, resulting in inefficient utilization of resources. Third, although government intervention achieves expected goals and high efficiency, it brings about unexpected negative effects. Fourth, it takes more than a single government to resolve some externalities or international economic and trade issues, such as nuclear contamination and international trade disputes. From the perspective of traditional economics, several factors contribute to government failure: Deficiencies in public decision-making, low efficiency in implementation of public policies, uncertainties in public policies, rent-seeking, inherent defects of governments in economic regulation.

The author will not comment here on the above views. Instead, I will attempt to analyze and evaluate the role of regional governments in allocating the three types of resources and in economic development based on practical experience.

Every country or region has three types of resources and how to allocate these resources defines how effective a government is. As mentioned above, for non-operative resources (livelihood economy), government policies should follow the principle of "guaranteeing basic needs, ensuring fairness and justice, raising effectiveness and efficiency"; for operative resources (industrial economy), the government should support the market in accordance with the principle of "planning and guiding, support and coordination, supervision and management"; for quasi-operative resources (urban economy, and even space economy and marine economy, etc.), the government not only deploys resources and supervises the market, but also competes in the market. So in allocating the three types of resources, national or regional governments should adopt policies according to the features of each type of resources for balanced and rapid development of the social economy. Such policies are within the range of government duties, and also a necessary making of an effective government.

The government should play its due role in the market economy. However, there can be government failure anyway, including the following three kinds. First, *inadequate support for livelihood economy* can result in government failure. Some governments, without any effort to guarantee basic social needs or to raise effectiveness and efficiency of livelihood economy, take livelihood economy as a burden and fail to acknowledge the important role of an equitable and just livelihood economy on building a steady and harmonious environment which is friendly for starting up and doing business, living, and tourism. Such failure arises from ignorance. Second, *lack of industrial polices* can result in government failure, including lack of "planning, guiding and supporting" policies as well as "coordination, supervision and management" policies on industrial economy. Without these policies, or highlighting some policies while neglecting others, things might get out of control or will result in inappropriate interventions. Such failure comes from lack of proper administration. Third, *gap in urban construction* can result in government failure. For example, there are few or even no policies and measures to boost regional economic growth through urban construction (investment in and construction of software and hardware infrastructure, and even development and operation of smart cities), or even if there are some infrastructure projects, but their scales are so little and structure so poor that the government neither participates in the competition nor cares to regulate them. Or the government might participate in the competition but goes beyond the market rules because it has only administrative purposes in mind, invests without considering returns, focuses only on construction while neglecting operation, and considers only public interests and ignores economic benefits, which will lead to massive wastage of urban infrastructure resources, poor operation of urban construction, disordered urban management, etc. Such failure stems from lack of vision.

Regional governments across the world have both quasi-macro and quasi-micro attributes (also in economic globalization), and along with enterprises, they constitute the dual entities in market competition. It is a common topic for governments around the world to lead with foresight and work out ways for conceptual, technological, organizational and institutional innovation so as to avoid or reduce market failure and function as an effective government in an efficient market. The integration of an effective government and an efficient market will boost comprehensive, scientific and sustainable development of the global economy.

9.3 Dual entities of market competition

9.3.1 Both regional governments and enterprises participate in resource distribution

According to traditional western economics, national governments and regional governments alike should do what the market cannot do or cannot do well, which means governments step in only in conditions of market failure, which shows the passivity of governments in performing its duty in safeguarding market order. However, as analyzed above and as shown by practice, in the modern market systemic system, national governments and regional governments have both quasi-macro and quasi-micro attributes. Take regional governments as an example. Regional governments on one hand plays a macro role on behalf of the nation in administrating and regulating the local economy and on the other hand deploys resources on behalf of local enterprises and individuals in market economy and compete with other regional governments through conceptual, technological, organizational and institutional innovation to maximize regional economic profits at the micro level.

"Quasi" does not refer to any specific category, but to some extent, features some special characteristics or functions. When comparing regional governments and enterprises, it is obvious that regional governments are not enterprises, but behave like one at some degree. The "quasi-micro" attributes of regional governments, as mentioned in Chapter 4, are manifested in several aspects. First, regional governments are highly independent economically, which enables them to pursue maximum profits for the regional economy through conceptual, technological, organizational and institutional innovation. Regional administrators, through competition, will have pioneering spirits and foresighted vision, which is almost close to "entrepreneurship" as Joseph Alois Schumpeter upheld. Second, administration and management of regional governments can absorb advanced corporate management theories and practice and establish an efficient and effective internal operation and management mechanism. Third, regional governments should fully respect the decisive role of the market in resource allocation, play their due administrative role in accordance with market rules, and engage in "9-in-3" competition among regional governments so as to give full rein of its quasi-micro role.

Regional governments and enterprises are two different categories of market entities, with the former as dominant market players in mezzoeconomy and the latter principal market players in microeconomy. Regional governments and enterprises have profound differences in purpose of production, way of operation, management and evaluation standard, while they also share some similarities.

First, both regional governments and enterprises participate in resource distribution. As Ronald Coase argued, firms in essence is a resource allocation mechanism alternative to the market. Internal corporate management utilizes a series of measures in planning, organizational structure, human resources, and budgets in resource allocation with a view to maximized profits. For regional governments, they also have some public resources under their command and it is one of their duties to rationally and effectively allocate and utilize their resources for the maximum output. As mentioned in Chapter 4 and Chapter 5, the objective function of competition of regional governments is centered around the determination mechanism of government revenues. Under the principle of determining expenditures according to revenues, regional governments adjust investment, consumption and transfer expenditures through optimizing their fiscal expenditure structures and create a leverage effect through planning and guidance, making budgets, management and administration as well as relevant supporting policies in resource distribution. So we can see both regional governments and firms can play a part in resource distribution, only in different scopes and for different purposes.

Second, competition always exists among regional governments and enterprises and serves as an engine for regional economic growth. Competition among enterprises runs under market rules. In perfect competition, companies maintain a cutting edge in production cost in order to survive; in monopolistic competition, enterprises survive relying on their special values and core competitiveness; in oligopoly, it seems the market is dominated by oligarchs, but among them, there is still fierce competition. So competition among enterprises drives forward industrial development. Competition among regional governments also follow market rules. As discussed in Chapter 5, the "9-in-3" competition among regional governments mainly centers on: projects, industrial chains, imports & exports; infrastructure investment policies, talents and science & technology support policies, and fiscal and financial support policies; policy system efficiency, environment system efficiency and management system efficiency, which propels sustainable growth of industrial economy, urban economy and livelihood economy. So competition among regional governments is also a driving force for regional economic growth.

Third, both regional governments and enterprises operate under market rules. In market environment, enterprises need to constantly explore market rules and take good stock of the market trends to determine distribution of resources within enterprises. Only if enterprises obey market rules, keep a close eye on market fluctuations and make adjustments accordingly can they survive and thrive. So do regional governments. Only when they respect the rule that the market plays a decisive role in resource allocation, formulate effective industrial policies, participate in urban economic development as investors and competitors, can they steadily improve people's livelihood, drive forward regional economic and social progress with foresight and lead local regions to the top-notch level.

Fourth, primarily, both regional governments and enterprises distribute resources from the point of view of maximizing profits. As we have already analyzed how enterprises behave in pursuit of maximal interests, we will not go into details again. Regional governments, as independent competitors in the market, aim for maximized government revenues or namely maximized budgets, which more often than not, depend on regional fiscal revenues in association with the regional economic level and tax-sharing proportions of local governments. Tax-sharing proportions are usually fixed and fixed for quite a long time, so fiscal revenues are closely related to economic development level of a region. Therefore, regional governments, as market entities, inevitably will try to maximize their profits, for instance, by boosting regional economic output and taxation through conceptual, technological, organizational and institutional innovation. In this way, economic activities of regional governments are mainly subject to availability of regional resources, laws and regulations, institutions and social acceptability under market environment. The relations of these factors with regional government income can be illustrated as follows:

$$\begin{cases} Y = a \cdot b \cdot GDP \\ GDP = C + I + G + NX \\ C = f_1(G, A_i) \\ I = f_2(G, B_i) \\ NX = f_3(G, D_i) \\ st\colon G = f_4(R, Z, F, E) \end{cases}$$

Y: Fiscal revenues of a regional government, namely total government incomes minus revenues deducted through the tax-sharing scheme

a: The proportion of fiscal revenues of a regional government in total government incomes

b: The proportion of total government incomes in regional GDP

GDP: Referring to regional GDP here

C: Consumption; *I*: Investment; *G*: Government expenditures; *NX*: Net exports

Ai: Factors affecting consumption apart from behaviors of the regional government

Bi: Factors affecting investment apart from behaviors of the regional government

Di: Factors affecting exports apart from behaviors of the regional government

R: Regional resources; *Z*: Institutional restraint; *F*: Legal restraint; E: Social restraint

In this model, *Y* represents fiscal revenues of a regional government, a stands for the proportion of fiscal revenues of a regional government in total government incomes, namely the tax-sharing proportion, which is fixed within a period of time, b is the proportion of total government incomes in regional GDP, which is related to local tax rates, and thus is also relatively fixed. So increases in fiscal revenues principally depend on the local GDP. So when the economy booms, the fiscal revenues of the regional government will be high. Therefore, the optimal way to maximize government revenues is to grow local economy and yield a high GDP. As analyzed in Chapter 7, regional governments no longer passively receive taxes, instead, they need to play an active and direct role in local economy through a series of policies to guide and adjust company investment, consumer consumption, and imports and exports so that they contribute more to the local GDP, and thus yield a high fiscal revenue for the local government. But of course, all economic issues strive to "find extreme values under constraints" and so the role of regional governments and the level of fiscal revenues of regional governments are still subject to various factors such as regional resources, institutions, laws and regulations, and public opinions.

9.3.2 Relations between the dual entities in market competition

First of all, it should be noted that competition among enterprises is mainly concentrated in industrial economy while competition among regional governments is primarily in urban economy.

The dual entities in market competition operate in two separate ranges, one within the range of enterprises and the other regional governments, which are independent yet correlated, and together constitute the dual entities in market competition. Competition among enterprises resides in the micro level only, while regional governments are obliged to create a sound market environment and regulate and administer the market to ensure open, equitable and just competition among enterprises from the perspective of policies, institutions and environment, rather than just participate in competition at the micro level like enterprises. Besides, regional governments have no right to directly interfere with enterprises' affairs at the micro level. As equal competitors in mezzoeconomy, regional governments compete with each other in terms of regional distribution of resources, economic efficiency and profits. In this regard, regional governments should respect enterprise competition under market rules and leave enterprises outside of competition among regional governments.

Meanwhile, competition among regional governments rely on competition among enterprises while regional governments also guide, regulate and supervise enterprise competition. Competition of enterprises is a basic attribute of market economy and an important impetus for market economy. Without enterprise competition, there would be no market economy. While competition among regional governments, based on enterprise competition, support enterprise competition from aspects like market environment, policies and administration efficiency. Without enterprise competition, competition among regional governments would become strife of administrative power. So in the modern market economic system, competition among enterprises promotes competition among regional governments, which shows the soundness of the modern market system. Competition among regional governments is manifested in areas such as projects, industrial chains, imports and exports, talents, science and technology, capital, as well as policy, environment and management efficiency, which foresightedly leads enterprise competition. The relation between competition among regional governments and competition among enterprises can be illustrated as follows in Figure 9.1.

Figure 9.1 shows the independent yet correlated relation between

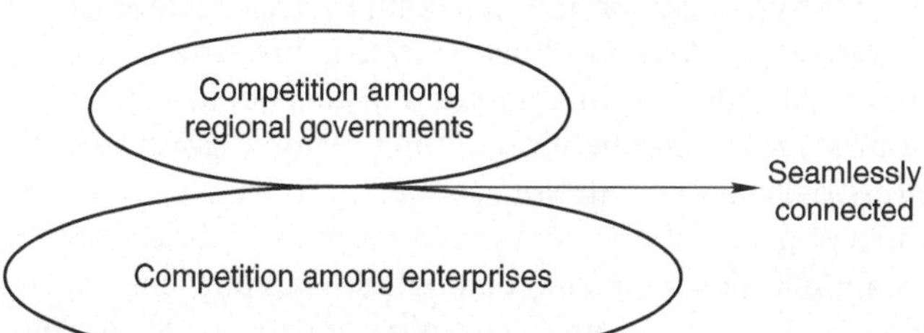

Figure 9.1 The relation between competition among regional governments and enterprises.

competition among regional governments and competition among enterprises. They are separated from each other, yet due to the foresighted leading role of regional governments, they are mutually supportive and closely related. How to distinguish the boundaries between the two is the key in dealing with their relations.

Besides, the core of enterprise competition is about resource allocation under conditions of resource scarcity while the center of competition of regional governments is resource allocation based on resource generation.

As analyzed in Chapter 2, the fundamental issue of enterprise competition at the micro level is about how to allocate resources under conditions of resource scarcity with its focus on price determination mechanism. Its major theories include those on equilibrium price, consumer choice, price determination of production factors, perfect competition and imperfect competition, general equilibrium, the game theory, and market failure. Research on competition among regional governments at the mezzo level concentrates on resource allocation on the basis of resource generation with the focus on major economic variables affecting regional competition, namely the revenue and expenditure of regional governments. Major theories in this field include the Resource Generation Theory, the Dual Attributes Theory of Governments, the Regional Government Competition Theory, the Theory of Resource Allocation in Four Development Stages, the GFL, the New Economic Engine Theory, the DEMC as well as the "Double Strong Forms" Theory of a mature market economy. So enterprises, regional governments as well as states, the research subject of macroeconomics, constitute the major forces of market competition in the modern market system (see Figure 2.1 in Chapter 2).

Competition among enterprises at the micro level and competition among regional governments at the mezzo level are both driving forces in the modern market economy and enterprises and regional governments are the dual entities in market competition which fuel up sustainable growth of regional economy or national economy.

In addition, both competition among enterprises and competition among regional governments end up in compliance with the 80/20 rule.

Professor of Business Administration at the Harvard Business School Michael E. Porter depicts four stages of national competitive development in *The Competitive Advantage of Nations*: Factor-driven, investment-driven, innovation-driven and wealth-driven. In Chapter 6 of this book, the author also illustrates the four stages of competition among regional governments: dominated by the industrial economy, urban economy, innovative economy, and competition and cooperation. From both economic theories and in practice of world economic development, competition among enterprises and among regional governments end up in compliance with the 80/20 rule. Or to put it in another way, in competition among enterprises and among regional governments, if enterprises and regional governments can develop a foresighted vision and adopt measures for conceptual, technological, organizational and institutional innovation for scientific and sustainable development, they are bound to distinguish themselves in industrial or regional development, while the rest would be left behind. Among all of them, 20% of the leading enterprises or regions will seize 80% of market shares and profits while the outdated 80% could only take the rest 20% (see Figure 7.2).

But of course in reality, driven by the dual entities in market competition, conceptual, material, organizational and institutional mechanism are shared to all enterprises and regions across countries as public goods, which brings development opportunities to backward companies and regions and also enables the outcomes of advanced enterprises and regions to be shared to more people. So, growth of enterprises or regions will be increasingly balanced. But it should be noted that as shown by both economic theories and practice, such balanced development is achieved in a gradient growth model.

9.3.3 Laws of regional competition

Laws reveal the inherent correlation of things and determine future trends. Laws possess the qualities of inevitability, universality, objectivity and eternity.

From above, we know that enterprises and regional governments are the dual entities in modern market economy and competition among enterprises and among regional governments are two engines boosting the development of industrial economy, urban economy and livelihood economy. In the practice of world economic development, these two varieties of competition follow three laws.

First, the congregating effect of the 80/20 rule. (1) There coexist competition among enterprises and competition among regional governments in the market. In microeconomics, the focus of study is about resource allocation under conditions of resource scarcity and enterprises play a dominant role in resource distribution. In contrast, mezzoeconomics considers resource allocation on the basis of resource generation and regional governments are responsible for it (macroeconomics studies resource utilization of nations on the basis of optimal resource allocation). So in market economy, they play different parts in the development of industrial economy and urban economy. Hence, competition among enterprises and among regional governments are independent yet correlated and complementary in modern market economy. (2) Competition among enterprises and among regional governments has different development paths. Competition among enterprises has four stages, which are respectively factor-driven, investment-driven, innovation-driven and wealth-driven, and result in perfect competition, monopolistic competition, oligopoly and monopoly. So in its development course, competition among enterprises is gradually growing weak. In the "9-in-3" Competition Theory, the competition evolves from dominated by industrial economy, to urban economy, then innovative economy and finally by competition and cooperation, which is actually growing strong. (3) Competition among enterprises and among regional governments worldwide end up following the 80/20 rule. In market economy, regional economic development is primarily growth through competition, which manifests a gradient model of economic development (see Chapter 6). Progress such as concentration of industrial chains, city clusters and improvement of social well-being is mainly seen in developed regions. So driven by the dual entities of enterprises and regional governments, regional economic development all over the world is displaying a concentration trend of progress in areas such as industrial agglomeration, formation of city clusters and improvement of people's livelihood in advanced nations or regions, demonstrating a gradient distribution pattern. So the congregating effect of the 80/20 rule is, to some extent, a reflection of the 80/20 rule.

Second, the equilibrium law of gradient changes, which exerts its influence in three phases. (1) In resource allocation, there coexist resource scarcity and resource generation. Resource scarcity is the prerequisite of enterprise competition while resource generation makes possible competition among regional governments. With progress of economic development, competition extends from enterprises to regional governments, from microeconomy to mezzoeconomy, from industrial resources to urban resources or even international resources such as space resources, marine resources and polar resources, so that economic growth worldwide will make substantial headway towards balanced development. (2) In terms of resource generation, there are "positive" resources (primordial resources and derivative resources) and "negative" resources (inverse resources), which can conflict with each other. Development of positive resources will be new fields of competition among enterprises and regional governments, which can propel economic progress and create new economic growth areas while development of negative resources can cause problems for regional economic growth and social harmony. When they conflict and restrain each other, regional economy can enjoy balanced growth. (3) Targets of regional economic growth are increasingly diverse. This is a necessary step in economic transition from factor-driven to investment-driven, innovation-driven, and wealth-driven. Economic growth no longer focuses on investment, consumption and export only, but more importantly strives for balanced growth of industrial development, ecological environment, social welfare and urban construction. In this way, regions nationwide will be heading for comprehensive and balanced development suitable for living, business and tourism, which motivates social progress in an all-round way. In pursuit of diverse development goals and adopting support policies and measures, regional governments find their way to balanced regional development, which on one hand promotes balance among industrial development, urban construction and social welfare within one region, and on the other hand, paves way for a balanced trend of industrial development, urban construction and social welfare across regions. The latter usually demonstrates equilibrium with gradient changes, so I call it "the equilibrium law of gradient changes." This is a subject worth further study.

Third, coordination law of competition and cooperation. (1) Coordination in policy. Enterprise competition adjusts the allocation of industrial resources while competition among regional governments adjusts allocation of urban resources and other generative resources through participating in project competition in the form of SOEs, joint ventures and joint-stock enterprises. So it is crucial to follow the principle of competitive neutrality, introduce proper industrial policies, adopt supporting measures and formulate policies in coordination with other regions and nations to boost new types of industrialization and urbanization, construction of smart cities, investment on scientific projects, infrastructure and agricultural modernization. So actually, competition among enterprises and among regional governments inevitably will result in coordination in policies. (2) Coordination in innovation, which is mainly in three aspects: large scientific projects which requires huge investment, takes long construction cycles and involves high risks; development of new scientific technologies; provision of conceptual, material, organizational and institutional mechanism as public goods to different sectors, regions and nations. In the transition of economic development mode and as social transformation deepens, regional coordination in innovation is an irresistable trend. (3) Coordination in rules. As said in Chapter 8, the law of regional economic competition, equity and efficiency, the common governing principle across regions, cooperation and win-win results, and regional security norms, peace and stability, will be listed high on working agenda of all participants in market competition as regional economic development further proceeds. So the essence of the coordination effect of competition and cooperation is to help market players foster advantages in talents, capital, information and technology through industrial, investment and innovation platforms to realize coordination in competition policies, innovation and rules so as to break down barriers, realize effective cooperation and common development and achieve their development goals at various stages of regional economic development. The fundamental target of coordination of competition and cooperation is for common growth and win-win cooperation, which has been an inevitable trend of the world.

In order to fully understand laws of regional economic competition from a practical point of view, we will cite part of *Report on Integration of Chinese Cities* released by China Development Research Foundation.

This report utilizes ACEP index in analyzing regional integration. Here A represents economic agglomeration, which equals the proportion of regional GDP in national GDP times regional economic density. The higher A is, the more concentrated are various industries and economic activities in urban agglomerations. C is about regional connectivity, which is measured by passenger volumes and freight volumes. The higher C is, the more connected are economic relations within the region. E stands for economic equalization, which equals one minus Gini coefficient of regional per capita GDP. The higher E is, the more balanced is economic development in the region. P is policy coordination, which equals one minus Gini coefficient of per capita fiscal expenditure. The higher P is, the less cost of and gap in policy co-ordination and public service. Together, these four indicators constitute ACEP index, which ranges from 0 to 100. The higher ACEP is, the more integrated is the regional economy.

This report studied ACEP indexes of 12 city agglomerations from 2006 to 2015, including Beijing, Tianjin and Hebei region, the Yangtze River Delta region, the Pearl River Delta region, the central plain, Southern Liaoning Province, Shandong Peninsula, West Coast of Taiwan Strait, Wuhan region, Changsha, Zhuzhou and Xiangtan region, Chengdu and Chongqing region, the central Shaanxi plain and Haerbin and Changchun region, covering a total of 157 cities of prefecture level or above. Among the 12 agglomerations, the Pearl River Delta region ranked top every year from 2006 to 2015. In 2015, ACEP index of the region was 61.58, higher by 4.79 compared with the Yangtze River Delta region in the second place. So we will take the Pearl River Delta region and its ACEP index as an example in the following analysis.

First of all, economic agglomeration in the Pearl River Delta region was quite high. From 2006 to 2015, the indicator A contributed to around 50% of ACEP index annually, ranking eighth among the 12 agglomerations, but only second among its own four indicators of ACEP.

(1) GDP of the region, ranking third among the 12 agglomerations after the Yangtze River Delta region and Beijing, Tianjin and Hebei region (see Figure 9.2), accounted to a relatively high proportion in the national total GDP, while land area of the region was only the tenth among the 12 regions, which indicated high economic intensity of the region. So economic agglomeration was high in the Pearl River Delta region.

(2) From 2006 to 2015, the Pearl River Delta region ranked top in terms of population growth among the 12 agglomerations with an increase of about 20%, followed by Beijing, Tianjin and Hebei region and the Yangtze River Delta region with increases of over 10% (see Figure 9.3). When calculating the elastic coefficient of population growth to growth of regional per capita GDP, the elastic coefficient of the Pearl River Delta region (0.97) was significantly higher than that of the Beijing, Tianjin and Hebei region (0.68) and the Yangtze River Delta region (0.49), which shows population growth in the Pearl River Delta region remarkably boosted regional economic growth.

Second, regional connectivity in the Pearl River Delta region was on the rise. From 2006 to 2015, indicator C contributed to around 55% of the ACEP index annually, the second largest among the 12 regions and the top among its own four indicators.

Passenger volumes of the Pearl River Delta region increased from the fourth among the 12 city agglomerations in 2006 to the second in 2015, up by 312.52%, making it the fast-growing region in this regard. Freight volumes in the region grew by 159.20% in 2015 from the 2006 level. Substantial growth in passenger volumes and freight volumes reflected increasing

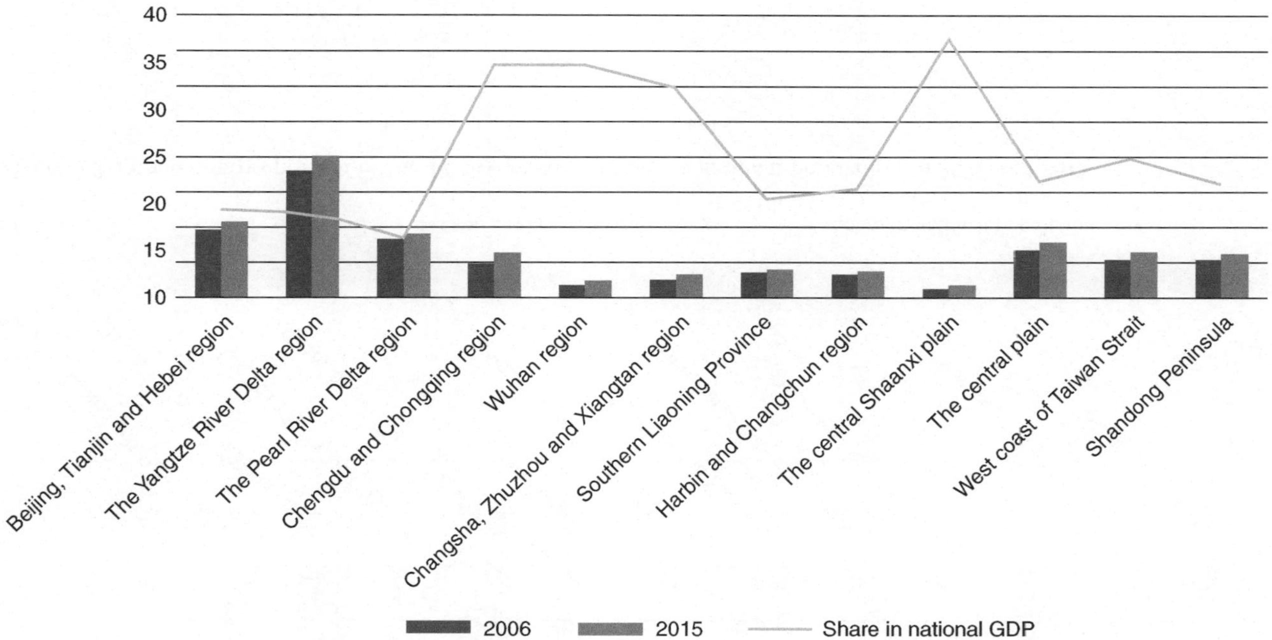

Figure 9.2 GDP proportion of the 12 city agglomerations in national total GDP in 2006 and 2015.

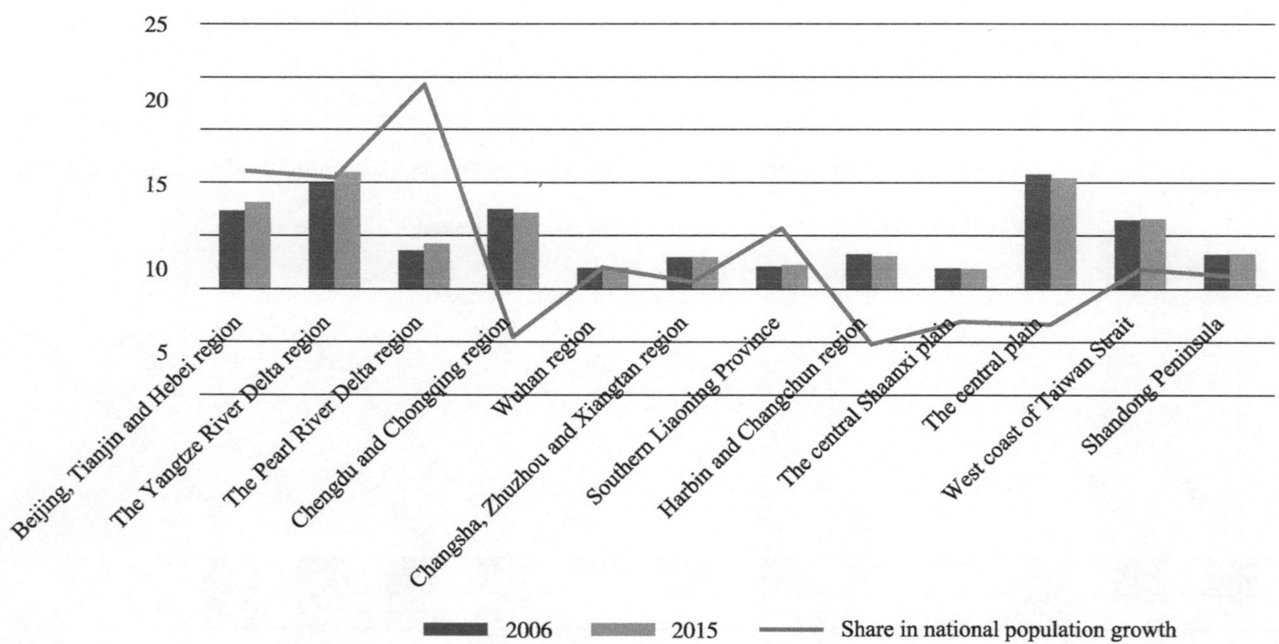

Figure 9.3 Population proportion of the 12 city agglomerations in national population in 2006 and 2015.

Table 9.1 Passenger Volumes and Freight Volumes in 2006 and 2015

	Passenger volume (2006)	*Passenger volume (2015)*	*Growth rate of Passenger volume*	*Freight volume (2006)*	*Freight volume (2015)*	*Growth rate of freight volume*	*Ratio of passenger volume to freight volume (2006)*	*Ratio of passenger volume to freight volume (2015)*
Beijing, Tianjin and Hebei region	103175	316569	206.83	168095	354868	111.11	0.61	0.89
The Yangtze River Delta region	324932	662576	103.91	311917	709702	127.53	1.04	0.93
The Pearl River Delta region	143849	593403	312.52	103201	267496	159.20	1.39	2.22
Chengdu and Chongqing region	217216	443732	104.28	115001	311423	170.80	1.89	1.42
Wuhan region	38627	76846	98.94	37291	82474	121.16	1.04	0.93
Changsha, Zhuzhou and Xiangtan region	75132	154317	105.39	62301	160000	156.82	1.21	0.96
Southern Liaoning Province	47432	94748	99.76	85322	196879	130.75	0.56	0.48
Haerbin and Changchun region	37161	86652	133.18	46354	85340	84.10	0.80	1.02

(Continued)

Table 9.1 (Continued)

	Passenger volume (2006)	*Passenger volume (2015)*	*Growth rate of Passenger volume*	*Freight volume (2006)*	*Freight volume (2015)*	*Growth rate of freight volume*	*Ratio of passenger volume to freight volume (2006)*	*Ratio of passenger volume to freight volume (2015)*
The central Shaanxi plain	31397	98813	214.72	23793	97779	310.96	1.32	1.01
The central plain	153130	378629	147.26	143905	592732	311.89	1.06	0.64
West coast of Taiwan Strait	127009	214847	69.16	96876	221334	128.47	1.31	0.97
Shandong Peninsula	127009	199854	57.35	96876	182343	88.22	1.31	1.10
Total	1426069	3320986	132.88	1290932	3262371	152.71	1.10	1.02

Unit: 10,000 people, 10,000 tons, %.

connectivity and close economic ties of the region. In terms of the ratio of passenger volumes to freight volumes, it went up from 1.39% in 2006 to 2.22% in 2015, showing faster growth rate of passenger volumes than freight volumes in the region (Table 9.1).

Third, the equalization of economic development among cities in the Pearl River Delta region is deepening. From 2006 to 2015, the indicator E's annual contribution to the ACEP index in the Pearl River Delta region, which was no more than 5%, was close to that of other agglomerations, and it ranked third among the four indicators.

This report investigated the Gini coefficient of regional per capita GDP of the 12 regions from 2006 to 2015 and the result shows apart from Shandong Peninsula, economic disparities among all the rest of the regions were narrowing down. Gini coefficient of regional per capita GDP in the Pearl River Delta region in 2015 declined by 16.24% compared with 2006, ranking fourth among the 12 regions. In contrast, the indicator E increased by 4.13%. Although this increase ranked only No. 7, the indicator E of the Pearl River Delta region was the third among all the city agglomerations, which indicates economic gap in the region was constantly shrinking and economic equalization was increasing (Table 9.2).

At last, policy coordination among cities in the Pearl River Delta region was inadequate. From 2006 to 2015, the indicator P contributed about -5% annually, the last but one among the 12 regions. So in terms of contribution to ACEP index, the indicator P ranked the last.

In 2015, with regards to Gini coefficient of per capita fiscal expenditure, the top three regions were Beijing, Tianjin and Hebei region, the Pearl River Delta region and the Yangtze River Delta region. Among them, the Pearl River Delta region saw an increase of 4.77% in 2015 compared with 2006, with a value of 0.3040, while other regions all witnessed decline compared with the 2006 level. Meanwhile, the indicator P in the Pearl River Delta region was 0.696 in 2015, down by 1.94% compared with 2006, so it was the only region with an increasing fiscal expenditure among the 12 regions (Table 9.3).

So it appears in terms of ACEP estimation, the Pearl River Delta region already ranked high in regional integration among city agglomerations. However, it also has some limitations like small inland area and limited growth space. If Hong Kong and Macao are integrated with the region and the development of the Guangdong-Hong Kong-Macao Greater Bay Area is coordinated, the ACEP index of the region would remarkably rise. According to estimates, the ACEP index in the Pearl River Delta region was 61.58 in 2015, while after incorporating Hong Kong and Macao, it would be 67.94, higher by 11.15 than the Yangtze River Delta region which was in the second place. It shows coordinated development of Guangdong, Hong Kong and Macao will further enhance integration of the Pearl River Delta region and it also indicates the rationality and necessity of promoting

Table 9.2 Changes in Economic Gap Among City Agglomerations from 2006 to 2015

	Gini coefficient of regional per capita GDP in 2006	*Gini coefficient of regional per capita GDP in 2015*	*Fluctuation in Gini coefficient of regional per capita GDP*	*Regional economic equalization in 2006*	*Regional economic equalization in 2015*	*Fluctuation in regional economic equalization*
Beijing, Tianjin and Hebei region	0.3227	0.2780	−13.86	0.6773	0.722	6.599734
The Yangtze River Delta region	0.2475	0.1955	−21.00	0.7525	0.8045	6.910299
The Pearl River Delta region	0.2027	0.1698	−16.24	0.7973	0.8302	4.126427
Chengdu and Chongqing region	0.2190	0.1791	−18.22	0.781	0.8209	5.108835
Wuhan region	0.3412	0.2887	−15.40	0.6588	0.7113	7.969035
Changsha, Zhuzhou and Xiangtan region	0.2676	0.2524	−5.68	0.7324	0.7476	2.075369
Southern Liaoning Province	0.1755	0.1309	−25.43	0.8245	0.8691	5.409339
Haerbin and Changchun region	0.2787	0.2749	−1.35	0.7213	0.7251	0.526827
The central Shaanxi plain	0.2211	0.2051	−7.24	0.7789	0.7949	2.054179
The central plain	0.2698	0.2292	−15.07	0.7302	0.7708	5.560121
West coast of Taiwan Strait	0.2602	0.2458	−5.54	0.7398	0.7542	1.946472
Shandong Peninsula	0.1522	0.1529	0.44	0.8478	0.8471	−0.08257

Table 9.3 Per Capita Fiscal Expenditure of City Agglomerations from 2006 to 2015

	Gini coefficient of per capita fiscal expenditure in 2006	*Gini coefficient of per capita fiscal expenditure in 2015*	*Fluctuation in Gini coefficient of per capita fiscal expenditure*	*Value of policy coordination in 2006*	*Value of policy coordination in 2015*	*Fluctuation in value of policy coordination*
Beijing, Tianjin and Hebei region	0.4435	0.3558	−19.76	0.5565	0.6442	15.75921
The Yangtze River Delta region	0.3860	0.2255	−41.58	0.614	0.7745	26.14007
The Pearl River Delta region	0.2902	0.3040	4.77	0.7098	0.696	−1.94421
Chengdu and Chongqing region	0.1923	0.1810	−5.84	0.8077	0.819	1.399034
Wuhan region	0.3013	0.1707	−43.34	0.6987	0.8293	18.69186
Changsha, Zhuzhou and Xiangtan region	0.1904	0.1361	−28.51	0.8096	0.8639	6.707016
Southern Liaoning Province	0.1691	0.1285	−24.03	0.8309	0.8715	4.886268
Haerbin and Changchun region	0.1380	0.0955	−30.74	0.862	0.9045	4.930394

(*Continued*)

Table 9.3 (Continued)

	Gini coefficient of per capita fiscal expenditure in 2006	*Gini coefficient of per capita fiscal expenditure in 2015*	*Fluctuation in Gini coefficient of per capita fiscal expenditure*	*Value of policy coordination in 2006*	*Value of policy coordination in 2015*	*Fluctuation in value of policy coordination*
The central Shaanxi plain	0.1515	0.1305	−13.85	0.8485	0.8695	2.474956
The central plain	0.2063	0.1163	−43.61	0.7937	0.8837	11.3393
West coast of Taiwan Strait	0.2355	0.1699	−27.82	0.7645	0.8301	8.580772
Shandong Peninsula	0.1650	0.1463	−11.29	0.835	0.8537	2.239521

coordinated development of the Guangdong-Hong Kong-Macao Greater Bay Area.

9.4 On "competitive neutrality"

In discussing the overview of economic behavior of regional governments, the author already put forward the view that regional governments deploy operative resources, non-operative resources and quasi-operative resources and regional governments engaged themselves in regional competition through SOEs or as stockholders of enterprises. The author also elaborated on the DEMC, which shows both enterprises and regional governments can participate in resource distribution in the market. So it seems regional governments not only compete with each other but also participate in industrial and urban economic projects through SOEs. So the principle of competitive neutrality is a necessary topic in regional economic development all over the world.

Before we go into details regarding "competitive neutrality," we first need to have a basic grasp of how developed economies improve business regulations through business environment evaluation mechanisms of some international organizations.

Currently, the *Doing Business* reports of the World Bank, the *Global Competitiveness Reports* of the World Economic Forum and the *Investment Climate Statements* of the US Department of State are some influential indicators of the business environment. These reports evaluate with different benchmarks and their data is utilized by nations and international firms. The *Global Competitiveness Reports* score macro business environment based on pillars such as institutions and infrastructure, as well as indicators directly linked to establishment, site selection, transportation and financial support of enterprises in the financial market. The *Investment Climate Statements* reports provide guidelines for American companies in overseas investment, helps them select the right investment locations and protect their interests abroad through targeted evaluation of business environment over other countries and regions. The reports cover issues such as dispute resolution, intellectual property rights and information disclosure. *Doing Business* reports are the most important publications among them and have been adopted by some developing countries in compiling their own business climate reports. For instance, *Ease of Doing Business: An Enterprise Survey of Indian States* was released by the Indian Department of Industrial Policy and Promotion based on *Doing Business* reports.

There are three major methodologies for *Doing Business* reports.

First, developing indicator sets. The World Bank sets up teams for developing indicator sets and after 16 years' exploration, the 11 areas of of regulations, including 43 specific indicators have been adopted in measuring the advantages and disadvantages of a nation or a region (Table 9.4).

Second, ease of doing business score. The ease of doing business score

Table 9.4 What *Doing Business* Measures—Areas of Business Regulation

Business stage	*Indicator set*	*What is measured*
Starting a business	Starting a business	Procedures, time, cost, and paid-in minimum capital to start a limited liability company for men and women
Getting a location	Dealing with construction permits	Procedures, time, and cost to complete all formalities to build a warehouse and the quality control and safety mechanisms in the construction permitting system
	Getting electricity	Procedures, time, and cost to get connected to the electrical grid; the reliability of the electricity supply; and the transparency of tariffs
	Registering property	Procedures, time, and cost to transfer a property and the quality of the land administration system for men and women
Financing	Getting credit	Movable collateral laws and credit information systems
	Protecting minority investors	Extent of disclosure index, extent of director liability index, ease of shareholder suits index, extent of shareholder rights index, extent of ownership and control index, and extent of corporate transparency index
Daily operation	Paying taxes	Payments, time, and total tax and contribution rate for a firm to comply with all tax regulations as well as postfiling processes
	Trading across borders	Time and cost of documentary compliance and border compliance for import and export
When problems arise	Enforcing contracts	Time and cost to resolve a commercial dispute and the quality of judicial processes for men and women
	Resolving insolvency	Recovery rate for a commercial insolvency and the strength of the legal framework for insolvency

captures the gap of each economy from the best regulatory performance observed on each of the indicators. An economy's ease of doing business score is reflected on a scale from 0 to 100, where 0 represents the lowest and 100 represents the best performance. The gap of each economy from the best regulatory performance is the ease of doing business score of the economy. In addition, one can both see the gap between a particular economy's performance and the best performance at any point in time and assess the absolute change in the economy's regulatory environment over time as measured by *Doing Business*.

Third, various channels and approaches in data collection and verification. The *Doing Business* data is based on a detailed reading of domestic laws, regulations and administrative requirements as well as their implementation in practice as experienced by private professionals, such as lawyers, accountants, judges and government officials as well as well-known consulting firms and industrial associations.

The international community's high attention on the business environment requires us to attach importance to the issue of "competitive neutrality." Competitive neutrality emphasizes that SOEs and private enterprises compete fairly in the market and that the government should provide a level playing field, eliminate distortions in the allocation of resources in favor of SOEs, and enhance the competitiveness of all market participants through the market forces in resource allocation.

In the 1990s when SOEs under the ownership of the Australian Federal Government and state governments took hold of massive means of production, Australia introduced the framework of competitive neutrality for reforms on ending preferential policies for SOEs. In 1991, the Australian Government decided to formulate a national-level competition policy, which was reviewed by the mass in the following year. In 1993, Australia released the *Hilmer Report*, which touched on the concept of "competitive neutrality." The report covers six reform objectives on national competition policy, including the competitive neutrality of competition between state-owned and private enterprises, the anticompetitive behavior of enterprises, and undue restrictions on competition caused by regulations. In the following year, Australia initiated a national reform on competition policy. In 1996, the Australian Government issued the "Competitive Neutrality Policy Statement," which set out stricter competitive neutrality measures, including corporate reform on SOEs, tax neutrality, debt neutrality, profitability requirements, regulatory neutrality, price reflecting full cost and complaint mechanisms, which were incorporated into the national competition policy.

The core of the Australian competitive neutrality framework is to ensure significant government businesses and private businesses compete fairly in the market. SOEs can engage in competition, pursue profits and earn normal rates of return, but may not use their status as government businesses to seek favorable resources or policy preference.

Later on, OECD launched competitive neutrality research since 2009, which pointed out eight main individual elements in obtaining competitive neutrality, including operational form of government business, identifying costs, commercial rate of return, accounting for public service obligations, tax neutrality, regulatory neutrality, debt neutrality and outright subsidies, and public procurement.

At present, the concept of competitive neutrality is not only limited to government businesses and private businesses within a country, but is also widely present in international trade. For example, the United States and the European Union have incorporated the principle of competitive neutrality into their bilateral trade regime. Besides, the 2012 US *Model Bilateral Investment Treaty* strengthened regulations over SOEs and highlighted the principle of competitive neutrality and sustainable development. *Statement of the European Union and the United States on Shared Principles for International Investment* issued in 2012 also incorporated "the principle of a level playing field" which aimed to promote the competitive neutrality, and requested the European Union and the United States to support the OECD's efforts in the area of competitive neutrality. At the same time, developed countries and regions have also made efforts to create a level playing field by promoting the governance structure of "common governance of both the industries and relevant statutory authorities," enhancing intellectual property rights protection and establishing sound taxation mechanisms.

With a basic understanding of the development of competitive neutrality, we can see that the essence of the principle is that all actions taken by governments should be neutral in their impact on market competition between SOEs and other business sectors, which means government conduct should not give any "undue competitive advantage" to any actual or potential market participants, especially SOEs. Competition is the soul of the modern market system, and a fair and orderly competition environment is always the "infrastructure" that keeps the market sound and vigorous. The principle of competitive neutrality is designed to protect the entire competition process of a market, rather than any single market player.

Treating SOEs based on the principle of competitive neutrality actually aims to create an environment to develop an equitable and just market so that each market participant finds their own place, the superior thrive and the inferior is eliminated, and the market plays a decisive role in allocating resources. The target of this principle is consistent with the goals of current SOE reform in various countries, which both strive to foster SOEs as independent market players that can independently operate, assume sole responsibility for their profits or losses, compete at their own risks, impose self-discipline and grow their businesses. The purpose of establishing the principle of competitive neutrality is to ensure equity and justice in the market through equal competition between public and private businesses, thereby ensuring the accuracy of a series of market signals such as prices, the smooth exchange of information, maximizing the rational allocation of resources and stimulating market vigor and vitality, thus "fueling up" economic transformation.

In order to have a deep understanding over the principle of competitive neutrality, we will take tax neutrality as an example. Tax neutrality is one of eight main individual elements in obtaining competitive neutrality identified by OECD. Tax neutrality indicates that government taxation does not distort the normal operation of market mechanisms, or rather, does not affect private sectors' original resource allocation. To put it simply, it means that the government should not increase or should refrain from increasing excess burden on taxpayers beyond their tax liabilities, which has two implications: First, government taxation should be limited within the range of tax liability of the society, without imposing additional burdens on taxpayers or the society; second, government taxation should avoid disturbing the normal functioning of the market economy, in particular, should not replace the decisive role of the market mechanism in resource allocation. *International VAT/GST Guidelines Value Added Tax* issued by OECD in February 2013 clearly states that "OECD jurisdictions with a VAT impose the tax at every stage of the economic process and allow deduction of taxes on purchases by all but the final consumer so as to ensure tax neutrality." It shows if government taxation changes consumers' consumption for maximum utility, or firms' behavior in pursuit of maximum profits, and the society changes the original (pre-tax) resource allocation of private sectors, such changes are considered tax non-neutrality.

Here the concept of excess burden is concerned. Excess burden of taxation is produced during the process by which the government transfers social resources from taxpayers to government sectors through taxation, which imposes an extra burden on taxpayers in addition to their due tax liabilities. It is mainly manifested in two aspects: First, government taxation reduces taxpayers' expenditures and increases government expenditures, and if the economic losses of taxpayers caused by taxation exceed the increased social and economic benefits brought about by taxation, there is an excess burden on resource allocation; second, taxation changes relative prices of goods, which has an adverse effect on taxpayers' consumption and production, and thus creates an excess burden on economic operation (Figure 9.4).

The excess burden of taxation is proposed by Arnold Harberger based on Alfred Marshall's cardinal utility theory and is commonly measured by the

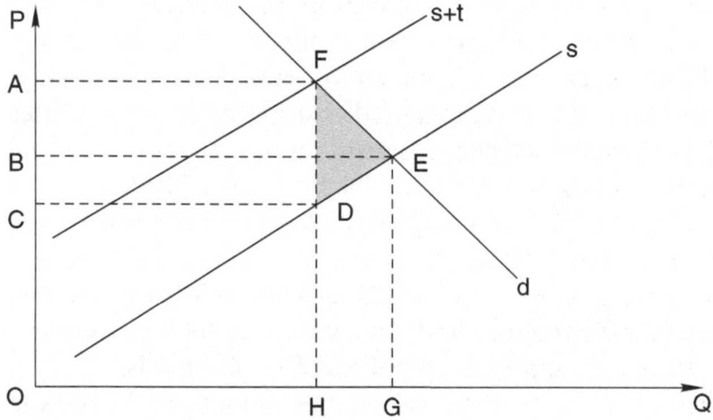

Figure 9.4 Excess burden of taxation.

area of the associated Harberger triangle as shown in Figure 19. Here d represents the demand curve for a kind of goods and s the supply curve. Before taxation, the demand and the supply reach an equilibrium at E, with the production as OG and price as OB. Let's assume the government imposes a specific duty of FD, the supply curve S will move up to s+t, the equilibrium point will shift to F, production to OH and price to OA. Its tax revenue is CD (sales volume) times DF (tax rate), namely the area of ACDF. The loss in consumer surplus due to taxation is ABEF and the loss in producer surplus is BCDE. Together, the losses are ACDEF, which is clearly larger than the government tax revenue (ACDF). So the area of FDE is the excess burden of taxation. This shows that the burden on taxpayers includes not only the tax payable of ACDF, but also the excess burden generated by the increase in prices and decrease in production (consumption) due to government taxation. Based on consumer surplus, the theory of excess burden of taxation shows that excess burden distorts consumers' consumption choices over dutiable goods and other related goods. On the basis of this analysis, we can propose three ways to reduce excess burden: Taxing goods with zero elasticity of demand, levying ad valorem tax on commodities and taxing on income.

After theoretical discussion over the principle of competitive neutrality, now we should consider how to apply this principle in practice in order to build a level playing field for the dual entities in market competition. On one hand, evaluation mechanisms on business regulations of various countries or international institutions should recognize the objective position of SOEs in history and at present while on the other hand, countries and relevant international institutions should improve and apply the principle of competitive neutrality to build an open, equitable and just business environment for the dual entities in market competition in the modern market economy.

We know that the flourishing emergence of SOEs began after World War II. With the transformation of general monopoly capitalism to state-monopoly capitalism, western countries started to intervene and regulate economic activities across the board. At the same time, driven by the new wave of technological revolution, the production scale of enterprises kept expanding and the market economy based purely on free competition caused social instability. Since 1945, the British Government nationalized a string of basic industries and the Bank of England; The French energy sector, insurance sector, financial sector and some large companies were taken over by the state; The number of SOEs founded by the Japanese Government skyrocketed from seven by the end of the World War II to 114 in the mid-1970s; the American Government also jumped on the bandwagon of establishing SOEs. These SOEs were mainly from the fields of energy, infrastructure and science and technology development, among which some were important suppliers of public goods.

Meanwhile, in order to revitalize their national economies and promote their own industrialization, developing countries have also witnessed two waves of nationalization. The first was in the late 1950s to mid-1960s, following the rise of national liberation movements, which targeted primarily on the then colonial enterprises and economic management institutions of colonies, such as customs, banks, taxation agencies as well as large enterprises owned by the then colonizers which were powerful enough to monopolize or manipulate a country's livelihood. This nationalization campaign was actually a follow-up to the national liberation movements in the economic field. The second one occurred in the 1970s, when developing countries, encouraged by the victory of oil-producing countries in the Middle East in their fight in regaining sovereignty over their oil resources, set in motion a trend of restoring ownership over natural resources. During this trend, some countries nationalized foreign-owned enterprises that actually manipulated backbone industries of their economies, and regained sovereignty over some mining, agricultural and fishery resources.

Currently, in terms of layout of state-owned business, SOEs across the world are increasingly concentrating on a few important strategic sectors. With regards to corporate ownership, most SOEs are under mixed ownership, by ways of going public, for example. In Forbes annual list of the world's 2,000 largest public companies that covers over half of the aggregate world economy, SOEs account for a significant part. In the fiscal year 2010–2011, 204 among the 2,000 largest listed companies were SOEs, which came from 37 countries, with China ranking first (70), followed by India (30), Russia (9), the United Arab Emirates (9), Malaysia (8) and a total of 41 from OECD countries. The 204 SOEs spanned across 35 sectors and registered a total sales volume of $3.6 trillion, equivalent to 10% of that of the 2,000 largest listed companies combined.

According to data, both developing countries and western developed countries represented by OECD, have a certain number of large SOEs, which play an important role in global economic development. It is fair to say that SOEs are an important channel for regional governments to participate in market competition. So to investigate on regional government competition, or the dual entities of market competition, it is necessary to clarify the special attributes of SOEs and how they comply with the principle of competitive neutrality in the market.

To sum up, the author, from the perspective of the six pillars of the modern market systemic system, proposes the following approaches with a view to improving and promoting the principle of competitive neutrality in light of current international practice or experience.

First, in the market factor system, the principle of competitive neutrality shall be promoted in terms of factor acquisition, cost confirmation, business operation, debt neutrality and subsidy constraints.

Second, in the market organization system, the principle of competitive neutrality should be practiced in allowing access permits, choosing business modes, shouldering obligations for public service and promoting fair competition among various forms of businesses.

Third, in the market legal system, the principle of competitive neutrality should be implemented in market value orientation, transaction, contractual behavior and intellectual property rights, especially in IPR protection and tax neutrality.

Fourth, in the market supervision system, the principle of competitive neutrality should be followed in investment promotion, bidding, government procurement and review and supervision over institutions, businesses, markets and mechanisms.

Fifth, the market environment system mainly includes the real economy as the foundation of the market economy, corporate governance structure and social credit system. It is now essential that the principle of competitive neutrality is carried out in the regulation of legal systems, fiduciary relationships, credit instruments, credit intermediaries and other relevant credit issues.

Sixth, market infrastructure mainly covers market service networks, supporting equipment and technology, various market payment and settlement systems and information technology systems. The principle of competitive neutrality should be strengthened with regard to standards for utilization of these various kinds of infrastructure in regional, national and even international markets by different market forces.

At present, it is of paramount importance and admits of no delay to enforce the principle of competitive neutrality in application standards of social credit systems and market infrastructure across regions and nations.

Notes

1 Gu, X. (2017, January 5). Rediscovering market failure: Nobel Laureate Joseph Stiglitz talks about industrial policy. *The Paper*. https://www.thepaper.cn/newsDetail_forward_1594001.

2 Gu, X. (2017, January 5). Rediscovering market failure: Nobel Laureate Joseph Stiglitz talks about industrial policy. *The Paper*. https://www.thepaper.cn/newsDetail_forward_1594001

3 The "463" Plan: from 2008 on, to promote the shareholding system transformation or launch of public listing of at least 100 enterprises within four years, and the successful listing of 60 home or abroad, and to reach a gross financing of RMB 30 billion yuan.

4 The Supplement VI to CEPA, signed on May 9, 2009 and effective on Oct. 1 of the same year, aims to further enhance the level of economic and trade exchanges and cooperation between the mainland and the Hong Kong SAR. According to the supplement, the mainland shall further relax the market access conditions in 20 areas, namely, legal, construction, medical, research and development services, real estate, placement and supply services of personnel, printing, convention and exhibition, public utility, telecommunications, audiovisual, distribution, banking, securities, tourism, cultural, maritime transport, air transport, rail transport and individually owned stores. Many of the specific policies were piloted in Guangdong Province.

5 Jing, S. (2011). Intelligent Foshan: Path of transformation under the logic of power division. *China Nongovernmental Science Technology and Economy*, *7*, 50–55.

10 "Double strong forms" theory in a mature market economy

10.1 Forms of efficient markets and effective governments

10.1.1 Efficient markets

The concept of an efficient market was first proposed by Eugene Fama in 1970. Fama believed that when prices of securities can fully reflect the information available to investors, the securities market is an efficient market, where investors can only expect a normal rate of returns corresponding to investment risks no matter what securities are chosen randomly.

According to information available to investors, Fama put forward three forms of efficient markets in his Efficient Market Hypothesis (EMH): The weak form, the semi-strong form and the strong form. In the weak form of an efficient market, all the information concerning past prices is already fully reflected in the current prices, so technical analysis on historical prices by means of moving averages and candlestick charts is ineffective. Apart from information on previous prices in the securities market, the semi-strong form of efficient market also has all the public information available in news coverage, such as annual and quarterly reports of securities companies, though fundamental analysis based on public information such as financial statements of enterprises is also ineffective. In the strong form of efficient market, there exists not only all public information but also all insider information, such as internal information held by senior managers in enterprises. If the hypothesis of the strong form of efficient market holds water, all the above information would already be fully reflected in the current prices, then even investors with access to insider information cannot always obtain abnormal gains.

So, Fama put forward the premise for an efficient market by assuming a perfect market, where first, there is no friction in the entire market, namely no transaction costs and taxation, and all assets can be completely separated and traded without restrictive provisions; second, the whole market is fully competitive, and all market participants are price takers; third, there is no information cost; last, all market participants receive information simultaneously and all of them are rational and pursue maximum utility.

DOI: 10.4324/9781003244837-10

However, these assumptions can hardly hold water in reality. The presence of market frictions indicates that a completely efficient market is impossible and investors must also take transaction costs, opportunity costs, taxes and other costs into account. All these make the premise of an efficient market difficult to be realized, so the Efficient Market Hypothesis can hardly find applications in practice.

Here the author won't comment on whether it is reasonable of Fama to evaluate market efficiency with the amount of transaction information available concerning prices. But I do agree with his methodology of dividing the modern market into the strong form, the semi-strong form and the weak form of efficient markets. I think that this methodology can be further extended from the securities market to the whole modern market economy so that on the basis of differences in the growth and maturity level of market systems of countries across the world, efficient market can be divided into three levels according to how complete the functions of the six pillars of the modern market system are as follows: (1) A market with only market factor system and market organization system belong to the weak form of efficient market. Such was the case of the United States from its founding in 1776 to 1890. (2) On the basis of the market factor system and market organization system, if a nation gradually establishes and improves the market legal system and market supervision system, it would evolve to the semi-strong form of efficient market, for instance, the United States from 1890 to 1990. (3) On the basis of the semi-strong form of efficient market, only when a nation builds the market environment system and market infrastructure can it be transformed into the strong form of efficient market, such as the case of the United States since the 1990s.

The division into the strong form, the semi-strong form and the weak form of efficient markets based on the growth and maturity level of the six pillars of the modern market system takes reference from and further develops the methodology employed by Fama in the Efficient Market Hypothesis, which not only can reflect the realities and genuine progress of economic development of countries across the world but also helps clearly differentiate market types, guide market practice and evaluate its effectiveness scientifically. Construction of a modern market system and improvement on market functions play important roles in promoting economic progress, urban construction and social welfare; thus, nations worldwide are making active explorations for breakthroughs in this regard.

10.1.2 Effective governments

Through the above analysis over the modern market economy, we can grasp three levels of connotations behind "market." First, as the rational core of market, market rules play a widely guiding role in mechanisms of commodities, factors of production, prices, supply and demand, and competition in industrial economy or resource generation as "an invisible hand." Second, as market platforms, circulation markets, which include various tangible regional markets and intangible online markets, as well as all commodities, factors of production, projects, talents, technology and funds (including foreign exchange) that are circulating and traded in markets, are constantly cycling under the guidance of the "invisible hand" in stages including production, circulation, transaction and consumption. Third, in the market mechanism, the six pillars of the modern market system are the basis of sound and orderly operation of the market, which guarantees its openness, equity and justice. But of course, when some aspect or some stage of the mechanism is inadequate or incomplete, the market can still work and market rules can still function. But deficiencies of a certain part of the market system will cause fragility to the market and lead to economic crisis and even worldwide economic recession due to market failure and eventually the market can be devastated or even overturned.

According to the growth and maturity level of market systems, we categorize a market with only a market factor system and market organization system as "the weak form of efficient market." On this basis, as the market gradually improves its market legal system and market supervision system, it would become "the semi-strong form of efficient market." After its market environment system and market infrastructure are put in place, the market would be established as "the strong form of efficient market." In this chapter, the focus of discussion will be the three types of effective governments that correspond to the three forms of efficient markets, "the weak form of effective government," "the semi-strong form of effective government" and "the strong form of effective government."

In Chapter 3, we talked about the three types of resources in economic operation in reality: Operative resources, non-operative resources and quasi-operative resources. As discussed in Chapter 4, operative resources (in industrial economy) should be allocated based on the principle of "planning and guiding, support and coordination, supervision and management"; allocation of non-operative resources (in livelihood economy) should follow the rule of "guaranteeing basic needs, ensuring fairness and justice, raising effectiveness and efficiency"; quasi-operative resources (in urban economy) shall be allocated based on the principles of "abiding by market rules, safeguarding economic order and participating in regional competition." In Chapter 5, we touched on government competition in the broad sense and in the narrow sense. In the broad sense, governments propel competitions over operative resources through supporting policies, which can invigorate the industrial economy and prompt its coordinated development, thereby driving forward growth of the regional industrial economy. By promoting competitions over non-operative resources through supporting policies, governments strive to fuel up the growth of livelihood economy, safeguard social stability and optimize regional business and investment environment. By strengthening competitions over quasi-operative resources through supporting policies, governments push forward investment, development and construction of urban economy in pursuit of comprehensive and sustainable development of the regional society and economy.

Corresponding to the above analysis, we can categorize effective governments into three types. The first type of government is only concerned with the distribution of non-operative resources (public welfare resources related to social welfare) and relevant supporting policies, which could be called the weak form of effective government. Governments of this category confine their role to the basic social welfare while having neither a clear understanding of nor actions on the distribution of operative resources and related policies and are short of a clear vision of or measures on participating in competition over quasi-operative resources. The second category of governments focus on the distribution of non-operative resources and operative resources and related policies, which are known as the semi-strong form of effective government. In addition to performing basic public duties such as social security, these governments also pay attention to market operation. In case of market failure, these governments can utilize policy instruments to mobilize effective demand or effective supply, implement regulation and intervention at the macro level to prevent massive economic recession and heavy losses and damages to the economy. At the same time, such governments can formulate economic strategies to set out and guide industrial layout, support and regulate production and operation, and supervise market competition under the principles of openness, equity and justice, regulate commodity prices, contain unemployment, so as to promote the dynamic equilibrium between aggregate supply and aggregate demand. However, they are in lack of adequate understanding over quasi-operative resources, so such resources are not clearly distinguished and are short of supporting policies. The third group of governments not only regulate the distribution of non-operative resources and operative resources and adopt relevant supporting policies, but also participate in and promote the distribution of quasi-operative resources, which are a strong form of effective government. These governments guide, regulate, forewarn economic development and based on the market mechanism, utilize measures of planning, investment, consumption, prices, taxation, interest rates, exchange rates, laws, etc., for conceptual, technological, organizational and institutional innovation. Such governments strive to improve the economic environment through effective distribution of operative resources; enhance economic vitality and coordination through effective distribution of non-operative resources; build a cutting edge to promote comprehensive, scientific and sustainable development of the society and the economy through effective distribution of quasi-operative resources. A strong form of effective government is a necessary path to success for nations in competition in the global market system.

10.2 Potential economic growth rate and real economic growth rate

As elaborated above, the modern market system incorporates the market factor system, the market organization system, the market legal system, the market supervision system, the market environment system and market infrastructure as six pillars. Economic resources can be divided into three categories: Operative resources, non-operative resources and quasi-operative resources. Different combinations of them can result in different combinations of effective governments and efficient markets in the market economy.

To sort out these various combinations, we need first to understand two important economic indicators: Potential economic growth rate and real economic growth rate.

Potential economic growth rate refers to the highest possible growth rate of aggregate goods and services produced by a nation in the modern market system, or in other words, the highest economic growth rate that a nation can produce when all of its various resources realize optimal allocation. It requires, first, an efficient market, in which the basic functions (ensured by the market factor system and market organization system), the basic market order (guaranteed by the market legal system and market supervision system), and the environmental foundation (constituted by the market environment system and market infrastructure) in the modern market system are sound, and second, an effective government, which can effectively regulate operative resources, non-operative resources and quasi-operative resources and introduce relevant supporting policies and mechanisms. So it appears potential economic growth rate is the growth rate that a government can achieve when it makes the best use of the three types of resources under a sound modern market system, which is realized under the combination of "the strong form of effective government + the strong form of efficient market."

The real economic growth rate measures the economic growth of a nation's Gross National Product (GNP) from one period to another, adjusted for inflation and expressed in real terms as opposed to nominal terms. The growth rate measured by the end of a base period is the nominal growth rate while measured at constant market prices of the base period, it is the real economic growth rate. The real economic growth rate reflects the actual rate of economic growth, a dynamic indicator of fluctuations of economic development in a nation within a certain period of time.

Due to differences in the maturity level of market development and government capabilities across the world, there exists the combination of "the weak form of effective government + the weak form of efficient market," such as most middle-income or low-income nations; "the semi-strong form of effective government + the strong form of efficient market," like the United States; and also "the strong form of effective government +

the semi-strong form of efficient market," such as China, which still needs to further improve its market competition order, credit system and infrastructure. There is still a certain gap between the real economic growth rate in all these nations and the potential economic growth rate under the combination of "the strong form of effective government and the strong form of efficient market."

This gap is where the economic potential of various economies lies, and measures taken to bridge this gap are the source of vitality for economic progress and policies or systems adopted to narrow the gap are where innovation for economic growth across the world originates. The mode of "a mature market economy = an effective government + an efficient market" is the optimal combination of the government and market, the best mode nations have explored through constant practice, and also the necessary path to realizing the potential economic growth rate of the world economy.

In economic reality, there are times when aggregate social demand falls short of aggregate social supply, or aggregate social demand exceeds aggregate social supply. From the combinations of "effective governments and efficient markets," we can find the root causes of economic problems from the perspective of the six pillars of the market system and how the government distributes the three types of resources and chart out courses for solutions.

10.3 Washington consensus and the middle-income trap

In the late 1980s, the world economy was trapped into recession and economic growth across the world was sluggish with an inadequate impetus for growth, weak demand, declining population growth, twists and turns in economic globalization, financial market turmoils and a continuous downturn in international trade and investment. Faced with the gloomy economic situations, in 1989, the American Institute for International Economics invited institutions such as the International Monetary Fund, the World Bank, and the Inter-American Development Bank to a conference in Washington D.C., and hence came the "Washington Consensus." There were ten reforms originally set out by the "Washington Consensus." (1) Fiscal Discipline, which aimed to discourage high fiscal deficits, curb high inflation and stabilize macroeconomic development. (2) Reordering public expenditure priorities to important long-term growth supporting sectors like basic health and education and infrastructure. (3) Implementing tax reform policies to broaden the tax base and adopt moderate marginal tax rates. (4) Liberalizing interest rates. (5) Encouraging competitive exchange rates. (6) Adoption of free trade policies. (7) Liberalization of inward foreign direct investment. (8) Privatization of state enterprises. (9) Deregulation. (10) Development of property rights.

The core of the Washington Consensus is to minimize the role of the government and accelerate privatization and liberalization. In theory, it advocates a perfectly free market economy that minimizes the role of the government and upholds that as long as the market can allocate resources freely, economic growth can be ensured. With respect to policies, its measures mainly include expediting liberalization of the market and domestic and foreign trade, accelerating privatization of SOEs, as well as reducing fiscal deficits, strictly restricting loans and issuance of currencies in order to realize macroeconomic stability.

Originally, the Washington Consensus was a set of economic policy recommendations for Latin-American countries that faced debt crises and Eastern European countries for political and economic transformation. During some specific times, the ten policy measures of the Washington Consensus did play an effective role in stimulating the economic development of various nations. However, they not only neglected the importance of improving the six pillars of the modern market system but also lacked knowledge in recognizing the importance of governments' role in distributing the three types of economic resources, hence featuring "the weak form of effective government + the weak form of efficient market." In this combination, the government has basically no regulatory control over the economy, the market development is far from sound, the legal system is missing, disorder prevails, and the market competition mechanism is often impeded. Such theoretical propositions, policy measures and modes certainly cannot sustain themselves and are bound to fall into difficulties.

In 2006, the World Bank introduced the concept of "middle-income trap." In the words of the World Bank, "After exceeding the poverty trap of $1,000 gross domestic product (GDP) per capita, many emerging market countries head rapidly to the middle income 'take off stage' of $3,000 per capita GDP, but as they reach the middle-income range, they experience long-term economic stagnation."

At this stage, these countries are facing two dilemmas. On one hand, the costs of resources, raw materials, labor force, capital, and management remain high. On the other hand, they have difficulties innovating due to lack of core cutting-edge technologies and are stuck in the middle and low ends of the industrial chain without any competitiveness. The decline or stagnation of economic growth leads to further employment difficulties, shortage of social public services, fragile financial system, polarization between the rich and the poor, rampant corruption, loss of faith, and social unrest, etc. Consequently, these countries are trapped in the middle-income stage for long periods and are unable to shift to high-income status.

Latin American countries that adhered to the Washington Consensus to promote economic reform have also become typical examples of countries caught in the middle-income trap. Argentina's per capita GDP already exceeded $1,000 in 1964, and rose to over $8,000 by the late 1990s, but fell to over $2,000 in 2002, before rising to over $12,000 in 2014. Mexico was already a middle-income country in 1973, with a per capita GDP of $1,000. In 2016, it was still only an upper-middle-income country with a per capita GDP of over $8,000. Despite decades of effort, there are many similar Latin

American countries that have not exceeded the per capita GDP threshold of $15,000 to become developed countries.

We can take Argentina as an example to analyze the root causes of stagnation in Latin American countries. First, there were huge fluctuations in real economic growth rate. During the 45 years from 1963 to 2008, Argentina's per capita GDP grew at an average of only 1.4% annually and saw negative growth for 16 years. In 1963, Argentina's per capita GDP was $842, which already reached the level of middle-income and high-income countries at that time. However, after 45 years, it grew to only $8,236 in 2008, still at the same income level. Second, the driving force of technology was inadequate. In terms of the proportion of R&D expenditure in GDP in Argentina, it was 0.41% in 2003, ranking beyond top 40 in the world. As for R&D personnel, in 2006, there were only 1.1 R&D personnel in every 1,000 people in Argentina. From the perspective of quality of labor forces, in 2007, 29.5% of labor force attained college education or above, which was not quite advantageous. Third, it suffered from wide income disparities and serious social conflicts. In the mid-1980s, Argentina's Gini Coefficient was around 0.45, close to 0.5 in the late 1990s and grew to 0.51 in 2007. Maldistribution was reflected not only in property income but also in wage levels. Besides, due to poor urban infrastructure and public services, Argentina's public security kept worsening and social conflicts were severe. Finally, government management was ineffective. Argentina suffered from long-term macroeconomic instability, sharp fluctuations in exchange rates, skyrocketing inflation, long-time accumulated fiscal deficit and various problems in the supply-side economy. However, the legal and economic measures adopted by the government at the macro level were too weak and only addressed symptoms rather than root causes when problems arose, which resulted in widespread economic and social imbalance.

So it seems that the Washington Consensus and the "shock therapy" it advocated have both failed, for the following reasons. First, an efficient market features perfect competition, orderly legal supervision and a sound social credit system. But the Washington Consensus focused only on competition and improvement of the basic functions of the market, namely the market factor system and market organization system, but neglected improvement of the basic order in the market, namely the market legal system and market supervision system, as well as the foundation of the market environment (including the market environment system and market infrastructure). As a result, the market economy from the perspective of the Washington Consensus was a free market economy, rather than a modern market economy with sound market systems. Moreover, effective governments abide by market rules, maintain market order and participate in market competition, while the Washington Consensus only recognized the role of the government in non-operative resources by supplying public goods and utterly ignored that governments also need to "plan, guide and support" competition over operative resources (industrial resources) besides the responsibilities to "coordinate, supervise and manage" them. It was also short of the knowledge that apart from promoting competition over and utilization of quasi-operative resources (urban resources), governments also need to be a part of market competition. Only those that formulate effective policies to support the distribution of the three types of resources belong to the strong form of effective governments in a mature market economy. Henceforth, the "de-regulation" in the Washington Consensus was essentially anarchism, and had obvious defects compared with the theory of "a mature market economy = an effective government + an efficient market." Furthermore, for the real economic growth rate to approach or reach the potential economic growth rate, apart from improving the modern market system, it is crucial to strengthen government capacity-building, including institutional arrangements and construction, as well as the transformation of development mode, which were all void in the Washington Consensus. To strengthen capacity-building, governments shall not only comply with market rules, but also need to steer the course of its development and participate in market competition. But this requires a sound institutional environment and transformation of development modes. The so-called institutional environment construction includes not only strengthening legislation, law enforcement and judicial systems related to the market economy, and reinforcing legal education, but also identifying supervisory watchdogs, ranges and ways for effective supervision over market institutions, businesses, and implementation of policies and regulations as the market economy requires, along with establishing social and institutional norms conducive to reform and development of government organizations. Transformation of development modes means that we should transform from Adam Smith's approach of "market (the invisible hand) + supply-side economy (regulation of commodities, prices and supply)" or Keynes' mode of "government intervention + demand-side economy (driven by investment, consumption and export)" to a modern mature market economy of "government leading (intervention) + supply-side economy (a new engine of the supply-side structural reform)," namely "the strong form of effective government + the strong form of efficient market," so that government foresighted leading plays a sweeping role in every aspect and during the entire process of market economic activities.

10.4 Combinations and assessments of "effective governments + efficient markets"

The relationship between the government and the market has always been one of the core disputes in economic research, with its focus on the role of the government in resource allocation in the market economy and its influence on industrial development, urban construction and social welfare.

Let's take a brief review over the main ideas of various economic schools. First, mercantilism at the early stage of capitalism advocated government intervention in economy, prohibition of outflow of gold and silver and increases of inflow of gold and silver. Mercantilism was based on the idea that a nation's wealth and power were best served by increasing trade surplus. Henceforth, it upheld government regulation of agriculture, commerce and manufacturing, foreign trade monopoly, protection of the domestic market through high tariff rates and other trade restrictions, and supplying domestic manufacturing industry with raw materials from and access to markets of colonies. This theory injected impetus for the rapid development of early capitalism. Second, after the rise of classical economics, allocating resources through the market became the prevailing view. Both Adam Smith's economic liberalism and David Ricardo's comparative cost theory confined the role of the government to a very limited range, whose function was to guarantee efficient operation of the market. Third, Keynesianism, which emerged in the 1930s, argued that the nation should adopt expansionary economic policies and promote economic growth by increasing demand and that the government should not only guarantee the functioning of the market but also intervene in economy through monetary and fiscal policies to ensure a balance between supply and demand in the economic system. At last, in the 1970s and 1980s, economists represented by Milton Friedman and Arthur Betz Laffer advocated government noninterference and proposed solutions such as improving supply to ease economic crises…

In effective allocation of the three types of resources, a common problem faced by the contemporary world, we find that the relationship between the government and the market is not simply a relationship in contradiction. The division of the weak form, the semi-strong form, and the strong form of efficient markets can not only be measured quantitatively, but also reflects the true historical process, while the categorization of the weak form, the semi-strong form, and the strong form of effective governments can reflect the true performance of nations in market economy and also sort out the relationship between the government and the market. In theory, there exist at least nine combinations of the two (see Figure 10.1).

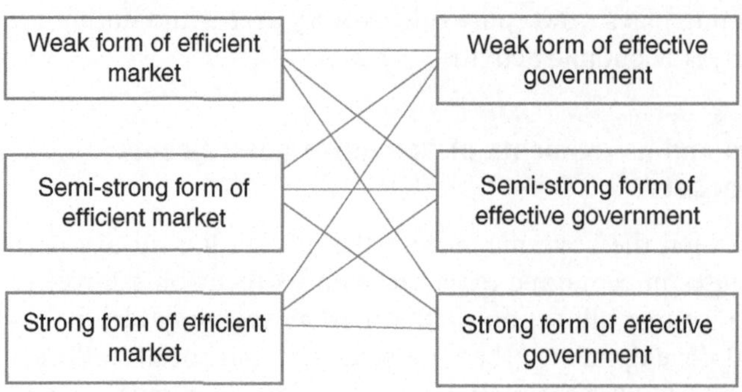

Figure 10.1 Nine combinations of effective governments and efficient markets.

First, the weak form of effective government + the weak form of efficient market, which is often seen in middle- or low-income nations, features basically no regulation of the government over economy, an incomplete market, poor market competition mechanism, inadequate legal system and disorder. Second, the weak form of effective government + the semi-strong form of efficient market. Such a mode can hardly exist in reality because there must be market legal system and supervision system in the semi-strong form of efficient market while a weak form of effective government is unable to build such systems. Third, the weak form of effective government + the strong form of efficient market, is a purely theoretical assumption that can find no real case in reality. Fourth, the semi-strong form of effective government + the weak form of efficient market, under which the government can play a sound role in distributing non-operative resources and providing basic public goods, and even begin to have the capability to distribute and support operative resources, though still not very good at grasping market trends, nor capable of independently solving problems in market operation. The experience of China from 1978 to 1984 when reform and opening up was just introduced bore much resemblance to this mode, which belongs to the early stage of market economy. Fifth, the semi-strong form of effective government + the semi-strong form of efficient market often occurs in a semi-mature market economy. Under this mode, the government can plan and guide industrial layout, support and regulate production and operation on one hand and endeavor to constantly improve market supervision mechanism, legal system, environment system, etc., on the other hand. Such mode is prevalent in nations of mid-term development stages of market economy, such as China before its entry into the WTO. Sixth, the semi-strong form of effective government + the strong form of efficient market is very much the case of the current United States. During the economic development of the USA, the market plays a decisive role in the distribution of resources, while the government also plays an important role in the distribution of non-operative resources. However, due to institutional or ideological constraints, the USA has been ambiguous or inconsistent in allocating operative resources and distinguishing and developing quasi-operative resources, hence difficult to make breakthroughs in this regard, resulting in lack of systematic and foresighted planning in its overall economic growth and urban upgrading. Seventh, the strong form of effective government + the weak form of efficient market, which barely exists in reality, because the strong form of effective government is at least equipped with the semi-strong form of efficient market. Besides, it should be noted that nations with planned economies do not belong to this mode. Eighth, the strong form of effective government + the semi-strong form of efficient market, which is very much akin to today's China. The Chinese economy is generally regarded as a gradually maturing market economy led by the government. Though China has already registered remarkable economic achievements, it also faces challenges in further improving market competition, market order, market credit and market infrastructure. Ninth, the strong form of effective government + the strong form of an efficient market, is the favorite or optimal combination of a government and a market, which shall be a target nations across the world strive for in theory and practice and also a necessary path to a truly mature market economy.

10.5 "An effective government + an efficient market" = a mature market economy

As seen from above, a strong form of effective government essentially has the following features. First, it is able to effectively distribute non-operative resources and introduce supporting policies, promote social harmony and stability, and enhance the economic environment. Second, it can effectively distribute operative resources and introduce supporting policies, maintain openness, equity and justice of the market, and effectively improve the overall productivity of society. Third, it is capable of effectively distributing quasi-operative resources and participating in the competition, promoting comprehensive and sustainable development of urban construction, social welfare and economic growth. The effectiveness of a strong form of effective government resides in its integrating of distributing the three types of resources, introducing supporting policies for them and fully capitalizing on them to realize social and economic targets. There are three criteria for a strong form of effective government: Respecting market rules; maintaining economic order and stabilizing economic development; effectively distributing resources and participating in regional competition.

As for the strong form of an efficient market, it indicates sound operation of the market (ensured by market factor system and market organization system), basic orders (guaranteed by market legal system and market supervision system) and a sound market foundation (constituted by market environment system and market infrastructure). The efficiency of a strong form of efficient market relies on the functioning of the six pillars of the modern market system and displays itself in the integration of perfect competition in production, a level playing field and a friendly business environment. There are three benchmarks for a strong form of efficient market: Perfect market competition, orderly legal supervision and a sound social credit system.

As discussed in Chapter 7, the strong form of effective government possesses at least three qualities in real economic development. First, keeping up with the times, which means the government urgently needs to keep abreast with new technologies. New resources, new instruments, new industries and new business modes derived from rapid technological development will manifest a huge impact on the traditional government administration system. New technologies bring not only new demands and high efficiency in social production but also various problems in government administration. Therefore, in order to fulfill its function in industrial development, urban construction and social welfare, or to play a proper role in distributing non-operative resources, operative resources and quasi-operative resources, the government must advance with the times in its governing philosophy, policies and measures. Second, to conduct all-round competition, which means a strong form of effective government needs to lead with foresightedness, innovate in concept, technology, organization and institution, and participate in the whole process and all fronts of competition in areas of social welfare (by optimizing the allocation of public goods and effectively improving economic environment), industrial development (by leading, supporting, regulating and supervising market players and effectively enhancing production efficiency) and urban construction (by following market rules and participating in project construction). An all-around competition is based on enterprise competition but is not limited to traditional competition over commodity production. Instead, it covers the whole process of planning, introducing policies and measures, and final production of outcomes to realize comprehensive and sustainable social and economic development of a nation. Third, disclosure of government information, including decision-making, implementation, management, services, key issues (areas) of public concerns. Open and transparent disclosure of government affairs can guarantee the right to be informed, participate, express and supervise of all parties in society, and enhance the effectiveness of resource distribution in industrial development, urban construction and social welfare. A strong form of effective government, which is transparent, innovative, clean, service-oriented and features governing by rule of law, can stimulate market vitality and social creativity for the benefits of all nations and the entire humanity.

The relationship between the government and the market is as complex as the Goldbach's conjecture in economics. Great achievements in industrial development, urban construction and social welfare made by the organic combination of effective governments and efficient markets have already been testified by successful cases at home and abroad, though there still exist lag in theory and contradictions between theory and practice, which still require further exploration for theoretical innovation. Here are some examples.

The first is the "Singapore Consensus," which helped promote overall social progress of the country with a total area of only 718.3 km^2 and a total population of around 5.5 million. In 1960, per capita GDP of Hong Kong SAR and Singapore were $405 and $427, respectively; by 1980, $5,700 and $4,927, respectively; and by 2013, $38,358 and $56,389, respectively, with Singapore far exceeding Hong Kong SAR. During this period, Singapore successfully realized five economic transformations: Establishing labor-intensive industries in the 1960s, building resource-intensive industries in the 1970s, shifting to capital-intensive industries in the 1980s, committing to technology-intensive industries in the 1990s and focusing on knowledge-intensive industries after entry into the 21st century, during which process, the government was the principal driving force.

The success of Singapore demonstrates the government's duties and roles in attracting and nurturing business. The Singaporean government has developed an industry-oriented corporate service mechanism to vigorously facilitate economic development. For example, the Singapore Economic Development Board (EDB), as a government agency responsible for strategies that enhance Singapore's position as a global center for business, innovation and talent, conducts detailed strategic discussions every three years on key industries to be introduced. Once key industries are identified, the EDB will set up a professional industry-oriented framework and establish a service system and send personnel to provide one-on-one full service for key clients and endow them with flexibility on government policies and ensure full service to clients. Specialized industrial screening and personal services have led to rapid progress in key sectors such as electronic information, biotechnology and healthcare. Besides, Singapore's government, while dominating economic development, has also endeavored to drive forward social progress and effective governance. The Housing Development Board (HDB) of Singapore, for example, is well known for addressing housing problems for people. On one hand, it enjoys preferential government policies to improve housing conditions and accelerate housing construction while on the other hand, it has introduced market mechanisms to ensure adequate financial backup. The combination of the forces of the government and the market, and that of economic development policies and social development policies, effectively promoted balance between efficiency and equity, development and stability, and propelled economic growth, urban upgrading and overall social progress. What the world commends as the "Singapore Consensus" is precisely the result of "an effective government + an efficient market," which leads the nation towards comprehensive and sustainable growth.

The second is about the economic takeoff of the Pearl River Delta and the emergence of Guangdong-Hong Kong-Macao Greater Bay Area, which are both epitomes of the "Chinese Dream." As reported by a Russian journalist called Pepe Escobar, Shenzhen was just a barren fishing village north to Hong Kong in 1979. In the early 1990s, the Pearl River Delta just began to emerge as China's largest labor-intensive manufacturing center. Today, the Pearl River Delta, represented by cities like Guangzhou, Shenzhen, Foshan and Dongguan, is accelerating its development of high-end industries in the value chain and building itself a world-class national manufacturing innovation center and national science and technology innovation center, as well as a first-class international metropolitan cluster based on its urbanization strategy. Its fascination with innovation and endeavor to promote urbanization in the Pearl River Delta is expediting and leading China towards a new social and economic model. The Pearl River Delta has accomplished in just 20 years what the west achieved in 200 years. The driving force behind such achievement in industrial development, urban construction and social welfare lies in the combined efforts of "the market + the government," a reconstructed model of innovative market economy. Now, the Pearl River Delta is continuing its efforts in exploring coordinated development of the government and the market for new breakthroughs in industrial development, urban construction and social welfare.

At present, the nine cities in the Pearl River Delta, including Guangzhou, Shenzhen, Zhuhai, Dongguan, Huizhou, Zhongshan, Foshan, Zhaoqing and Jiangmen, are joining hands with Hong Kong SAR and Macao SAR in building the Guangdong-Hong Kong-Macao Greater Bay Area. Speaking of bay areas, Tokyo, New York and San Francisco bay areas will pop up in one's mind. These three areas are all key economic and cultural centers of their nations respectively. The Tokyo Bay Area is the headquarters of many Fortune Global 500 companies, such as Toyota, Sony and Mitsubishi; the San Francisco Bay Area boasts Internet giants like Apple, Google, and Facebook; whilst the New York Metropolitan Area has gathered a large number of financial institutions, making itself the heartland of global finance. The Greater Bay Area of Guangdong, Hong Kong and Macao aims to rival Tokyo and New York bay areas. In 2016, the GDP of the Greater Bay Area was about $1.38 trillion, comparable to that of the ROK, which ranked 11th in the world economy; Its cargo capacity reached 65.2 million TEUs (20-foot equivalent unit), exceeding that of the Tokyo, New York and San Francisco bay areas combined; In terms of airport passenger throughput, it topped all bay areas by a total of 186 million person-times; The total value of imports and exports in the Greater Bay Area stood at around $1.8 trillion and foreign direct investment $102.91 billion, accounting for 5.9% of global FDI inflows.

China's "Government Work Report" in 2017 stressed to go ahead with the initiative of Guangdong-Hong Kong-Macao Greater Bay Area, striving to build it into a first-class international bay area and a world-class city cluster. Specific measures include the following. First, boosting infrastructure connectivity and coordinated development of ports, airports and rapid transportation networks as well as infrastructure for imports and exports. Second, speeding up the development of logistics and shipping and building the Greater Bay Area a world-class shipping cluster that includes accelerating construction of free trade ports, vigorously developing intermodal logistics systems and upgrading shipping services of the region. Third, promoting innovation in science and technology and resource-sharing, and building an international innovation center for science and technology. In addition to strengthening science and technology infrastructure, establishing a transfer and transformation mechanism of scientific and technological achievements, encouraging youth innovation and entrepreneurship, and promoting science and technology finance, it is also vital to vigorously encourage outsourcing of science and technology services and cooperation on intellectual property protection. Fourth, driving forward integrated development of manufacturing industries and building a pilot zone of "Made in China 2025" initiative, which will facilitate synergy of manufacturing industrial chains, reinforce industrial informatization, promote international cooperation in production capacity and incentivize equipment manufacturing industry to go global. Fifth, enhancing innovation in financial sectors and building an international financial hub, which includes measures to foster and strengthen shipping finance, science and technology finance, promote the integration of industry and finance, expedite the construction of financial platforms, and promote offshore finance and onshore finance to converge. Sixth, strengthening the integration of the bay area and building a friendly environment for living, business and tourism. The rise of the Guangdong-Hong Kong-Macao Greater Bay Area, which has already manifested substantial progress, has created a new development pattern and served as a new model of regional economic development, which is attributed to the dual roles of "an effective government + an efficient market."

The third example is the case of US government, which is yet to be deciphered. To date, the United States is still the most powerful economy in the world. In economic theory, the United States upholds economic liberalism, while at some critical moments of domestic and international economic development, the American government has repeatedly turned to government intervention and succeeded, thus shaping the largest economy in the past, at present, and possibly even in the future. Here are some cases.

1 The American monetary and financial system was established by Alexander Hamilton. Hamilton, the first secretary of the Treasury serving during George Washington's administration, committed his efforts in building the national financial system under the support of his President. During his term, he endeavored to establish the national credit scheme, improve the financial system, set up a complete financial management system, and managed to create favorable conditions for the development of industry and commerce, hence putting in place the five pillars of the American financial system: a unified government bond market, a central-led banking system, a unified mintage system (bimetallism), a taxation system based mainly on tariff and consumption tax, and financial and trade policies encouraging growth of manufacturing industries. Together, they laid a solid foundation of the modern financial system of the country, which grew to lead the global economy. Therefore, Hamilton is considered by some as the greatest secretary of the Treasury of the country. In this regard, we need to consider: Why did Hamilton, a figure over 200 years ago, already emphasize so heavily on "national credit?" Why did he think that it was necessary for the USA to build a strong federal government in order to build the nation into a prosperous and powerful economy?
2 President Franklin D. Roosevelt's New Deal, implemented since 1933. It mainly aimed to increase employment and stimulate consumption and production through vigorous construction of infrastructure projects. Here are some specific measures under the program. First, the Civilian Conservation Corps (CCC) work program, which hired young men, aged 18–25, to work in woods and fields to plant trees, prevent and control

floods, fight soil erosion, build roads and buildings, construct forest roads and trails and fight forest fire on the federal land. By the time the USA joined the battle of the World War II, a total of over 2 million young men were employed in the CCC. Together, they worked on more than 7.4 million acres of national forests and parks. Second, the Public Works Administration and the Civil Works Administration were established for long-term projects. The Civil Works Administration which aimed at civil engineering were responsible for 180,000 small-scale projects across the nation, including school buildings, bridges, dikes, sewerage systems, post offices and buildings of administration agencies, providing employment for four million people successively. Several new relief systems were also established subsequently. Among them, the most prominent were the Works Progress Administration (WPA), which received a grant of $five billion from Congress and the National Youth Administration (NYA) which provided work training for the youth of the nation. It was estimated that a total of 23 million people were employed by WPA and NYA, over half of the nation's total working population back then. Third, on the eve of World War II, the Federal Government had already invested $18 billion for various projects and direct relief. Under the New Deal, the American government built nearly 1,000 airports, more than 12,000 sports fields, and more than 800 school buildings and hospitals, which created vast employment opportunities for the American people. The Golden Gate Bridge and the Hoover Dam built under Roosevelt's New Deal are still American landmarks till this day.

3 The international financial system was established at the Bretton Woods Conference. In July 1944, the Bretton Woods Conference was convened in New Hampshire, the USA. Prior to the conference, John Maynard Keynes, the principal British negotiator, put forward his plan of an international reserve currency called the bancor, a powerful global central bank, and an International Clearing Union for international economic stability in the postwar world. In contrast, Harry Dexter White, representing the ascendant power of the USA as a chief international economist at the Treasury, in light of the logic that politics prevails over economy, managed to win over Keynes with his White Plan, which eventually led to the establishment of three committees working respectively on the establishment of the International Stabilization Fund, the International Bank for Reconstruction and Development, now known as the World Bank Group, and other issues on international financial cooperation. The subsequent International Monetary Fund (IMF), the World Bank (IBRD), and the Bank for International Settlements (BIS) all originated from his vision. Here what is worth considering is why the international financial system of the Bretton Woods Conference, a result of wrestling of power of 44 nations more than 70 years ago, is still exerting its impact today?

4 The dollar-dominated international currency system reinforced by the Marshall Plan, which, led by the USA, began in April 1948 and ended in 1951. During this period, the Organization for European Economic Cooperation (OEEC) was established to administer the predominantly US-funded Marshall Plan for post-war reconstruction on the continent and a counterpart fund was set up to turn the foreign aid into reserves of the domestic currency. The USA's aid to Europe included funds, technology and personnel, etc. Among them, funds flowed from the USA to European countries, which were utilized as foreign currency to purchase American goods. Apart from Germany which used such funds for reinvestment in private enterprises, the majority of European countries had to fill deficits with the funds and thus basically had no capability to repay the debts. In this process, the US dollars stayed in Europe and became "eurodollars." From bimetallism to the "gold standard," currency system gradually developed from the "gold and silver bimetallism," to pegging the exchange rates of all currencies to the US dollar, which was pegged to gold (with a fixed exchange rate: $35 to 1 ounce of gold), and then to the "fixed exchange rate system of US dollar to other currencies" (the dollar was separated from gold on August 15, 1971), and to the "floating exchange rate system of US dollar to other currencies" (established in 1976 by the Jamaica Agreement), and eventually to the petrodollar, which is used to pay oil-exporting countries in exchange for oil, the international currency system was dominated by dollar so that the US dollar has been a strong currency in the international economy.

5 The American response to the 2008 financial crisis. The Federal Reserve, the Department of the Treasury, the Federal Deposit Insurance Corporation (FDIC), the Securities and Exchange Commission (SEC), the US Congress, and relevant federal agencies, such as the Department of Housing and Urban Development (HUD), were all fully committed in coping with the financial crisis and various measures were taken. First, the Federal Reserve, as the central banking system independent from the federal government and free from partisan disputes, adopted both the traditional radical monetary policy and unconventional currency policy, which effectively eased the impact of the financial crisis and stabilized the financial market through market approaches. Second, when the monetary policy of the Federal Reserve failed to ease the widely influencing and increasingly serious crisis, the Bush Administration timely introduced government intervention measures. Created and run by the Treasury, the Troubled Asset Relief Program (TARP) was implemented under the funding of the government in aid of major financial institutions and some large enterprises. Third, after Barack Obama took office, he took a string of steps to stabilize the financial market, enhance supervision and regulation, rapidly cut taxes in numerous areas, increase government spending and deficits to boost economic growth, along with the rescue programs adopted by the Bush Administration. Fourth, in

order to tackle the financial crisis, safeguard financial stability and reinvigorate the economy, both houses of Congress managed to build a sound legal environment through timely legislation. For instance, under the Bush and Obama Administration, Congress passed a series of acts such as the Emergency Economic Stabilization Act of 2008 (EESA), Economic Development Revitalization Act of 2008, Economic Development Revitalization Act of 2009, American Recovery and Reinvestment Act of 2009 (Recovery Act), as well as one of the most important economic reform and regulatory acts since the Great Depression in 1929, the Dodd-Frank Wall Street Reform and Consumer Protection Act (the Dodd-Frank Act). So it seems in response to the 2008 financial crisis, the United States has made every effort to address the crisis and achieve substantial results by adopting a number of measures, including monetary policy, fiscal policy, regulatory policy, economic revitalization programs and legislation, to maintain the stability and development of the financial market.

6 The $2 trillion infrastructure plan was proposed by Donald Trump in 2019. The program was put forward by the Trump Administration in order to create a new engine of economic growth through infrastructure construction such as highways, bridges, tunnels, airports, schools, hospitals, etc., so as to provide employment to millions of people and build the best highway and aviation system in the world.

In summary, laissez-faire has always dominated the American economy, and even the "Washington Consensus," a set of ten economic policy recommendations for South American countries, was introduced under this system. However, during economic operation in reality, the American government has not only repeatedly intervened in the economy, including livelihood economy and urban construction at home, through decisively formulating policies in support of industrial development at some critical moments, but also adopted forceful measures in intervening the international economy when necessary, and achieved success.

Although we say theory lags behind practice, theory, after all, originates from practice. The mode of a mature market economy, made up of a strong form of effective government and a strong form of an efficient market, even though has been proven by some successful cases, still leaves us many questions to answer. So it takes more effort to further study in this respect in order to explore an effective path to a mature market economy.

11 Several consensuses on governmental economic behavior

11.1 Review of mezzoeconomic theories

First, the Resource Generation Theory. Resource generation is relative to resource scarcity. Resources generated in resource generation are not produced as planned but are resources that already exist or resources generated with the progress of the times. They become dynamic from the original static state before they get economic and productive features. Resource generation covers at least three levels of resources. First, primordial resources, such as space resources, marine resources, polar resources and deep earth resources. When unexploited, they are static natural resources while once developed and exploited, they become dynamic and generative economic resources. Second, derivative resources. In the course of historical development, resources such as hardware and software urban infrastructure have gradually emerged as demanded by social and economic progress, so that quasi-operative resources are transformed into operative resources, which are derivative resources of an economic nature in the urban economy. Third, inverse resources, for example, carbon emissions and trading of carbon emissions, which do not originally exist, but are generated by the spillover effect of regional economic development. If such resources are not exploited, the negative externalities of the economy would run rampant in the society, while if exploited, the scope and extent of the negative externalities would be contained or curbed. Such resources are also generative resources with economic values.

Overall speaking, generative resources have four main characteristics: Dynamic, economic, productive and high risks. It is precisely because of its high-risk nature that the government must be the primary investor in the three types of generative resources mentioned above, at the same time, it should assume the responsibility for determining regulations of investment and development and pricing. Furthermore, the development of resource generation externally makes it possible for government competition.

Second, the Dual Attributes Theory of Governments. According to this theory, regional governments play a quasi-macro role with their public and mandatory power in performing their political, economic, urban and social

DOI: 10.4324/9781003244837-11

functions on the one hand while on the other hand, regional governments, acting as an agent of the regional economy, play a micro role to effectively distribute resources for maximum benefits of the regional economy through conceptual, technological, organizational and institutional innovation, so that right of jurisdiction of regional governments is transformed into the right of operation of the regional economy. The quasi-macro attribute of regional governments emphasizes coordination while the quasi-micro attribute highlights interests. So in terms of policy implementation, the principle of "planning and guiding, support and coordination, supervision and management" is practiced in the industrial economy, the principle of "formulating overall plans, participating in construction and conducting orderly management" is followed in the urban economy, and the principle of "guaranteeing basic needs, ensuring fairness and justice, raising effectiveness and efficiency" is complied with in livelihood economy. What supports the dual functions of regional governments is the fiscal revenue mechanism, in which fiscal income depends on the regional economic development level, economic policies and measures and efficiency of economic management. So, the nature of dual attributes of regional governments requires them to maximize fiscal revenues, and in turn, to improve the policy environment and adopt effective economic measures, which suggests an inherent inevitability of regional governments' participation in the competition.

Third, the Regional Government Competition Theory, namely the "Sheep's Horns Competition Theory" or the "9-in-3" Competition Theory. The level of regional economic development is determined by the number of regional economic projects, how complete industrial chains are and the volume of imports and exports; regional economic policies and measures are reflected in the amount of input of regional investment in urban infrastructure, the level of scientific and technological innovation of talents and support of financial instruments; regional economic management efficiency is manifested in efficiency of regional policy system, environment system and management system. Together, they constitute the "9-in-3" competition among regional governments (see Figure 5.1).

Broadly speaking, competition among regional governments is centered around supporting policies and measures for competition over operative resources (industrial economy), non-operative resources (livelihood economy) and quasi-operative resources (urban economy), which actually is "9-in-3" competition. In essence, it is a competition over government revenue, the objective function in industrial development, urban construction and social welfare. Narrowly speaking, regional government competition mainly refers to competition for investment, development and construction of quasi-operative resources (infrastructure resources), which substantially is a competition in investment strategies. Regional government competition differs from enterprise competition in nine aspects: The objective functions they compete for, the way they establish their objective functions, the path they realize their objective functions, their investment and financing mechanisms, their price-determining mechanisms, competition orientations, areas of competition, their roles in competition, as well as their management modes. The competitiveness of regional governments can be assessed quantitatively by comparing the input end (structure of fiscal expenditure) and the output end (regional performance) through the District Resource Planning (DRP) model. Through the "9-in-3" competition, regional governments will benefit from the scale effects, cluster effects and neighborhood effects, and the urban economic development will follow the 80/20 rule, which eventually will prompt investors to select regional governments by "voting with feet," which means through the flow of personnel, capital and goods, investors choose regions with favorable public environment and services to grow their business.

Fourth, the Competitive Economic Growth Theory. Through analysis over the growth periods dominated by competition in the industrial economy, urban economy, innovation-driven economy and competition and cooperation driven economy, this theory reveals that economic development in countries all over the world is boosted by the dual entities of competition, enterprises and regional governments, and that economic growth in all countries is primarily driven by competition. In this historical process, regional government competition has shown trends towards industrial effects, urban sprawl, innovation-driven and coordinated development, which ultimately demonstrates a gradient trend. On one hand, regional government competition is initiated in developed regions who lead in industrial, urban and innovative growth, while on the other hand, with progress of the times and with changes in regional economies internally and externally, regional government competition has gradually spread from developed regions to less developed regions. Developed regions have a leading advantage in government competition and are at the high end of the gradient pattern, while other regional governments are at the low end of the gradient pattern due to differences in competitiveness, policies and measures. During the objective process of historical development, there has been an increasing supply of ideological, material, organizational and institutional public goods, so economic development across regions is moving towards balance with gradient differences.

Fifth, the GFL. Regional governments should exercise "foresighted leading" in resource allocation, which means to do what enterprises cannot do or cannot do well while allowing enterprises to play their own part. The GFL requires governments to follow market rules and rely on market forces to guide, adjust and forewarn the growth of the industrial economy, coordinate, participate in and maintain the order of urban economic development and guarantee, safeguard and improve livelihood economy. It requires governments to utilize policies on planning, investment, consumption, pricing, taxation, interest rates, exchange rates, legislation, etc., as well as conceptual, technological, organizational and institutional innovation to effectively push forward structural reforms on the supply side or the demand side with a view to forming a leading edge in economic growth and facilitating scientific and sustainable development of the regional economy.

GFL includes four stages: Leading in concept, organization, technology and institution, and overall leading. In theory, foresighted leading in concept is the key to competitiveness for factor-driven economic growth, organizational leading the key to investment-driven economy, technological and institutional leading the key to innovation-driven economy, and overall leading the inevitable choice for wealth-driven economy. In practice, the formulation and implementation of competition policies of regional governments play a critical role. The competition policy system of regional governments should cover policy targets, policy content, expected objectives, instruments, effects and time lag. Among them, policy instruments (tools) benefit from spillover effects from fiscal, financial, environmental, efficiency and legal instruments, which together form the externalities of regional supply-side and demand-side effects, regional economic stock and incremental effects, and externalities from disequilibrium to equilibrium, thus making economic growth across regions conform to "the 80/20 rule." Government foresighted leading enables regions to distinguish themselves from regional government competition and regional economic competition so as to make them part of the winning minority in the 80/20 rule.

Sixth, the DEMC. The horizontal market system consists of the industrial economy, urban economy, and international economy (such as space economy, marine economy, polar economy, earth exploration economy), etc. While the vertical market system includes market factor system, market organization system, market legal system, market supervision system, market environment system, and market infrastructure. In the modern market system, enterprises are the major market players in the industrial economy and regional governments the major market players in the urban economy as well as the principal investors in developing generative resources. Therefore, there are DEMC: enterprises mainly in the industrial economy and regional governments mainly in the urban economy. Enterprise competition centers on optimized resource allocation under conditions of resource scarcity, while regional government competition strives for optimized resource allocation on the basis of resource generation. The role of the dual entities in the modern market economy manifests three rules in the development practice of nations around the world, including the congregating effect of the 80/20 rule, the equilibrium law of gradient changes and the coordination effect of competition and cooperation. At the same time, due to participation in the competition of regional governments and their SOEs, we must also emphasize the principle of competitive neutrality. From the perspective of the six pillars of the modern market system, regional governments should, based on the principle of competitive neutrality, create a level playing field for the DEMC. At present, it is extremely important to formulate and constantly improve the principle of competitive neutrality for the application standards of market credit systems and market infrastructure across regions and nations.

Seventh, the "Double Strong Forms" Theory of a mature market economy. Efficient markets can be categorized into three types, the weak form, the semi-strong form, and the strong form and so do effective governments. Together, they can produce nine combinations. A mature market economy must be the combination of a strong form of effective government and a strong form of efficient market that shall be the target economic breakthroughs aim at and the necessary path nations worldwide should follow for sustainable development. For a strong form of effective government, it must respect market rules, safeguard economic order and keep economic development on a stable track, and effectively distribute resources and participate in regional competition. While a strong form of effective market also has three criteria. It should allow full competition, feature orderly legal supervision, and put in place a sound social credit system. The "double strong forms" mechanism in a mature market economy will help clarify the complicated relationship between the government and the market so as to concretely improve industrial development, urban construction and social welfare in nations around the world.

Eighth, the New Economic Engine Theory. Generative resources include primordial resources, derivative resources and inverse resources. Generative resources have four main characteristics: Dynamic, economic, productive and high risks, which requires the government to be the primary investor in generative resources. At the dawn of the era of urbanization-led economic growth, countries around the world should build new investment engines (through promoting supply-side structural reform, increasing investment in infrastructure and science and technology projects, and enhancing financial and fiscal support), new innovation engines (by driving forward ideological innovation, material innovation, organizational innovation and mechanical innovation, namely innovation in concept, technology, management and rules), as well as new rule engines (by maintaining the rules of international security order of "peace and stability," rules of international economic competition of "equity and efficiency," and rules of international common governance of "cooperation and win-win results)." Such new engines are structural engines on the supply side, rather than trade engines on the demand side. To achieve new growth in this century, countries around the world must equip themselves with new economic engines.

11.2 Mezzoeconomics and China

Through the previous discussion, we have made it clear that microeconomics studies the economic behavior and its results of individual agents (producers, consumers and firms) as its subject of research; the fundamental issue in microeconomics is about how to allocate resources under conditions of resource scarcity with its focus on price determination mechanism and relevant major microeconomic theories. Macroeconomics studies economic behavior and relevant results of a national or regional economy as a whole; it considers utilization of national resources and their optimal use, with the focus on the mechanism of determination of national income, and relevant major macro-economic theories. In contrast, mezzoeconomics concentrates on economic behavior and the results of regional agents (regional governments); its fundamental issue is about resource allocation on the basis of resource generation with the focus on major economic variables affecting regional competition, namely the revenue and expenditure of regional governments; major theories in this field include the Resource Generation Theory, the Dual Attributes Theory of Governments, the Regional Government Competition Theory, the Competitive Economic Growth Theory, the GFL, the New Economic Engine Theory, the DEMC as well as the "Double Strong Forms" Theory of a mature market economy, among which the Regional Government Competition Theory, the DEMC, the "Double Strong Forms" Theory and the GFL are disruptive innovations in modern economics or even the entire economic system, which are based on Chinese experience but are affecting the whole world.

The American economist, Milton Friedman, commented that whoever accurately explained China's reform and development would win a Nobel Prize in Economics. China's economic development has become a special phenomenon in the world economy. Theoretical research and empirical analysis over the Chinese economy will certainly become one of the important achievements of world economic research. By far, various schools of economics have put forward different explanations for China's unique experience of success through reform and opening up.

First, the new institutional economics (NIE). The first one is the Coase Theorems on property rights. According to the second theorem of Coase, if bargaining becomes costly, then property rights matter significantly. In the words of Coase, "If bargaining is costly and information is imperfect, then liability rules help to achieve optimality and the party that has the least costly way of dealing with the harmful effects of an externality should be made responsible for paying the costs associated with the externality." From the practice of China's reform, we can see that the extension of terms of farmers' contracted farmland in rural areas and circulation of farmers' rights to operate contracted farmland, ownership reform in urban China, as well as measures to invigorate large enterprises while relaxing control over small ones are all closely associated with the theorem. During its reform and opening up, China is moving in the direction of clarifying property rights and protecting property rights. According to Qiren Zhou, a professor of economics at Peking University, by clarifying property rights, institutional costs have been cut significantly and economic performance has improved remarkably. The second is the transaction cost approach upheld by economists such as Oliver E. Williamson. Transaction cost is a core concept in new institutional economics. The efficiency of transactions represents the efficiency of economic operations. The lower the transaction costs, the higher the efficiency of economic activities. Therefore, the system with the smallest transaction costs is the most effective one. A string of reform measures China adopted aims to reduce transaction costs. For instance, at the micro level, companies gradually establish and constantly improve their corporate governance structure with a view to decreasing internal organizational costs and external supervisory costs. At the macro level, government reforms in economic and social management, including "deregulation," reforms in commercial systems and introduction of negative lists, all strive to cut transaction costs. The third is the institutional change theory of Douglass North. North categorizes institutional changes into two types: Induced institutional changes and imposed institutional changes. The former is a bottom-up reform while the latter is a top-down change. Coase believes that the reason why China's reform has achieved remarkable success is that there exists two different paths of reform: Top-down reform imposed by the government (through top-level design) and bottom-up induced revolutions (grass-root-level innovation), which complement each other. In practice, reform measures are first piloted in some regions before they are rolled out nationwide, usually from the countryside to cities, from coastal regions to the hinterland, thus forming a gradual reform model that combines induced and imposed institutional changes. Fourth, the theory of *xian* (county) competition proposed by Steven N.S. Cheung, a Hong Kong-born American economist. Steven N.S. Cheung believes that the *xian*-competing system is the chief reason why China was able to sustain rapid growth during some very difficult times in the 1990s, and is also an important factor for China's economic success in the early 21st century. He holds that *xians* are effectively business firms of the first order. Business firms of the same nature compete, and this is another reason for the intense competition among *xians*. Because of *xian* competition, the concentration of industries by type in particular locations is very pronounced and privatization of state enterprises has been pressed to proceed faster. Besides, *xian* competition has also been a force to reduce corruption. So competition among *xians* makes the Chinese economic miracle possible. In fact, *xian* competition can also be extended to local governments at various levels. Chinese Vice Premier He Liu once pointed out that each successful province and even each successful region in China has its own unique development mode, which incentivizes different variables to play their part and contribute to economic development. Different as they are, they share similarities in nature. Fifth, the cultural factor theory advocated by He Liu. Liu believes that it seems that capital, labor, technology and geographical advantages are factors determining economic growth, but in fact, ultimately it is culture and customs that are the key to success. So we must explore the reform path in a gradual manner and in accordance with the Chinese culture. Tian Zhu, Professor of Economics, Santander Chair in Economics, Associate Dean and Director of EMBA Programme at CEIBS, also believes that a high savings rate and a high level of civic education are indeed the driving force behind the rapid growth of China's economy, which primarily has its origin from the Chinese culture which values savings and education.

Second, the development economics. The first one is the open economy theory upheld by Hollis B. Chenery. According to his two-gap model, opening up to the outside world and introducing foreign capital play an important role in realizing economic take-off for developing countries.

From the perspective of China's reform and opening up, the significance of opening up is no less than reform. As He Liu pointed out, opening up allows China to take advantage of the best practice of economic development of the human society in a timely manner and greatly benefit from the global division of labor. Opening up also plays an important role in affecting, shattering and devastating the outdated mechanism of the planned economy. After adopting a series of measures to increasingly deepen reform, such as export-oriented economic policies, the establishment of special economic zones, a sharp depreciation of the RMB, and accession to the WTO, China has been able to establish close ties with the international community and fully enjoy the dividends of globalization so that China's economic system is integrated into the global division of labor. Based on China's comprehensive comparative advantages such as low labor costs, China rapidly upgrades its technology and improves economic operation, which has led to a massive wave of industrialization. The second is Alexander Gerschenkron's model of late-comer economic development. According to this theory, China's rapid development after 1978 has benefited from its late-comer advantages. Developing countries can invent new industries and new technologies themselves, or they can learn from high-income countries and capitalize on mature technologies which are better than those they currently use and enter into mature industries with higher added value than theirs. In this way, developing countries can greatly reduce the costs and risks of technological innovation and industrial upgrading and achieve rapid growth. However, according to Xiaokai Yang, a Chinese-Australian economist, attention should be paid to the disadvantages of latecomers. It is easy for latecomers to imitate technologies, but it is more difficult to imitate mechanisms because reforms on mechanisms will hurt vested interests. As a result, although developing countries can realize rapid growth in the short term, many hidden problems will be incurred in the long term, which may even lead to failures. The third is the "dual economy" development model proposed by W. Arthur Lewis. One of the special features of China's reform and opening-up is that it makes full use of its demographic dividend. On one hand, during the reform, labor-intensive industries expanded rapidly, which absorbed massive employment, and the rural labor force migrated at an unprecedented scale, so that China's advantages in the labor force were transformed into a comparative advantage of the Chinese economy. On the other hand, with a high proportion of working population and a high employment rate, the total social saving was huge and so was surplus in economic activities, which drove up a high savings rate in China at the time. The realization of a high savings rate, apart from being boosted by the population dividend, could not have been possible without a sound environment and market mechanism for savings and investment through reform measures. The fourth is the three-stage development model proposed by Michael E. Porter and Klaus Schwab in *Global Competitiveness Report*. According to them, economic development can fall into three stages, factor-driven (per capita GDP less than $2,000), efficiency-driven phase (per capita GDP $3,000 to $9,000) and innovation-driven stage (per capita GDP greater than $17,000). At the beginning of reform and opening up, factors of production including internal and external labor force, capital and land were fully mobilized through reform, which propelled rapid economic expansion, thus allowed China to smoothly shift from the factor-driven stage to the efficiency-driven stage. However, the basic role of the market in resource allocation was not given full play and more emphasis was put on the role of the government than the market. So there was still space for improvement in terms of efficiency. Now, some large cities and wealthy provinces have entered into the innovation-driven stage and some enterprises have been as advanced as those in developed countries, which charts the course for future development of the Chinese economy.

Third, the transitional economics. In the process of China's transition from a planned economy to a market economy, there have been issues such as "costs of reform" as proposed by Gang Fan, one of China's most prominent economists and one of China's most active reform advocates. Compared with radical reform, progressive reform incurs higher costs, but less friction, so the total cost is relatively small. After weighing the benefits and costs of reform, China chose the path of progressive reform, which thus has always been associated with economic interests, compensations and alternatives. First, reform measures are advanced from easy ones to difficult ones. Reform measures usually started from areas with small frictions and low risks in rural areas and once succeeded, were promoted to urban areas, which is what Coase called the "marginal revolution." The second is to resolve reform obstacles through economic compensation. At the early stage of reform, China chose the path of "Pareto improvement," which means when relaxing the unplanned system, proper "interest compensation" was given to the planned economy. For example, when raising the prices of agricultural products, subsidies for non-staple food were given to urban residents and prices of industrial products related to agricultural products were also allowed to increase correspondingly. Later on, an "alternative" strategy was adopted to cultivate a new and more efficient economic system (non-state economy) in place of the old system, thereby effectively easing the conflict of interests within the old planned system. The third is to adjust the market relationship through the "dual-track price system," which represents one of the special features of China's economic reform. Through the dual-track system, market relations were established outside the planned system, laying a solid foundation for the market economy. Besides, various other reform measures have been formulated, such as the dual-track exchange rate system, the dual-track wage system, the dual-track housing system and the reform on the social insurance scheme. The fourth is to transfer reform costs through decentralization. Before the reform, the national power was highly centralized while local governments had limited autonomy. In order to effectively promote reform, the central government decentralized its power to local governments, recognized local interests, mobilized local enthusiasm, and forged a competitive relationship between local governments, thus making local governments a powerful engine of reform. Fifth, promoting comprehensive institutional innovation through pilot programs. In line with the path of progressive reform, pilot programs were adopted at the onset of reform and once ready, were promoted across the board. A typical example is the establishment of special economic zones, which is conducive to accumulating experience and reducing risks. At the same time, the demonstration effect of pilots can propel institutional innovation, thereby greatly reducing the costs of reform when it is implemented.

Fourth, the neoclassical economics. According to Xiaonian Xu, Honorary Professor at CEIBS, reform and opening up have actually followed two paths. The first path is to drive economic growth by improving the efficiency of resource utilization, which can be called the "Smithian model" while the second path is to propel economic growth through increased resource input, which can be called the "Keynesian model." Xu believes that in around the first half of reform and opening up of about two decades, the rapid growth of the Chinese economy was attributed to market mechanisms and private forces rather than policy-driven investment, as well as improvement of efficiency of resource allocation and utilization instead of increases in the amount of resources invested. Since the mid-1990s, China has turned to the "Keynesian model" of government intervention. Keynesian policies stimulated short-term demand, but were unable to boost long-term growth and dependence on stimulus was easily developed. Since the government has limited capability to put in resources and could not always raise a loan nor issue currency, apart from the impact of "the law of diminishing marginal returns on capital," policy-driven economic growth cannot sustain itself. From the perspective of neoclassical economists such as Paul R. Krugman, the success of China's reform and opening up mainly lies in the government's targeted selection of the neoclassical "prescription" and took it in a gradual manner. Take the exchange rate system as an example. In the era of the planned economy, the RMB was severely overvalued and became the main cause of China's "hunger for international currencies." After reform and opening up, the government began to adopt a dual-track exchange rate system, under which the RMB was still overrated in the official exchange rate, which was mainly used to control imports and cut costs of imports, while the market exchange rate basically followed market rules and was used to encourage exports. This is a typical mercantilist policy and a flexible application of neoclassical economic principles. Since 1994, the dual-track exchange rate system was unified and the price of the RMB against the dollar was fixed at 8.25 yuan until 2005, after which, the RMB entered into an era of managed floating exchange rates, but still striving to be stable. The fixed exchange rate system has greatly fueled China's exports and accelerated China's industrialization process at the expense of rising worker wages.

Other cases in point also include the dual-track price system, SOE reforms and industrial policies. Selective application of "prescriptions" of neoclassical economics is actually not unique to China, but is a common practice of successful economies in East Asia.

Fifth, the political economics. Focusing on relations between the government and the economy, political economics holds that in the process of reform and opening up, the government plays an extremely important role in three aspects. One is the neutral central government theory proposed by Yang Yao, professor at the China Center for Economic Research and Dean of the National School of Development at Peking University. A neutral central government can introduce systems and policies that are conducive to long-term development. At the beginning of the reform, the central government abandoned the obsession with class struggle, and instead implemented measures on economic construction. Through a series of meetings of the central authorities and a string of five-year plans, the central government has adopted systems and mechanisms conducive to economic growth. As Vice Premier He Liu pointed out, the government attaches great importance to the guiding role of the national development strategies, strives to maintain macroeconomic stability and values the advantages of China's political system in pulling together strength and wisdom on major undertakings, which is one of the greatest experiences of the reform and opening up. The second is the decentralization theory upheld by Weiying Zhang, a Chinese economist and former head of the Guanghua School of Management at Peking University. It is one of the special features of China's fiscal structure to endow local governments with rights of government revenues and also one of the contributors to its success. According to Zhang, decentralization to local governments has mobilized the enthusiasm of local officials to develop local economy, and regional competition has promoted the market-oriented transformation of the entire economy and thus is one of the most important driving forces of China's reform and progress. Daokui Li, Mansfield Freeman Chair Professor of the School of Economics and Management of Tsinghua University, argues that through administrative decentralization and promotion of market economy, local governments and emerging entrepreneurs are motivated to emerge, forming a trend to push forward China's economic and social development as a whole. The third is the official selection theory proposed by Barry Naughton. According to Naughton, leaders are racing to promote their supporters to key positions in order to get a key vote when necessary. The ability of a leader to promote his staff, as well as the ability to hinder his opponents from promoting their staff, is critical for building and consolidating his power. This two-way accountability system triggered fierce competition for promotion. Officials, especially local officials, launched a series of contests among each other, including in indexes of GDP, which greatly stimulated growth potentials.

Back to research on mezzoeconomics. The multidimensional mezzoeconomic theory stems from the practice of China's reform and opening up, and it also finds applications in resolving economic problems China meets in reality. It is fair to say that the establishment of mezzoeconomic theory is inextricably linked to China's experience. First, from the theoretical perspective, at least six aspects of the core economic theory the author attempts to establish in the field of mezzoeconomics come from the forefront of China's practice in reform and opening up. (1) The Resource Generation Theory and categorization of three kinds of regional resources, which originated from the author's experience in serving the Foshan Municipal Government. As a regional government, Foshan separated and redefined the role of industrial development, urban construction and social welfare, and made applications in practice accordingly in as early as 2004. (2) The establishment of the GFL. This theory can be traced back to achievements made by the Shunde District in Foshan in the process of reform and opening up and it was put into practice in 2005 for the sustainable economic development of the district. (3) The Dual Attributes Theory of Governments. This theory is based on an analysis over the economic behavior of the Shenzhen Municipal Government and has been further updated and improved as Shenzhen's reform and opening up constantly deepens. (4) The Regional Government Competition Theory, or the "9-in-3" Competition Theory. It is rooted in comparative analysis over cities in the Pearl River Delta region and it is also an overview of their practice in reform and opening up. (5) The DEMC and the "Double Strong Forms" Theory of a mature market economy. These two theories not only originate from reasonable thinking over China's four-decade reform and opening up, but also are backed up by the great achievements already made in China. (6) The New Economic Engine Theory. This theory is based on China's success in reform and opening up and sustainable development and puts forward concepts of new investment engines, innovation engines and rule engines, which explores a new path for sustainable development of the world economy. Second, from the point of view of research subjects, regional governments' competition in China can be seen in at least two fronts. One is the "9-in-3" competition, which outlines a clear picture of regional governments' contest in economic development, policies and measures as well as management efficiency. Besides, regional governments tend to establish SOEs as the backbone in competing for projects, resources for building complete industrial chains and imports and exports. These two modes of competition are interconnected and complementary in practice, hence comes the topic of competitive neutrality. Third, in chronological order, China's reform and opening up has grown by leaps and bounds and transformed from factor-driven, investment-driven to innovation-driven. Various forces have driven forward the sustainable growth of the Chinese economy, among which competition is a major contributor, as the competition among enterprises and among regional governments are double driving forces for the growth. Fourth, from the perspective of space, the major playing field of reform and opening up is extending from coastal regions to the hinterland

and from special economic zones to the whole nation. With the formation of dual entities in the market and as government foresighted leading comes into play, the socialist market economy with Chinese characteristics is making substantial strides to a mature market economy featuring a strong form of effective government and a strong form of an efficient market. The Chinese economy has already come under the global spotlight with its way of economic solution. The socialist economics with Chinese characteristics, combining an effective government and an efficient market, will revolutionize the global economic system.

In the face of the practice of China's reform and opening up, the academic community has debated for over four decades regarding three economic issues, yet without conclusions. First, at the national policy level, how do the government and the market get along with each other? Second, under the market system, how do private and state-owned enterprises get along with each other? Third, in private sectors, how do oligarchs and small and micro enterprises get along with each other? As mentioned previously, economists at home and abroad have already had their voices heard. Among various theories and views, mezzoeconomics, which stems from China's economic practice, has its answers to the above questions. Mezzoeconomics has a relatively short history of research and development. It was initially put forward by Dr. Hans-Rudolf Peters, a German professor of national economics in the mid-1970s. In the mid-1980s, Chinese scholar Mr. Shenzhi Wang published *Mezzoeconomics* (Shanghai People's Press, 1988) which elaborated upon Peters' idea and further expounded on the research scope of mezzoeconomics as sector economy, regional economy and collective economy. In 2011, the author published *Foresighted Leading: Theoretical Thinking and Practice of China's Regional Economic Development*, which was published by the German publishing company Springer in English two years later. In 2013, the author co-published with Jianwei Qiu *Government Foresighted Leading: Theory and Practice of the World's Regional Economic Development*, whose English edition was published by the British publisher Routledge in 2017. In 2015, co-authored with Wenjing Gu, the author's *Mezzoeconomics: Innovations and Developments in Theoretical Configuration of Economics* came out and was published in English by American Academic Press in 2018. In 2017, again co-written with Wenjing Gu, the *Regional Government Competition* came off the press and made its English publication by Routledge in 2019. The latest book *New Economic Engine—Effective Government and Efficient Market* made its publication in 2019. These publications have set up the theoretical framework of mezzoeconomics and opened up a broad space for further growth by elaborating on the GFL, the Dual Attributes Theory of Governments, the DEMC, and the "Double Strong Forms" Theory of a mature market economy. These mezzoeconomic theories have helped resolve economic problems China meets in economic development and have also charted the course for global economic development and the establishment of a new global economic governance system.

11.3 Mezzoeconomics and the world

Theoretical problems and practical conflicts of the world economy still center around the core issue of "the relationship between the government and the market." In China, we are exploring government foresighted leading; in the USA, the American government is making attempts to improve the domestic and international economy; the Singaporean government has already been promoting integrated development of an effective government and an efficient market; Germany, Japan and India are all making efforts to strengthen the role of governments in the economy; the USA and China have confronted each other for many times under the framework of the WTO. All the practice reflects the urgency to further study the above issues. Specifically, we need to make clear: In a modern market economy with a sovereign as a whole, should the government, the market, and the society each act in their own way? Or have the government and enterprises already become the dual entities of the modern market economy?

Mezzoeconomics, which takes regional governments and resource allocation on the basis of resource generation as the focus of research, provides answers to the above questions in at least seven aspects.

First, there are generative resources in all countries around the world, including primordial resources, derivative resources and inverse resources. Due to high risks associated with investment, development and operation of such resources, in reality, governments, including that of the USA, are their primary investors.

Second, within a country, resource generation spans across investment, development and construction of urban software and hardware infrastructure and facilities for the construction of smart cities. Internationally, it mainly includes investment and development of space resources, marine resources, polar resources and deep exploration resources. In reality, governments, including that of the USA, are all facing competition for projects in this regard at home and abroad.

Third, there exists industrial-economic competition with enterprises as the primary forces and urban and international economic competition with governments as principal players in countries worldwide. Therefore, economic growth inevitably will be driven forward by competition.

Fourth, faced with competition, governments around the world have formulated policies and measures to improve their industrial development, urban construction and social welfare through fiscal, financial, environmental, efficiency and legal instruments. So, it is an important topic for governments to introduce policies and measures based on the principle of competitive neutrality from the perspective of the six pillars of the modern market system, namely market factor, organization, legal system, supervision, environment and infrastructure systems.

Fifth, new engines of global economic growth include not only new investment engines in the field of resource generation but also new innovation engines on concept, technology, organization and institution, as well as new rule engines on ideological, material, organizational and institutional public goods. Governments around the world must face head on to this reality and capitalize on these new economic engines.

Sixth, according to the 80/20 rule, the final pattern of world economic development should be in a gradient model of balance, and the world economy should move towards growth through both competition and co-operation, and gradually realize a shared economy of win-win cooperation. Based on this view, governments around the world should follow market rules and do things that companies cannot do or cannot do well so as to guide, adjust and forewarn the growth of the industrial economy, co-ordinate, participate in and maintain the order of urban economy, and guarantee, safeguard and improve livelihood economy with policy instruments for coordinated innovation and sustainable development of the national economy. In this way, government foresighted leading will become an objective requirement for governments around the world and an inevitable trend they must follow.

Seventh, in the modern market economy, there exist three forms of effective governments: The weak form, the semi-strong form and the strong form. According to development levels of different countries (based on how complete and sound the six pillars of the modern market system are), there are also three forms of efficient markets: The weak form, the semi-strong form and the strong form. Combinations of effective governments and efficient markets result in differences in the economic progress of countries in the world today. A mature market economy must be one that combines the strong form of effective government and the strong form of an efficient market, which is not only an objective requirement in the process of resource generation, exploration and development but also a necessary path to scientific and sustainable growth for the world economy.

The rationality of mezzoeconomic theories will effectively help resolve world economic problems and substantially propel the sustainable economic growth of countries around the globe.

Epilogue

Since 2019 I have started lessons on mezzoeconomics for undergraduate and postgraduate students in the School of Economics, Peking University, School of Economics, Fudan University and Lingnan College, Sun Yat-sen University, with a view to addressing issues unable to be explained or resolved by microeconomics and macroeconomics. It was during this time that the first draft of this book basically took shape. In this book, I attempt to bring together my experience in and thoughts from the academia, business and official posts to discuss the economic behavior of regional governments and its significance, on which basis the long-neglected mezzoeconomics in economic research is further elaborated in order to illustrate China's practice of the recent four decades during reform and opening up and also try to identify new growth engines for the world economy.

My courses on mezzoeconomics are also based on key ideas illustrated in this book (attached is a copy of the course description on mezzoeconomics at Peking University). When teaching at some of the best universities in China, I'm able to discuss with promising young scholars on mezzoeconomic issues that have undoubtedly played an important role in helping me further improve this book. Hence, I would like to express my heartfelt gratitude to Peking University, Fudan University and Sun Yat-sen University for providing me with such platforms. My sincere thanks go to the Peking University Press for many years of support and to Professor Zhao Huimin of Sun Yat-sen University for her efforts in mathematical models employed in this book. I would also like to thank Wang Xianchao and Zhao Yaru for their hard work in editing the book, as well as Liu Xin and Li Yaqun for their precious contribution to the English translation of the book.

This book attempts to explore some innovations in terms of ideas, range of research and theoretical system. I hope it could stand the test of time and also look forward to feedback from society!

Yunxian Chen
Guangzhou, Guangdong
June 25, 2019

Summer Course of School of Economics, Peking University | 2019 "Scholar Lectures" Series

Mezzoeconomics

Course description

The research on economics has for a long period of time focused on micro and macro levels. However, between them, there exists an elusive branch of economics that is not covered by either microeconomics or macroeconomics, the mezzoeconomics, in which field, regional governments are the principal market players. This course elevates regional economics to the level of mezzoeconomics, and examines theories and practice of regional governments, so as to utilize the new theoretical framework of mezzoeconomics to answer questions that cannot be effectively explained and resolved by microeconomics and macroeconomics.

Syllabus

Lecture 1
Introduction on mezzoeconomics
Lecture 2
Resource Generation Theory and categorization of three types of resources
Lecture 3
Dual Attributes Theory of Governments
Lecture 4
Regional Government Competition Theory
Lecture 5
Government Foresighted Leading Theory (GFL)
Lecture 6
New Economic Engine Theory
Lecture 7
Dual-Entity of Market Competition (DEMC)
Lecture 8
"Double Strong Forms" Theory of a mature market economy
Lecture 9
Mezzoeconomic system and development prospect

Profile of Professor Chen Yunxian

Chen Yunxian, born in October 1955 in Shanghang, Fujian Province, is a senior economist with a PhD in economics at Peking University, a guest professor and researcher at Harvard University, Hong Kong Polytechnic University, Peking University and Sun Yat-sen University, Commissioner of Financial Advisory Committee of Guangdong Province, honorary dean of

International School of Business Finance and Advanced Institute of Finance at Sun Yat-sen University and former vice governor of Guangdong Province. He is awarded a special allowance by the State Council.

Since 1988 Chen studied economics at School of Economics, Peking University as a student of Xiao Zhuoji, a renowned Chinese economist, and obtained a PhD. In 1991, Chen founded GF Securities and since 2003 started to assume political posts, working as Secretary of Shunde District Committee of Foshan City in Guangdong Province, Executive Vice Mayor, Mayor and Secretary of the Foshan Municipal Committee of the Communist Party of China, Chairman of the Standing Committee of the Foshan Municipal People's Congress and Vice Governor of Guangdong Province.

He has furthered his study at the University of Massachusetts Boston, Harvard Business School, John F. Kennedy School of Government, Yale University and Rotman School of Management, University of Toronto.

Major academic publications

Chen Yunxian. *On Securities Investment*, Peking University Press, 1991.

Chen Yunxian. *On Investment Banking*, Peking University Press, 1995.

Chen Yunxian. *On Risk-Return Tradeoff*, Peking University Press, 1998.

Chen Yunxian. *Exploration on Financial Theory and Practice*, China Finance Publishing House, 1999.

Chen Yunxian and Zhang Mengyou. *An Investigative Study on the U.S. Financial System*, China Finance Publishing House, 2001.

Chen Yunxian. *Evolutional Explorations in Ways of Monitoring and Handling Financial Crisis in America*, China Finance Publishing House, 2013.

Chen Yunxian. *Exploration on China's Financial Reform and Development*, China Finance Publishing House, 2017.

Chen Yunxian. *Eight Highlights of Finance in China*, China Finance Publishing House, 2018.

Chen Yunxian. *National Finance*, Peking University Press, 2018.

Chen Yunxian. *Foresighted Leading: Theoretical Thinking and Practice of China's Regional Economic Development*, Peking University Press, 2011.

Chen Yunxian and Qiu Jianwei. *Government Foresighted Leading: Theory and Practice of the World's Regional Economic Development*, Peking University Press, 2013.

Chen Yunxian and Gu Wenjing. *Mezzoeconomics*, Peking University Press, 2015.

Chen Yunxian and Gu Wenjing. *Regional Government Competition*, Peking University Press, 2017.

Chen Yunxian. *Government Foresighted Leading: Theory and Practice of the World's Regional Economic Development*, Springer-Verlag Berlin Heidelberg, 2014.

Chen Yunxian and Qiu Jianwei. *Foresighted Leading: Theory and Practice of the World's Regional Economic Development*, Routledge, 2017.
Chen Yunxian and Gu Wenjing. *Mezzoeconomics*, American Academic Press, 2018.
Chen Yunxian and Gu Wenjing. *Regional Government Competition*, Routledge, 2019.

Course arrangement

Time: 9:00 am–11:00 am, July 1–5, 8–10, 2019.

Location: School of Economics

Assessment: Essay

Course-Choosing: This course is one of the series of quality courses of the School of Economics and is open to all undergraduate and postgraduate students of the school. Students who are interested in taking the course can join the course directly. After completing all the learning assignments and assessments in the summer, please select "Scholar Lectures Series" online (1 credit) in the fall semester, and the school will assess grades based on your attendance and essays submitted in the summer courses for "fail" or "pass."

Special Note: For postgraduate students, the credit of this course will not be included in required credits, but will be displayed on your school report cards.

Bibliography

Acemoglua, D., Golosova, M., & Tsyvinski, A. (2008). Markets versus governments. *Journal of Monetary Economics, 55*(1), 159–189.

Burnham, D., & Bennett, E. (1993). *Plan of Chicago* (1st ed.). New York: Princeton Architectural Press.

Chen, G. (2017). *Public finance* (9th ed.). Beijing: China Renmin University Press.

Chen, Y. (2011). *Foresighted leading: Theoretical thinking and practice of China's regional economic development*. Beijing: Peking University Press.

Chen, Y. (2018). *National finance*. Beijing: Peking University Press.

Chen, Y., & Gu, W. (2015). *Mezzoeconomics: Innovations and developments in theoretical configuration of economics*. Beijing: Peking University Press.

Chen, Y., & Gu, W. (2017). *Regional government competition*. Beijing: Peking University Press.

Chen, Y., & Qiu, J. (2013). *Government foresighted leading: Theory and practice of the world's regional economic development*. Beijing: Peking University Press.

Cheung, S. N. S. (2009). *The economic system of China*. Beijing: China Citic Press.

China News. (2017, April 1). Japanese experts: Trump's economic policies are like Roosevelt's "New Deal." http://www.chinanews.com/gj/2017/04-01/8189095.shtml.

Fama, E. F. (1970). Efficient capital markets: A review of theory and empirical work. *The Journal of Finance, 25*(2), 383–417.

Grimsey, D., & Lewis, M. K. (2004). *Public private partnerships: The worldwide revolution in infrastructure provision and project finance*. Edward Elgar Pub.

Gu, X. (2017). Rediscovering market failure: Nobel Laureate Joseph Stiglitz talks about industrial policy. *The Paper*, https://www.thepaper.cn/newsDetail_forward_1594001.

Hongye, G. (Ed.). (2018). *Western economics* (Macro section, 7th ed.). Beijing: China Renmin University Press.

Hongye, G. (Ed.). (2018). *Western economics* (Micro section, 7th ed.). Beijing: China Renmin University Press.

Huang, J. (2018, June 14). How major economic schools explain China's reform and opening up. *China Economic Times*.

Jia, T. (2014). SOEs worldwide concentrate on a few important strategic sectors. *China Economic Times*, August 8.

Keynes, J. M. (2016). *The economic consequences of the peace*. New York: Skyhorse Publishing Inc., P136.

Keynes, J. M. (2018). *The general theory of employment, interest, and money*. Palgrave Macmillan.

Krugman, P. R. (1983). New theories of trade among industrial countries. *The American Economic Review*, *73* (2), 343–347.

Lewis, W. A. (1955). *The theory of economic growth*. London: Allen and Unwin.

Nanfang Daily. (2016, October 31). It is time to make "Aerospace" a big business. http://epaper.southcn.com/nfdaily/html/2016-10/31/content_7593559.htm.

Pan, M., & Han, L. (Eds.). (2015). *Government economics* (4th ed.). Beijing: China Renmin University Press.

Pigou, A. C. (2013). *The economics of welfare*. New York: Cosimo Classics.

Porter, M. E. (2011). *The competitive advantage of nations*. New York: Free Press.

Rosen, H. S. (2013). *Public finance* (10th ed.). New York: McGraw-Hill Education.

Ross, I. S. (2010). *The life of Adam Smith*. New York: Oxford University Press Inc., pp. 240, 254, 333.

Rudiger, D., Fischer, S., & Startz, R. (Eds.). (2017). *Macroeconomics*. New York: McGraw-Hill Higher Education.

Samuelson, P. A., & Nordhaus, W. D. (2010). *Economics*. New York: McGraw-Hill/Irwin, P4.

Sifeng, Z. (Ed.). (2015). *Public economics*. Beijing: China Renmin University Press.

Smith, A. (1976). *The theory of moral sentiments*. New York: Oxford University Press.

Smith, A. (1977). *An inquiry into the nature and causes of the wealth of nations*. Chicago: University of Chicago Press.

Song, J. (2011). Smart Foshan: Transformation path under power division. *China Nongovernmental Science Technology and Economy*, (7), 50–55.

Stiglitz, J. E. (1989). *The economic role of the state*. New York: Blackwell Pub.

Sun, J. (Ed.). (2016). *Urban economics*. Beijing: China Renmin University Press.

Varian, H. R. (1992). *Microeconomic analysis* (3rd ed.). New York: W. W. Norton & Company.

Wolf, C., Jr. (1993). *Markets or governments—choosing between imperfect alternatives (a Rand research study)*. London: The MIT Press.

Xingzhi, X. (Ed.). (2016). *Industrial economics* (2nd ed.). Beijing: China Renmin University Press.

Index

Note that the italicized "*f*" after the page number refers to a figure and the italicized "*t*" refers to a table.